African Guerrillas

African Guerrillas

Edited by
CHRISTOPHER CLAPHAM

JAMES CURREY
OXFORD

FOUNTAIN PUBLISHERS
KAMPALA

INDIANA UNIVERSITY PRESS
BLOOMINGTON & INDIANAPOLIS

First published in Europe
and the Commonwealth by
James Currey Ltd
73 Botley Road
Oxford OX2 0BS

and in North America by
Indiana University Press
601 North Morton Street
Bloomington
Indiana 47404

First published in Uganda and East Africa by
Fountain Publishers
P.O. Box 488
Kampala

ISBN 0–85255–815–5 (James Currey paper)
ISBN 0–85255–816–3 (James Currey cloth)
ISBN 0-253-21243-X (Indiana paper)
ISBN 0-253-33466-7 (Indiana cloth)

British Cataloguing in Publication Data
African guerillas
    1. Guerrilla warfare – Africa 2. National liberation
    movements – Africa 3. Government, Resistance to – Africa
    4. Africa – politics and government – 1960–
    I. Clapham, Christopher
    322.4'2'096'09045

Library of Congress Cataloging-in-Publication Data
African guerillas / edited by Christopher Clapham.
    p.   cm.
    ISBN 0-253-33466-7 (alk. paper). — ISBN 0-253-21243-Z (pbk. alk. paper)
    1. Africa. Eastern—Politics and government—1960 2. Insurgency—
Africa, Eastern—History—20th century. 3. Guerillas—Africa.
Eastern—History—20th century. 4. Liberia—Politics and
government—1980– 5. Insurgency—Liberia—History—20th century.
6. Guerillas—Liberia—History—20th century. 7. Sierra Leone—
Politics and government—1961– 8. Insurgency—Sierra Leone—
History—20th century. 9. Guerillas—Sierra Leone—History—20th
century. I. Clapham, Christopher S.
DT365.8.A37 1998
322.4'2'096—dc21   98-15631
1 2 3 4 5 03 02 01 00 99 98

Typeset in 10½/11½ pt Bembo by Long House Publishing Services, Cumbria, UK
Manufactured in Britain
for Villiers Publications Ltd, London N3

Contents

Preface   vii
About the Authors   ix
Abbreviations & Acronyms   xi
Map   xiv

1 CHRISTOPHER CLAPHAM   1
Introduction: Analysing African Insurgencies

2 DAVID POOL   19
The Eritrean People's Liberation Front

3 JOHN YOUNG   36
The Tigray People's Liberation Front

4 DOUGLAS H. JOHNSON   53
The Sudan People's Liberation Army
& the Problem of Factionalism

5 DANIEL COMPAGNON   73
Somali Armed Units
The Interplay of Political Entrepreneurship
& Clan-Based Factions

6 PASCAL NGOGA   91
Uganda: The National Resistance Army

7 HEIKE BEHREND   107
War in Northern Uganda
The Holy Spirit Movements of Alice Lakwena,
Severino Lukoya & Joseph Kony (1986–1997)

8 GÉRARD PRUNIER   119
The Rwandan Patriotic Front

9 WM CYRUS REED   134
     Guerrillas in the Midst
     The Former Government of Rwanda &
     the Alliance of Democratic Forces for
     the Liberation of Congo-Zaire in Eastern Zaire

10 STEPHEN ELLIS   155
      Liberia's Warlord Insurgency

11 IBRAHIM ABDULLAH & PATRICK MUANA   172
      The Revolutionary United Front
      of Sierra Leone
      A Revolt of the Lumpenproletariat

      Bibliography   195
      Index   202

Preface

In recent years, the guerrilla phenomenon has gained increasing importance in Africa, as widely varied groups across the continent have resorted to insurgent warfare in pursuit of state power, and of other goals which may be economic or even spiritual in nature. As the institutional infrastructure of African states has decayed, so armed insurrection in the countryside has displaced military coups launched by the state's own armed forces as the principal threat of violent overthrow facing many of their leaders.

The inaccessibility of the areas in which they usually arise, and the exceptional levels of violence and social disruption that accompany them, have made guerrilla movements in Africa extremely difficult to study. As a result – outside the southern part of the continent, where they have been closely associated with 'liberation war' against colonial and white minority regimes, and with those regimes' attempts in turn to destabilize their neighbours – they have failed to receive a level of analytical attention that remotely corresponds to their importance. This book, which draws on case studies from across tropical Africa, from the Horn through Central Africa to coastal West Africa, attempts the first comparative study of African insurgencies that has yet been undertaken. All of the individual studies have been contributed by authors with extensive fieldwork experience in the areas in which these movements have formed and operated; and while regional and even global factors have certainly played an important role in the spread of guerrilla warfare in Africa, one theme that emerges very strongly from all of the case studies is that the indigenous social base on which the insurgency is constructed has been of critical importance. Varying circumstances have correspondingly produced a range of often very different movements, with the result that this volume clearly indicates the dangers of excessive generalization. There are nonetheless a set of common themes which are explored in the introductory chapter.

In exploring these themes, the authors of this book were very greatly assisted by the opportunity for most of us to meet during a two-day conference at the Afrika-studiecentrum at Leiden in the Netherlands in January 1997, at which we presented early drafts of our papers and discussed the linkages between them. We are most grateful to the Afrikastudiecentrum, and its director Gerti Hesseling, for hosting the conference and meeting the travel costs of its participants.

Christopher Clapham
Lancaster

About the Authors

Ibrahim Abdullah teaches History at the University of the Western Cape, Cape Town, South Africa.

Heike Behrend is Professor of Anthropology at the Institute of African Studies, University of Cologne. She is author of *Alice und die Geister: Krieg im Norden Ugandas* (Munich: Trickster, 1993), an English translation of which is forthcoming from James Currey Publishers.

Daniel Compagnon, formerly Director of the Institut Français de Recherche en Afrique (IFRA) at Harare, Zimbabwe, wrote his PhD in political science on the regime of Mahamed Siyaad Barre (1969–91), and has conducted extended research on Somali affairs. An acknowledged specialist on the Somali opposition to Siyaad Barre's rule, he was also briefly involved in conflict resolution efforts at the beginning of the international intervention in Somalia, as a member of a think-tank convened by the Life and Peace Institute at Uppsala, Sweden, at the request of the United Nations.

Christopher Clapham is Professor of Politics and International Relations at Lancaster University; a specialist on the Horn of Africa, he is also author of *Africa and the International System: The Politics of State Survival* (Cambridge University Press, 1996), and editor of *The Journal of Modern African Studies*.

Stephen Ellis is a senior researcher at the Afrikastudiecentrum, Leiden, Netherlands, was formerly Editor of *Africa Confidential*, and is now co-editor of *African Affairs*. He is the author, with Tsepo Sechaba, of a study of Umkhonto, the ANC and the South African Communist Party in exile called *Comrades against Apartheid* (James Currey and Indiana University Press, 1992). He is shortly to publish a book on the Liberian war with Hurst Publishers.

Douglas Johnson, a specialist on the Southern Sudan, is a Senior Associate Member at St Antony's College, Oxford. He is the author of *Nuer Prophets* (Oxford University Press, 1994) and editor of the Sudan volume in the British Documents on the End of Empire Project series, to be published by the Stationary Office. He is completing *The Root Causes of Sudan's Civil Wars*.

Patrick Muana is a social anthropologist at the University of Sheffield.

Pascal Ngoga, a Rwandan by origin, recently completed a PhD thesis on the National Resistance Army at Lancaster University.

David Pool is a lecturer in Government at Manchester University, and has written extensively on Eritrea and the EPLF. He is the author of *Eritrea: Towards Unity and Diversity* (Minority Rights Group, 1997), and is currently completing a study of the EPLF.

Gérard Prunier is a researcher at the Centre National de Recherche Scientifique, Paris, and the author of *The Rwanda Crisis 1959–1994: History of a Genocide* (Hurst, 1995).

Wm Cyrus Reed is Director of African Studies and Associate Professor of Political Science at the American University in Cairo. His principal research interests focus is the intersection between the domestic and international activities of guerrilla movements, and their transition from movements to governments. In 1997/8, he was a Visiting Scholar at the African Studies Program at Indiana University, where he completed a book on the role of the ADFL and the RPF in the transformation of the Congo and Rwanda.

John Young teaches political science at Addis Ababa University; he is the author of a book on the TPLF, *Peasant Revolution in Ethiopia* (Cambridge University Press, 1997).

Abbreviations & Acronyms

ADFL	Alliance of Democratic Forces for the Liberation of Congo–Zaire
AFL	Armed Forces of Liberia
AFRC	Armed Forces Revolutionary Council (Sierra Leone)
APC	All People's Congress (Sierra Leone)
BMA	British Military Administration (Ethiopia)
CAR	Central African Republic
CDR	Coalition pour le Défence de la République (Rwanda)
CF	Commander of Forces (Uganda)
CMA	Civil/Military Administrator (Sudan)
CO	Commanding Officer (Uganda)
DP	Democratic Party (Uganda)
ECOMOG	ECOWAS Monitoring Group
ECOWAS	Economic Community of West African States
EDU	Ethiopian Democratic Union
ELF	Eritrean Liberation Front
EPDM	Ethiopian People's Democratic Movement
EPLA	Eritrean People's Liberation Army
EPLF	Eritrean People's Liberation Front
EPRDF	Ethiopian People's Revolutionary Democratic Front
EPRP	Ethiopian Peoples' Revolutionary Party
ERA	Eritrean Relief Association
EXFAR	(Former) Armed Forces of Rwanda
FAN	Forces Armées du Nord (Chad)
FAR	Forces Armées Rwandaises
FAZ	Zairean Armed Forces
FBC	Fourah Bay College (Sierra Leone)
FCT	Frontline Coordination Team (Uganda)
FGOR	Former Government of Rwanda
FLCS	Front de libération de la Côte des Somalis
FLN	Front de Libération Nationale (Algeria)
Frelimo	Frente de Libertação de Moçambique
Frolinat	Front de Libération Nationale (Chad)

Fronasa	Front for National Salvation (Uganda)
HSM	Holy Spirit Movement (Uganda)
HSMF	Holy Spirit Movement Forces
IDU	Internal Defence Unit (Sierra Leone)
KY	Kabaka Yekka (Uganda)
LPC	Liberia Peace Council
LRA	Lord's Resistance Army (Uganda)
Magrivi	Mutuelle des Agriculteurs et Eleveurs du Virunga (Farmers and Livestock Raisers Cooperative of Virunga)
MAP	Mass Awareness and Participation (Sierra Leone)
MDR	Movement Démocratique Républicain
MLLT	Marxist–Leninist League of Tigray
NDA	National Democratic Alliance (Sudan)
NFDLF	Northern Frontier District Liberation Front (Somalia)
NIF	National Islamic Front (Sudan)
NPFL	National Patriotic Front of Liberia
NPRC	National Provisional Ruling Council (Sierra Leone)
NRA	National Resistance Army (Uganda)
NRC	National Resistance Council (Uganda)
OAU	Organization of African Unity
OFDA	Office of Foreign Disaster Assistance (United States)
OLF	Oromo Liberation Front (Ethiopia)
OLS	Operation Lifeline Sudan
OPDO	Oromo People's Democratic Organization (Ethiopia)
PA	People's Assemblies (Eritrea)
PAC	Policy and Administrative Committee (Uganda)
PAIGC	Partido Africano da Indepêndcia da Guiné e Cabo Verde (African Party for the Independence of Guinea and Cape Verde)
Panafu	Pan African Union (Sierra Leone)
PC	Political Commissar (Uganda)
PDRY	People's Democratic Republic of Yemen
PLF	Popular Liberation Forces (Eritrea)
PMHC	Political–Military High Command (Sudan)
PRA	Popular Resistance Army (Uganda)
RANU	Rwandan Alliance for National Unity
RC	Resistance Council (Uganda)
Renamo	Mozambique National Resistance Movement
REST	Relief Society of Tigray
RPA	Rwandan Patriotic Army
RPF	Rwandan Patriotic Front
RRWF	Rwandan Refugees' Welfare Association
RUF/SL	Revolutionary United Front of Sierra Leone
SAF	Sudan Allied Forces
SNA	Somali National Alliance
SNM	Somali National Movement
SPLA	Sudan People's Liberation Army
SPLM	Sudan People's Liberation Movement

SPM	Somali Patriotic Movement
SSA	Somalia Salvation Alliance
SSD	State Security Defence (Sierra Leone)
SSDF	Somali Salvation Democratic Front
SSIA	South Sudan Independence Army
SSIM	South Sudan Independence Movement
TNO	Tigray National Organization
TPDF	Tanzania People's Defence Force
TPLF	Tigray People's Liberation Front
UFF	Uganda Freedom Fighters
UFM	Uganda Freedom Movement
Ulimo	United Liberation Movement for Democracy (Liberia)
UNITA	União Nacional para a Independência Total de Angola (National Union for the Total Independence of Angola)
UNLA	Uganda National Liberation Army
UNLF	Uganda National Liberation Front
UNOSOM	UN Operation in Somalia
UPA	Uganda People's Army
UPC	Uganda People's Congress
UPDA	Uganda People's Democratic Army
UPDCA	Uganda People's Democratic Christian Army
UPDF	Ugandan People's Defence Force
UPM	Uganda Patriotic Movement
USC	United Somali Congress
Uwonet	Uganda Women's Network
WMC	War Mobilization Committee (Uganda)
WNBF	West Nile Bank Front (Uganda)
WPE	Workers' Party of Ethiopia
WSLF	Western Somali Liberation Front
WWF	World Wildlife Fund

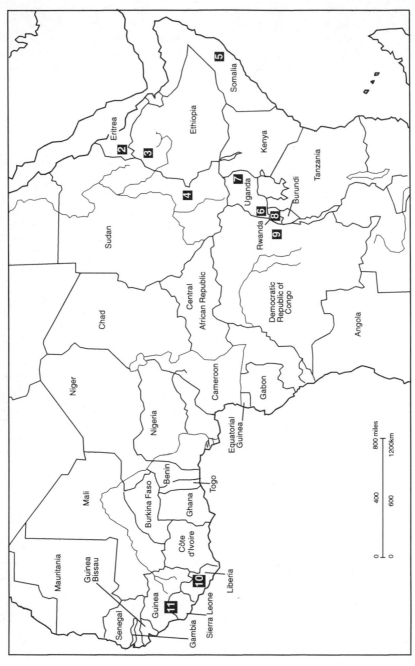

Map of middle Africa showing location of chapter case studies

1

CHRISTOPHER CLAPHAM
Introduction:
Analysing African Insurgencies[1]

This book seeks to assess an important but often neglected phenomenon in the politics of modern Africa: the development of armed movements, usually originating in the countryside and often attacking across state frontiers, which have sought to contest the power of African states, and have frequently established their own forms of rule, in territories from which the control of established states has disappeared. 'Guerrillas' is the most familiar term used to describe such movements, and one which we retain in the title of this book. Most of the movements with which we are concerned – the former government of Rwanda, whose activities are examined in Chapter 9, being the main exception – originated in classic guerrilla fashion as small armed bands in rural areas, guided by a political programme which, at least in their own eyes, sought some form of 'liberation'. Subsequently, these movements diverged, some of them – like the Eritrean People's Liberation Front (EPLF) – developing into large conventional armies which could no longer plausibly be described as 'guerrillas', whereas others fragmented into little more than predatory gangs. In most of this book the term 'insurgencies' is used, to include movements which may not qualify as guerrillas in a strict sense of the term, and to avoid some of the ideological and even romantic associations which 'guerrilla' has acquired.

Amongst the insurgencies that have emerged in modern Africa, this book concentrates on those that have been directed against independent African governments, which in some cases have continued in the absence of any effective government at all. We have excluded movements formed to wrest state power from colonial and settler regimes, as well as movements – notably the National Union for the Total Liberation of Angola (UNITA) and the Mozambique National Resistance (Renamo) – which were closely associated with the struggles across the 'front line' between white- and black-ruled Southern Africa. These movements had many elements in common with those with which we *are* concerned, but have been excluded from this book, not only because they raise rather different issues, but also

---

[1] I am grateful to other contributors to this book, and especially to Stephen Ellis, for comments on earlier drafts of this chapter.

because they have been covered extensively in the existing literature.[2] We have also excluded the insurgencies of North Africa and the Sahelian zone, from Western Sahara through Algeria and the various Touareg resistance movements to Chad. Apart from these, though this survey could not be fully comprehensive – the Horn of Africa alone has thrown up far too many groups for that – we have sought to cover the most important movements and a sample of others. Four chapters – on Eritrea, Tigray, Somalia and Southern Sudan – cover the Horn. Four more, on northern and southern Uganda, Rwanda and Zaire – deal with the insurgencies of East-Central Africa. Two chapters, finally, examine Liberia and Sierra Leone in West Africa.[3]

Historical Overview

'Guerrilla' warfare, which in European history has been largely defined in contrast to that conducted by the regular armies of established states, may be regarded as the normal form of warfare in societies without powerful states, and in this sense occupies a prominent place in the history of Africa. Only with the imposition on Africa of colonial territorial states, and the professional military forces which were needed to sustain them, does it become possible to distinguish 'guerrilla' or 'insurgent' warfare as a distinct form of conflict. Many of the insurgencies considered in this volume, directed as they usually were against the formally structured militaries of post-colonial states, exhibit evident legacies from pre-colonial modes of warfare.

In the post-Second World War era, insurgency became closely associated with the revolutionary doctrines of 'people's war' articulated by Mao Tse Tung, and was adopted in Africa as elsewhere as the most effective means of defeating the highly organized and heavily armed, but also cumbersome and alien armies of the major industrial powers and their local allies. Only to a very limited extent did this adoption incorporate the class analysis which is central to Mao's own approach, not least because few parts of Africa had rural class structures in any way comparable to China's; but it first emerged in relatively organized form – notably in the Mau Mau movement in Kenya from 1952 onwards, and in the Algerian war of independence from 1954 – as a mode of resistance not just to colonial rule, but to the alienation of land by white settlers. Subsequently, armed liberation movements became the normal expression of African demands for self-government in territories where colonial recalcitrance or white minority rule obstructed a peaceful transition to independence. Outside Guinea-Bissau, where the articulate leadership of Amilcar

[2] See notably David Lan, *Guns and Rain: Guerrillas and Spirit Mediums in Zimbabwe* (London: James Currey, 1985), Norma J. Kriger, *Zimbabwe's Guerrilla War: Peasant Voices* (Cambridge: Cambridge University Press, 1992), and Ngwabi Bhebe and Terence Ranger, *Soldiers in Zimbabwe's Liberation War* (London: James Currey, 1995), on Zimbabwe; William Minter, *Apartheid's Contras: an Enquiry into the Roots of War in Angola and Mozambique* (London: Zed Books, 1994), on Angola and Mozambique; Colin Leys and John Saul, *Namibia's Liberation Struggle: the Two-Edged Sword* (London: James Currey, 1995), on Namibia.

[3] A further West African insurgency which it has not been possible to include is the Mouvement des Forces Democratiques de la Casamance in Senegal; see Jean-Claude Marut, 'Solution militaire en Casamance', *Politique Africaine*, 58 (1995).

Cabral helped to achieve prominence for the African Party for the Independence of Guinea and Cape Verde (PAIGC), this in turn defined the major location for insurgent warfare as Southern Africa, notably in opposition to Portuguese colonialism in Angola and Mozambique, and to minority rule in Zimbabwe, Namibia and South Africa; in Angola and Mozambique, especially, insurgent opposition to the newly established African governments was then sustained with external aid after independence. The exceptional case of Cameroon, where the radical Union des Populations Camorounaises (UPC) resorted to armed opposition against a regime that was closely associated with the colonial power, also warrants a place on the record.[4]

Elsewhere, insurgencies directed against indigenous African governments grew initially out of failures in the decolonization settlements, which subjected a number of peoples and territories to states widely regarded as alien and illegitimate. This in turn helped to define a second major region of insurgency in the Horn of Africa. Sudan, where independence in 1956 immediately raised the issue of the relationship between the southern districts and the government in Khartoum, has some claim to be the first. Somali resistance to incorporation into Ethiopia was endemic, but took a more explicit form with the independence of the Somali Republic in 1960, and the creation of irredentist movements in Ethiopia, Kenya and Djibouti which were backed by the government in Mogadishu. In Eritrea, armed opposition to the Ethiopian government, which had taken over the territory under a UN-sponsored settlement in 1952, dated from the early 1960s.

Insurgencies resulting from failures in decolonization merge with those prompted by unrepresentative or autocratic regimes in independent states. There may not be a great deal to choose between Sudan, where a Moslem regime based in the north induced resistance from alienated Christians in the south; and Chad, where a regime based in the south eventually induced equivalent resistance from the Moslem north and east. Like Sudan, too, Ethiopia was a state whose 'ownership' by a particular segment of the population, in this case the Orthodox Christian and Amharic-speaking peoples especially of the central province of Shoa, was always liable to prompt resistance from other peoples who were excluded from, and alienated by, state power. Even in Senegal, one of the more mildly governed of African states, a sense of alienation in the southern region of Casamance was eventually to lead to armed resistance.

Some insurgencies, finally, can be ascribed to an experience of post-independence government so bad as to lead to a resistance born of desperation, and to the consequences of prolonged immiseration, exploitation and state decay. In Uganda, a tricky political legacy at independence was exacerbated by the political mismanagement of the Obote regime and culminated in the Amin dictatorship and the second Obote government. Somalia, behind the facade of a common national identity and culture, was riven by conflicts which were normally articulated in clan terms; in a region where arms and external support were readily available, the Siyaad Barre regime's attempt to maintain control by force was eventually contested in the same way. In Liberia, a small, peaceful and relatively prosperous country fell apart once

[4] For an excellent study, see Richard A. Joseph, *Radical Nationalism in Cameroon* (London: Oxford University Press, 1977).

the overthrow of the True Whig oligarchy was followed only by the crude kleptocracy and ethnic favouritism of the Doe regime; while in Sierra Leone, which consistently figures at the bottom of global quality-of-life indices, revolt was the ultimate resort of an alienated lumpenproletariat.

By the 1990s insurgent warfare had led to the ousting of incumbent regimes in several African states, and to the installation of successors which owed their origins to insurgency. Excluding cases of liberation from colonial or white minority rule, the first insurgency to seize power in an independent African state was Hissen Habré's Forces Armés du Nord (FAN) in Chad in 1979, after which there were further upheavals before Habré succeeded in establishing himself more firmly in June 1982. The second was the capture of Kampala by Museveni's National Resistance Army (NRA) in 1986, followed by the seizure of Addis Ababa by the Ethiopian Peoples' Revolutionary Democratic Front (EPRDF) and of Asmara by the EPLF in May 1991. In the interim, the National Patriotic Front of Liberia (NPFL) and the Somali National Alliance (SNA) in Somalia had overthrown the incumbent regimes of Samuel Doe and Siyaad Barre in September 1990 and January 1991 respectively, without being able to establish viable new governments. The capture of Kigali by the Rwandan Patriotic Front (RPF), in the aftermath of the genocide in July 1994, and the subsequent success of the Alliance of Democratic Forces for the Liberation of Congo-Zaire (ADFL), together with the war in Sudan, created a substantial block of insurgency-affected states across the centre of the continent.

These developments, from the independence era to the present day, occurred within a rapidly changing political environment, both globally and within the African continent. Although the global rivalries of the Cold War provided a supportive international setting for some insurgencies, both in the Horn and in Southern Africa, the conventions of African diplomacy in the first decades after independence clearly distinguished between legitimate 'liberation war' against the remaining white regimes and the illegitimacy of any challenge to the post-colonial order. The heavy emphasis on 'national sovereignty' and 'territorial integrity', built into such documents as the Charter of the Organization of African Unity, gave enormous international advantages to recognized central governments, and was bitterly criticized by such leaders as Yoweri Museveni and Issayas Afewerki once they had fought their way to power. In the post-Cold War context, with its emphasis on multi-party democracy and assumption that many of the problems of African states were the result of their own misgovernment, insurgencies were regarded more readily as the authentic expression of popular alienation, and their international acceptability increased accordingly. Rather than sending incumbent regimes the armaments with which to suppress them, the dominant states of the new global order were more likely to insist that they be incorporated into a new political settlement.

But as the legitimacy of insurgencies increased, the effectiveness of the states which they were fighting – and which they also sought to take over – diminished. The assumption of the elites who took over at independence, that they had inherited an instrument which they could use to shape the societies that they governed, proved to be seriously mistaken. The sources of the economic and political decay of African states have been the subject of a vast literature, and lie well beyond the scope of this volume.[5] They were most immediately reflected, not only in the new political conditionalities that enhanced the status of insurgencies, but also in structural adjustment programmes which sought to undermine the ability of governments to control the sources of economic patronage.[6] While on one hand this made the insurgents' task easier, since it undercut the main mechanism through which governments maintained political support, on the other hand it raised the question of whether such states were worth capturing at all. In an increasing number of cases, insurgents found it easier just to capture the trading networks on which states had depended, and use them for their own purposes.

Causes, Typologies, and Central Questions

This synopsis has ascribed causes to many insurgencies, which will be nuanced or amended in the individual case studies. It suggests that insurgencies derive basically from blocked political aspirations, and in some cases also from reactive desperation. In post-colonial states whose governments reflected a heavy level of urban bias, insurgencies could also often be associated, despite their normally urban intellectual leadership, with rural resistance to the exploitative exactions of centralized statehood. But even if the case studies indicate that these are plausible explanations, some thought nonetheless needs to be given to *why* the insurgent path opened up in each particular case. The ideologies or mythologies of the insurgent movements themselves understandably emphasize the history of oppression and exploitation which has driven the population involved to arms, and there is generally no call to disparage or dispute these: only extreme conditions are likely to induce people to attempt anything as risky and costly as guerrilla warfare. On the other hand – and here we face the problem that in concentrating on cases where insurgency *has* occurred, we necessarily ignore those where it has not – serious insurgency has broken out only in a minority of African states, though a significant one. Generalized explanations rarely capture what is distinctive about each case, and this distinctiveness may well explain why insurgency occurs in one case but not in others.

Sometimes, as in Somalia, a disposition to resort to insurgency may result from the structures or values of particular societies; in other words, where state structures are weak, and violence in pursuit of communal goals had been a normal feature of pre-colonial society, what is now defined as insurgency may merely be the continuation of such practices into the post-colonial era. Even in Ethiopia, where there was a strong tradition of statehood, this was accompanied by equally ancient traditions of rebellion or banditry. In societies in which raiding or pillage were established aspects of warfare, these were readily incorporated into the practices of insurgent armies, and the scope for them was often increased, in one way or

[5] See, for example, Donald Rothchild and Naomi Chazan, eds, *The Precarious Balance: State and Society in Africa* ((Boulder: Westview, 1988); James S. Wunsch and Dele Oluwu, eds, *The Failure of the Centralized State: Institutions and Self-Government in Africa* (Boulder: Westview, 1990); and Leonardo A. Villalon and Phillip A. Huxtable, eds, *The African State at a Critical Juncture: Between Disintegration and Reconfiguration* (Boulder: Rienner, 1997).

[6] There is a massive literature on structural adjustment; see Rolph van der Hoeven and Fred van der Kraaij, eds, *Structural Adjustment and Beyond in Sub Saharan Africa* (London. James Currey, 1994).

another, by the incorporation of Africa into the global economy.[7] Equally, few African states made provision for reasoned opposition to incumbent authorities (or 'voice', in Hirschman's famous categorization), and the normal way of expressing opposition in pre-colonial Africa was therefore 'exit', or withdrawing from the regime altogether. In post-colonial territorial states, where the opportunities for exit were reduced drastically, the inducement to resort to force was correspondingly enhanced.[8]

The causes (or precipitants) of particular insurgencies also derive from differing combinations of leadership or elite action, on one hand, or popular resistance on the other. The relationship between leaders and followers, which is critical to the analysis of any insurgency, is explored in greater detail later. It is commonly obscured in insurgent mythologies by an emphasis on 'the people' as the foundation for resistance; but although any effective insurgency requires a combination of elite leadership (usually by educated individuals of strikingly different background from that of the population among whom they operate) and popular support, there may be considerable variation in the significance of each. While in some cases the leadership may indeed only need to supply the match which sets the tinder-dry bush alight (the study of insurgency is replete with overworked metaphors), there may be others where insurgency results only from the deliberate and determined efforts of a small group of committed leaders to start it.

Any attempt to distinguish between different types of insurgency runs the risk of imposing oversimplified categorizations on movements whose character is both changeable and mixed, and several of the case studies draw attention to the dangers of trying to fit them into particular boxes; but the level of variance has been great enough to call for at least some attempt at classification. Writing about the international relations of African insurgencies,[9] I found it useful to identify four broad groups. The first, *liberation insurgencies*, set out to achieve independence from colonial or minority rule: Algeria, the Portuguese colonies of Angola, Guinea-Bissau and Mozambique, and the settler states of Zimbabwe, Namibia and South Africa. These are anti-colonial nationalist movements which took an insurgent form, owing to the refusal of incumbent regimes to concede majority rule; as already noted, they enjoyed a special standing in African international relations.

A second group, *separatist insurgencies*, seek to represent the aspirations and identities of particular ethnicities or regions within an existing state, either by seceding from that state altogether, or else by pressing for some special autonomous status. The classic examples of such insurgencies are in Southern Sudan and Eritrea, though the Somali irredentist movements against Ethiopia and Kenya also qualify. The original Front de Libération Nationale (Frolinat) resistance to the Tombalbaye government in Chad, and the Tigray People's Liberation Front (TPLF) opposition to the Mengistu regime in Ethiopia, are further potential candidates. So, on a smaller

---

[7] The work of Charles Tilly on plunder and the economics of warfare in Europe makes for fascinating comparisons with modern Africa; see, for example, Tilly, *Coercion, Capital and European States, AD 990–1990* (Oxford: Blackwell, 1990).

[8] See Jeffrey Herbst, 'Migration, the politics of protest, and state consolidation in Africa', *African Affairs*, Vol. 89, No. 355 (1990).

[9] Christopher Clapham, *Africa and the International System* (Cambridge: Cambridge University Press, 1996), Chapter 9.

scale, is the Casamance movement. Virtually all African insurgencies, however, draw to some degree on ethnic differentiation within the state concerned, even in cases like Uganda (and much more markedly Rwanda) where the movement makes no explicit claim on behalf of particular peoples or regions, and the boundaries of this group are necessarily fuzzy.

The third group, *reform insurgencies*, seek radical reform of the national government, and are most evidently represented by the NRA in Uganda and the EPRDF (itself descended from the regional TPLF) in Ethiopia, with the Zairean ADFL as a further possible example. Generally, Africa has lacked insurgencies committed to the revolutionary ideologies found in East and South East Asia, as well as in Latin America, for reasons which can most plausibly be ascribed both to differing levels of 'development' (and most evidently class formation), and to differing forms of external domination and regional conflict, especially within the context of the Cold War. In cases such as Angola and Mozambique, there was indeed an explicit commitment to Marxism-Leninism which in turn shaped the post-independence government, but the central 'project' of the insurgency was nonetheless anti-colonial liberation rather than domestic revolution. In the Ethiopian and Ugandan cases, however, and also in Rwanda and Zaire, insurgency was at least ostensibly directed towards the creation of a new kind of state, in place of that which it sought to overthrow. Some elements of the reform agenda were also present in the Sudan People's Liberation Army (SPLA), both in reaction to the Khartoum government's attempts to impose an Islamicist regime, and because an explicitly separatist programme alienated external supporters. Several of the leaders of these movements were former student radicals, with a commitment to 'liberation' and a thorough grounding in the work of Mao Tse Tung, who found an increased freedom of action in post-Cold War Africa.

The fourth type, *warlord insurgencies*, arise in cases where the insurgency is directed towards a change of leadership which does not entail the creation of a state any different from that which it seeks to overthrow, and which may involve the creation of a personal territorial fiefdom separate from existing state structures and boundaries. 'Warlord' remains a controversial term in African political analysis,[10] and some authors prefer not to use it; it has not only entered popular usage, however, but also denotes a significant phenomenon. Charles Taylor's would-be regime in Liberia, for example, scarcely differed from Samuel Doe's, while little separated Mahamed Faarah Aidid's SNA in Somalia from Ali Mahdi Mahamed's Somalia Salvation Alliance (SSA), or indeed the preceding regime of Mahamed Siyaad Barre. Though UNITA in Angola and Renamo in Mozambique could certainly be distinguished on ideological grounds from the governments which they opposed, their attempts to present themselves as capitalist (or, still more remarkably, liberal democratic) organizations owed more to their need to appeal to external backers than to any convictions of their own. These insurgencies have had the greatest difficulty in establishing effective regimes, even after the overthrow of their original opponents, and have readily resulted in state collapse. For such leaders, indeed, control of a state was desirable but not essential: leaders like Taylor or Aidid, or

---

[10] For an articulation of the concept with reference to Africa, see Roger Charlton and Roy May, 'Warlords and militarism in Chad', *Review of African Political Economy*, 45/46 (1989), pp. 12–25.

equally Savimbi, sought to take over the recognized national governments of their respective states, but could run their own quasi-governmental operations in the absence of fixed territories, formal governmental structures, or international recognition.

The differences between types of insurgency also bear on the critical differences between their outcomes. Some insurgencies have been organized effectively, and have proved capable at least of taking over and operating existing state structures, and in some cases even of reconstructing states which had virtually collapsed. Others, lacking such organization, have been the instruments of state collapse themselves. Explaining the difference between state-consolidating and state-sub-verting insurgencies is thus a challenge which no comparative analysis can ignore; and though neither this introduction nor the book as a whole may fully be able to meet it, it is at least possible to sketch out some of the explanatory variables that are involved.

One range of hypotheses essentially looks for explanation from the top down: it seeks answers in purposive action by insurgent leaders, and the skill and determina-tion with which they are able to shape their movements to their own design. Central to their success is their ability to articulate common goals to which the movement is committed, and to devise the organizational structures through which those goals can be fought for and eventually achieved. Such leaders are likely in turn to look for viable models of insurgent organization and strategy, among which in the modern world that of Mao Tse Tung has been pre-eminent. At its simplest, indeed, Maoism might be regarded as a 'kit' which, with appropriate allowance for local variations, insurgent leaders can take over and apply to their own situations.

Alternatively, explanations may be sought in the environment in which insurgencies have to operate. Formed in most cases 'in the field', and drawing a high proportion of their recruits from the peoples of the area in which they operate, insurgencies are intensely dependent on their relations with host societies and may be expected to reflect local structures and values; some of these may help to sustain statist ideologies and organizations, whereas others do not. Insurgencies may also be influenced by the national setting, and especially by the character of the regimes against which they are fighting: those which, as in Ethiopia or Rwanda, are challenging powerful and centralized regimes need to develop an equivalent organizational capacity if they are to succeed; whereas collapsing states, as in Somalia and Liberia, may be overthrown even by feebly organized opposition. International variables also play a part; during the Cold War, when many insurgencies were broadly Marxist in orientation, and the work of Mao Tse Tung enjoyed exceptional prestige, insurgencies which claimed to implement his ideal of people's war had both a status and sources of international support which disappeared in the ideological vacuum of the 1990s.

At all events, these considerations help to define a number of broad categories through which the variations between insurgencies may be explored. First, there are questions about the internal structure of the movement – its leadership, ideology, and organization. Second, there are questions about its relationship with the people amongst whom it operates. Third, there are questions about its relationships with the international system, which – especially in relatively small and open states, such as those of sub-Saharan Africa – may play a critical role. Finally, there are questions about outcomes: most basically, about the reasons for success or failure, but also about the nature of 'success', if this is achieved. The following sections will discuss each of these in turn.

Leadership, Ideology and Organization

All social explanation confronts the problem of the emphasis to be given to variables derived from the voluntary and purposive behaviour of individual people, as against those derived from the structural features of the settings in which they operate, but this problem is particularly acute in the case of insurgent movements. On one hand, these are organizations which owe a great deal to individual initiative: they are formed in opposition to established political structures, and allow their leaders a great deal of choice over how they should be organized and how they should operate. In many cases, the leader and the movement are so closely associated that it is hard to conceive of one without the other. On the other hand, insurgencies like other political movements are constrained by their settings, and in particular by their need to maximize access to both domestic and international support, so that the freedom of action open to their leaders is in practice limited. Depending on how these variables work out, movements may differ appreciably from one to another.

At all events, the leadership, structure and ideology of an insurgent movement tell us a great deal about it, regardless of whether these derive from the voluntary choices of a few individuals or are imposed by circumstance. Most of the leaders of the movements considered here were drawn from elite sections of society, as middle-level politicians, army officers or student radicals, and deliberately decided to pursue an insurgent route to power after alternatives were blocked. These origins do not determine directly the organizational effectiveness of the movements which they formed: both Museveni in Uganda and Taylor in Liberia were articulate and educated middle-level politicians, one of whom led a highly disciplined insurgency while the other became a classic 'warlord'. There is nonetheless no case in which uneducated leaders, such as Foday Sankoh in Sierra Leone or Joseph Kony in northern Uganda, were able to create disciplined movements with clearly defined political projects; education is at least a necessary, though not a sufficient, condition for organizational effectiveness.

Insurgent warfare exposes organizations to the supreme test of prolonged conflict, often accompanied by heavy casualties, and the ultimate indicator of their effectiveness is the way in which they develop or decay over time. The capacity of the EPLF to survive and adapt over some two decades of intensive conflict provides the extreme example, in sharp contrast, for example, to Somalia, where, as Compagnon shows, different organizations formed and fragmented with changing circumstances. One critical variable is whether a movement is capable of changing leaders peacefully (as the TPLF did on several occasions), or replacing them if they are killed or captured; or whether the leadership is so central to the movement that the loss of the leader entails the collapse of the organization. The ultimate test of leadership is dispensability, illustrated by the way in which the RPF kept going and achieved ultimate success, despite the death of its leader Fred Rwigyema on the second day of the campaign.

Leadership, in turn, is closely associated with ideology and organization: where members of the movement share a commitment to common principles and goals, and where the movement has an effective structure through which it seeks to achieve those goals, issues of personal leadership will be less critical. These organizational variables may be tested in a number of ways. Formal structures – command councils, hierarchies, military formations – provide one indicator: they may possess some autonomy of their own, or change at the whim of the top leader. The representatives of the movement outside the area of conflict may operate in a broadly bureaucratic fashion, or act as the individual emissaries of the leader. Recruits, or indeed officers or their equivalents, may receive formalized training not simply on military technicalities, but on the organization, aims and ideology of the movement; or they may be left to pick up the information that they need as they go along. Those movements, such as the NRA in Uganda or the TPLF in Ethiopia, which devoted a good deal of attention to these organizational matters proved to be more effective than those, such as the NPFL in Liberia or any of the Somali movements, which did not do so. At the extreme, the EPLF in Eritrea was marked (as Pool indicates) by an intense commitment to inculcating all of its members with an official 'history' which constituted the ideological charter of the movement, together with formalized structures for self-criticism and thorough training in the theory of liberation war derived from Mao Tse Tung.

Movements also differ markedly in coherence: in their ability to stay united on one hand, or their tendency to split on the other. Splits, indeed, are key indicators of the way in which a movement is organized: personalist movements are liable to split on personal lines, ethnic movements on ethnic lines, ideological movements on ideological lines. The defection from the ELF in Eritrea of those elements who subsequently formed the much more effective EPLF reflected their frustration with a movement whose Islamic affinities and dependence on support from radical Arab states were counterproductive bases for resistance in a territory evenly split between Moslems and Christians. Both in Eritrea and in Sudan, a history of division profoundly affected the determination of the EPLF and the SPLA to maintain a united organization in a fragmented host society. The defection of Prince Johnson's INPFL from Charles Taylor's NPFL in Liberia, on the other hand, or the numerous splits in Somalia, reflected only the calculation of subordinates in personalist organizations that they could do better on their own.

A further criterion which often shows up sharp differences between movements is the level of discipline maintained by their forces. Some movements, such as the NRA in Uganda and the closely associated RPF in Rwanda, were able to enforce such stringent levels of discipline that individuals responsible for rape or the murder of civilians were publicly executed. In others, and notably the different movements in both Liberia and Somalia, murder, rape and looting constituted much of the *raison d'être* of the insurgent forces themselves; though Charles Taylor did promulgate a code of conduct for the NPFL, its enforcement was both personalized and sporadic. Here again, the chain of causation is often uncertain. Did the leadership in some cases insist on a high level of discipline, while in others it was content to let its forces gratify themselves as they wished? Or were there in some cases underlying social structures which permitted the maintenance of a level of discipline that in others would simply have been impossible to enforce?

The differences between movements are especially clearly illustrated by the recruitment of children to fight in insurgent forces. Although these children often came from traumatic personal backgrounds, as war orphans or refugees, they behaved in startlingly different ways in different insurgencies. In Uganda and Ethiopia, they acted with a level of discipline well beyond that displayed (in Uganda, especially) by the 'regular' army, whereas in Liberia and Sierra Leone they were responsible for many of the most appalling atrocities. Though even twelve-year-olds cannot be regarded simply as so much human plastic whom insurgent leaders can mould as they wish, there is scope here to identify ways in which the organizational ethos of different insurgencies had a discernible effect on the individuals who took part in them.[11]

Relations with Host Societies

All of the literature on insurgent warfare places an enormous emphasis on the relationship between the insurgents and the people among whom they operate. This is most often assessed in terms of whether the insurgents and the 'host population' identify closely with one another, or whether the relationship is essentially one of control; but this is only one aspect of a relationship which needs to be conceived much more broadly. For a start, African insurgencies represent the most powerful and explicit challenge to the state structures established, in most cases, as a result of colonialism; and they provide the clearest available indicators of the extent to which it may be possible to establish any alternative, more closely based in the structures and values of indigenous societies, to the political order which Africa has inherited from its peculiar experience of state formation. This is not to say that insurgencies must necessarily draw from some uncontaminated well of African 'civil society'. The leaders of African insurgencies, like their equivalents elsewhere, are usually the products of 'Western' education, and the models which they seek to implement have been derived (often by way of Marxism-Leninism) from Western industrial society. They have also often had to adapt themselves to the demands of external backers, from the USSR and Cuba, on one hand, to the United States and apartheid South Africa on the other. Insurgent organizations must nonetheless be created on the ground, to an appreciably greater extent than any other form of African political organization, and it is plausible to assume that they must be constructed in large part from the social materials that they find there. Understanding insurgencies is thus to an appreciable extent a job for the political anthropologist.

African societies, in sharp contrast to the generalizing stereotypes which are often applied to them, differ very markedly from one to another, and these differences are equally evident in the insurgencies which they sustain. Insurgencies have none-theless occurred in virtually the full range of rural African social settings: it is not the case that some kinds of African society foster insurgency, while others do not. In northern Ethiopia and Rwanda, effective insurgencies were created in hierarchical societies with long traditions of statehood. In Somalia, they arose in a segmentary

---

[11] See Oliver Furley, 'Child soldiers in Africa', and Paul Richards, 'Rebellion in Liberia and Sierra Leone', both in Furley, ed., *Conflict in Africa* (London: I.B. Tauris, 1995).

pastoralist society with a strong egalitarian ethos. In Southern Sudan, they were based in cultures which had provided generations of anthropologists with case study material on stateless societies. In Liberia and Sierra Leone, they swept through areas in which small chiefdoms had been established in response to the administrative requirements of colonial or Americo-Liberian rule. A similar variety of settings can be found for the insurgencies of Southern Africa. Nor is there any evident correlation between insurgency and levels of 'development', or of incorporation into the global economy. While, at one extreme, rural Liberia has been deeply engaged in production for the world market, through both cash crops and minerals, Tigray in northern Ethiopia was overwhelmingly dominated by subsistence agriculture. Although levels of incorporation, as discussed below, clearly affected the resources available to sustain guerrilla warfare, they had no discernible influence on whether such warfare took place or not.

But even though the structure of indigenous society does not appear to have much bearing on the occurrence of insurgencies, it may nonetheless have a considerable impact on the kinds of insurgency that emerge from different kinds of society. The way in which insurgencies have to fit themselves into their social setting has been attested in numerous cases, most evidently in the way in which religious beliefs (in their broadest sense) are commonly incorporated into the structure and workings of the movement. In Zimbabwe, for example, Lan has shown how ZANU became associated with Shona spirit possession cults.[12] In Liberia, Ellis has suggested close parallels between the apparently mindless violence of the civil war and patterns of spirituality that are also exhibited in the Poro societies.[13] Behrend's chapter in this volume provides an extraordinarily detailed understanding of how Acholi religious beliefs shaped a succession of movements which – uniquely among those examined here – were explicitly conceived in religious terms. In Somalia, clans provide the language in terms of which insurgencies, like other political structures, are articulated.

It may thus be possible to detect in insurgencies the operation of those 'governmentalities' which Bayart has identified as standing at the heart of African political life.[14] Many of the attitudes and assumptions which in one way or another have a bearing on political organizations are deeply embedded in the cultures of particular societies; and these may be expected to have a special impact on insurgent organizations, given the relative weakness in their formation of the organizational models inherited from colonialism. Societal attitudes towards authority and leadership may be particularly important, and these in turn may differ sharply as between African societies with and without traditions of statehood, and equally as between pastoralist and agrarian societies. Differences between insurgent movements may thus be due not simply to the ideologies and organizational models set out by their leaders, and to the determination with which these are implemented, but to the receptivity to them of the host societies. Organization may in essence come, not from the top down, but from the bottom up.

Cultural criteria of this kind are both difficult to pin down and extremely

---

[12] See Lan, *Guns and Rain*.
[13] See Stephen Ellis, 'Liberia 1989–94', *African Affairs*, Vol. 94, No. 375 (1995).
[14] See Jean-François Bayart, *The State in Africa* (London: Longman, 1993).

frustrating to operationalize. Behavioural social scientists have characteristically sought to uncover them by means of attitudinal surveys, of the kind that have been used to suggest differences in commitment to democratic values in European societies.[15] Even if this exercise can be conducted with some degree of plausibility, and there have been very few attempts to conduct such studies of African guerrillas,[16] there are still considerable hazards in applying the results to specific political circumstances. It is all too easy to use supposedly entrenched cultural criteria to 'explain' what turn out to be no more than transient political phenomena. It is nonetheless striking that the most disciplined and effective African insurgencies have arisen in those societies – highland Eritrea, northern Ethiopia, southern Uganda, Rwanda – which have long established traditions of statehood; and that in societies which have lacked such traditions – Somalia, Liberia, northern Chad, Southern Sudan – insurgent movements have been far more liable to fragmentation and indiscipline.

A second perspective from which to view the relationship between insurgencies and host societies is by looking at how insurgency relates to the familiar disjunction between indigenous ethnicities and post-colonial statehood. Often crudely presented in terms of a dichotomy between 'tribalism', on one hand, and 'nation-building' on the other, this may more helpfully be examined in terms of the creation of alternative identities under the intense and often traumatic pressures of insurgent war. Any insurgency, dependent on mobilizing local-level support, almost necessarily must articulate concepts of identity which bind together its supporters and distinguish them from their adversaries. In many instances – Djibouti, Somalia, Liberia, for example – this process has intensified the differentiation between groups within the territorial state, and correspondingly undermined the bases for state reconstruction. In Ethiopia, the TPLF and subsequently the EPRDF explicitly articulated an idea of 'nationality' which formed the basis for a state structure built on the principle of ethnic federalism.[17]

Other insurgencies have sought to construct a 'national' or territorial identity which would provide a legitimizing basis for state construction or reconstruction. The most remarkable of these has been the EPLF in Eritrea. Already noteworthy as one of the most effective insurgencies of all time, maintaining its long resistance against a massive Ethiopian army backed by the Soviet Union, it achieved this feat within an ethnically fragmented territory whose population was about equally divided between Islam and Christianity: its determination *not* to reflect its indigenous social base, but instead to displace it with an ideology of 'Eritreanness', was critical to its success. In Uganda, though the NRA's social and military base lay in the kingdoms of the south, it nonetheless maintained a national identity and programme; it was

[15] See Almond and Verba, *The Civic Culture* (Princeton University Press, 1963); I have attempted a very broad survey of 'culturalist' approaches to third world politics in Clapham, 'The developmental state: governance, comparison and culture in the "third world"', in L. M. Imbeau and R. D. McKinlay, eds, *Comparing Government Activity* (London: Macmillan, 1996).

[16] The interviews carried out by Paul Richards in Sierra Leone are the only systematic attempt to ascertain the values and attitudes of African guerrilla fighters of which I am aware. They appear in *Fighting in the Rain Forest* (James Currey, 1996) and elsewhere.

[17] For a discussion of the alternative TPLF and EPLF approaches to ethnicity and state construction, see C. Clapham, 'Eritrean independence and the collapse of Ethiopian centralism', *Geopolitics and International Boundaries*, Vol. 1 No. 2 (1996).

much harder for the RPF in ethnically divided Rwanda to do the same.

We can revert, finally, to the issue which preoccupies most analysts of the relationship between insurgencies and host societies. To what extent is this a relationship of common interest, in which the population supports the insurgency, and the insurgents represent the aspirations of the population? To what extent, conversely, is it one in which the insurgents control and even exploit that population, in pursuit of interests which local people do not share? Despite the Maoist orthodoxy which emphasizes the identity of the two sides, this is a relationship which may work in very different ways in different cases. On one hand, one of the first priorities of insurgents must be to destroy the linkages between the regime and the host society, by killing or ejecting the regime's representatives in local society. Even if these are identified in insurgent rhetoric as 'stooges' or 'collaborators', they must have at least some links with local societies or they would not be able to do their job. Insurgency, too, imposes intense pressures on host societies, subjecting them both to the exactions of the insurgents (even in cases where these can impose effective discipline on their own members), and to the retaliation of the government. In some cases, as in Eritrea, the demands made on the host society in 'liberated areas' may be intense.

On the other hand, insurgents seek to establish themselves in regions where the regime has little support. Insurgent leaders usually (though not always) have their own origins among the host population, whose interests and identities they claim to represent. All of the better organized insurgencies place an overriding emphasis, in keeping with Maoist principles, on the need to build close relationships with host societies. This is achieved in part, certainly, by 'educating' these societies in order to adapt their perceptions to those of the insurgents, but in part also by impressing the insurgents themselves with the need to adapt to local mores. Meles Zenawi once told me that one of the first criteria applied by the TPLF to new urban recruits was their ability to live and eat like the local peasantry, without evident signs of revulsion.[18] In addition, insurgents have the enormous advantage of living among host populations on a day-to-day basis, whereas government forces are readily identified as alien and external. Measures taken by government forces to control insurgents often alienate host populations: there is nothing that so readily cements a relationship of solidarity between insurgents and host populations as the experience of being bombed together.

Much of the literature on insurgency in Southern Africa – the only region of the continent, as already noted, for which a substantial body of research is yet available – is noteworthy for the emphasis that it places on the control and even exploitation of host populations by insurgents, as against a relationship of solidarity. In cases, such as Kriger's analysis of the *chimurenga* in Zimbabwe, where insurgency was directed against white minority rule, this is particularly striking.[19] A study of Namibia by Leys and Saul likewise draws attention to the authoritarian and unrepresentative structure of the South West Africa People's Organization (SWAPO), though it was unable to establish 'liberated areas' in which its relations with host populations could be assessed; the 'two-edged sword' of the study's title was turned on one hand against

---

[18] Personal interview, January 1995.
[19] Kriger, *Zimbabwe's Guerrilla War.*

the South African occupying forces, on the other against its own internal opponents.[20] Less surprisingly, Minter's study of insurgency in Angola and Mozambique suggests that where an ill-disciplined government army fights an ill-disciplined insurgent movement, there may be very little to choose in terms of popular sympathy between the two of them.[21] This is not to suggest that such studies provide any general guidance on levels of popular support for African insurgencies: different movements differ enormously from one to another, and several of the authors of this volume, such as Young in his discussion of the TPLF, contest the application of such findings to their own cases. It is simply to indicate that levels of solidarity between insurgents and host populations must be open to empirical investigation, and that the mythology of solidarity asserted by the insurgent leadership cannot be taken at face value.

The International Politics of Insurgency

Virtually all insurgencies depend to an appreciable extent on external support, most obviously for access across the border of a neighbouring state which is prepared at least to turn a blind eye to its activities, but also for weapons, money, diplomatic backing and (especially in regions such the Horn which have been deeply affected by famine) even food. Given the small size and permeable borders of most African states, and their high levels of external dependence, the role of outside support is likely to be especially great in African insurgencies. In exactly the same way, African governments need external support in order to keep themselves going, and outside aid to insurgents is balanced by corresponding aid to incumbent regimes. Though insurgent mythologies characteristically play down or deny external involvement, while emphasizing the popular and domestic elements of the struggle, no account of insurgency can ignore consideration of the extent to which it is affected (and sometimes even guided) by international alliances.[22]

These alliances characteristically extend, through connections with neighbouring states whose regimes are hostile to the government of the 'target state' against which the insurgency is directed, to the global alliance structures which dominated international politics during the Cold War era. Alliances in turn indicate the shifting relationships of insurgencies to the international order, from an initial period in which they were almost necessarily associated with the cause of 'national liberation', and hence with the Soviet Union and its allies, through to 'contra' movements fostered by right-wing regimes (notably, in the African case, apartheid South Africa) in order to destabilize Soviet clients such as Angola. With the end of the Cold War, they have come to reflect alternative lines of cleavage, such as those created by militant Islam, or the rivalries between anglophone and francophone communities.

As the scale and scope of insurgencies have increased, simple cross-border support for particular movements has been overlaid by complex regional rivalries and alliances, in which constellations of governments and insurgencies have formed in

---

[20] Leys and Saul, *Namibia's Liberation Struggle.*
[21] Minter, *Apartheid's Contras.*
[22] I have attempted a fuller account of the international politics of African insurgencies in Clapham, *Africa and the International System*, Chapter 9.

opposition to one another. Especially in the Horn and East-Central Africa, the proliferation of insurgencies and the readiness of governments to ignore the once-cherished continental conventions of 'non-intervention' have blurred the distinction between government and insurgency. Regimes which, as in Eritrea, Ethiopia, Uganda and Rwanda, had come to power through insurgency, could scarcely be expected to refrain from supporting movements which they readily equated with their former selves. At the same time, supporters from the era of the liberation struggle, such as Sudan for the EPLF and the TPLF, were transformed into enemies once these movements captured power in Asmara and Addis Ababa, and found much more in common with the Sudanese opposition than with their own former backers. These external links in turn feed back into the structure of the insurgency itself. Though some insurgencies have maintained their own internal coherence and autonomy, others have been affected critically by the role of their outside backers; successive movements in Southern Sudan, for example, have tended to remain united when a single leader could monopolize access to external aid, and to fragment when one could not.

Further important 'externalities' derive from the relationship between insurgency and the international economy. Insurgents, like governments, depend on extracting resources from external trade, a process which in some cases serves to sustain the struggle, and in others provides the main *raison d'être* for the insurgency itself. Political power in Africa from the earliest times has derived in large part from control over long-distance trade, and in insurgent zones the struggle for control has entered a new phase. Insurgents seek to cut off governments from the exportable commodities, overwhelmingly derived from the rural areas, which these have used to sustain their urban lifestyles and supporters, and to divert these commodities to their own use; the linkages established with foreign companies by Charles Taylor in Liberia provide a particularly clear example.[23] Diamonds, ivory and even slaves have been captured in this way, along with the straightforward looting of anything that could be carried away, and a rapidly increasing level of involvement in the international trade in narcotics. But there is also an insurgent import economy, supplied in large part by humanitarian assistance, and by the non-governmental organizations through which the industrial world's relations with Africa are increasingly conducted. At its simplest, famine relief provides a resource which can be used to maintain control by insurgents (and, of course, governments) over local populations. More broadly, NGOs provide the most important vehicle for complex processes of 'asset transfer' that turn warfare into a profitable long-term operation.[24]

A final critical external resource is the control of language. Insurgents gain access to the outside world through their ability to express themselves in ways which that world will respond to, while those who cannot do so remain cut off from external sympathy and assistance. Politicians everywhere use different vocabularies to address different audiences, but the range required of insurgent leaders is particularly great, stretching from the mobilization of indigenous spirituality, on one hand, to the

[23] See William Reno, 'Foreign firms and the financing of Charles Taylor's NPFL', *Liberian Studies Journal*, Vol. 18, No. 2 (1993).
[24] See Mark Duffield, 'The political economy of internal war: asset transfer, complex emergencies, and international aid', in Joanna Macrae and Antony Zwi, eds, *War and Hunger: Rethinking International Responses to Complex Emergencies* (London: Zed Books, 1994).

matching mobilization of Western ideologies of development, democracy or human rights on the other. The capacity to manipulate these different languages provides one of the major advantages which elite politicians enjoy over their less-educated equivalents: Charles Taylor was able to address an international audience in persuasive tones over the BBC World Service, whereas Alice Lakwena, with no such linguistic facility, could readily be dismissed as 'crazy'. Jonas Savimbi in Angola, whose appeal to local ethnic sentiments and traditions included the burning of witches, simultaneously represented himself in the United States as an anti-communist democrat, and in South Africa as an ally of apartheid.[25]

Outcomes of Insurgency

Insurgency also has much to tell us about African statehood and government as a whole. Outside those territories in which it served as a distinctive form of national liberation movement directed against colonial or white minority rule, it has both followed from, and contributed to, deep-seated weaknesses in the structure of statehood inherited in most cases from colonialism. In some cases, as in Sudan, it has challenged the assumption that colonial territorial units, regardless of their internal composition or the artificiality of their boundaries, could be taken as the basis for independent statehood. In Eritrea, paradoxically, it has reconstituted just such a territorial unit which had been incorporated into a neighbouring state. In Liberia and Uganda, insurgency may be regarded as the ultimate political recourse under circumstances in which the existing basis for statehood had been destroyed by internal misgovernment. In Somalia, it may be questioned whether an indigenous basis for statehood existed at all.

But if insurgency can be related readily to the problems of African statehood, its relationship to any viable solutions to those problems is much less clear. In some cases, as for example in Uganda, Ethiopia and Eritrea, it does indeed appear to have provided, if not any ready-made solution, then at any rate a structure of government, a political breathing space and a set of ideas through which a solution could be attempted. In others, it has provided a means of establishing fragile and exploitative forms of rule which owe more to pre-colonial patterns than to any model of 'modern' statehood. Often, it has contributed immeasurably to the level of human suffering to which many parts of Africa have been prey, without offering any evident means through which the basic human needs of peace and welfare could be attained. In looking at insurgency, we are, ultimately, taking one particular slant on the complex processes through which Africa is – for better or worse – adapting to the decay of the post-colonial continental order.

Analysing Insurgencies

The analysis of insurgencies raises questions, finally, about the analysts themselves. All of the work of social scientists is in some degree self-regarding, and reflects not

[25] See Linda Heywood, 'Towards an understanding of modern political ideology in Africa: the case of the Ovimbundu of Angola', *Journal of Modern African Studies*, Vol. 36, No. 1 (1998).

an 'objective' reality but a set of questions and concerns which are deeply affected by the attitudes and values of its authors. The study of African politics has undergone rapid shifts in the sympathies and perceptions of its authors, but even within this field, the study of insurgencies is subject to an exceptional level of personal concern.

For one thing, insurgency itself is readily interpreted in terms of contested conceptions of African statehood. Those for whom 'liberation war' extended only to the struggle against white rule could not accord the same status to insurgencies directed against indigenous African regimes; these were instead to be condemned as a threat to the project of African nationalism, and could often plausibly be regarded as exemplifying the evils both of 'tribalism' and 'balkanization', and of 'neo-colonial' interference in the domestic affairs of the continent. For others, guided by a Maoist assumption that insurgents could only operate when they enjoyed the support of their host populations, any insurgency necessarily took on the tincture of liberation; and it is difficult to find any insurgency which did not attract the attention of at least a number of 'guerrilla groupies', characteristically educated Westerners imbued with romantic leftist attitudes to guerrilla warfare, who accorded it uncritical support. Both the recognition of misgovernment by African regimes sufficient to induce resistance, and the recognition of the levels of repression and brutality often engaged in by guerrillas themselves, called for major changes in perception.

Still more important, from the viewpoint of academic analysis, insurgency is exceptionally difficult to study from a distance. Any attempt to understand it almost necessarily involves close contact with the insurgents themselves, either by accompanying them into the field, or else at least by interviews with participants. In many cases, understanding and explaining behaviour which from an external viewpoint is readily dismissed as either crazy or evil requires both fieldwork skills and a dedicated effort at social imagination. All social action must in some degree be explained through the perceptions of the actors, and in the case of many insurgencies this involves an attempt to construct a framework of rational action under circumstances which appear to defy it. Explanation, of course, does not entail justification, but it does at times require scholars to get uncomfortably close to those whom they seek to understand.

Insurgent warfare, finally, has taken place amidst some of the most appalling scenes of human suffering which modern Africa has had to endure. At times, this suffering could most readily be attributed to the insurgents, at times to the governments against which they were fighting, and very often indeed to both. It is impossible for academic observers to remain indifferent to the human and moral dimensions of the events that they study, and difficult to assert that they should even attempt to do so; and a measure not only of sympathy for the victims of these events, but of tacit support for those who are seen as, at any rate, less guilty than their opponents, is an inescapable part of the exercise. This volume accordingly approaches a variety of often very different insurgent movements from a diversity of standpoints. It makes no claim to an objectivity which is conceptually, and not just in practice, impossible to attain. But it does seek to enhance understanding of a phenomenon or set of phenomena which urgently call for it.

2 DAVID POOL
The Eritrean People's Liberation Front

The Eritrean People's Liberation Front (EPLF) has proved one of the most durable and successful liberation movements in the Third World. It secured *de facto* independence for Eritrea in 1991, even though it had undergone a serious internal crisis shortly after its foundation, was involved in two civil wars with its rival, the Eritrean Liberation Front (ELF), and, with very limited external support, fought an Ethiopian army supported by the Soviet Union and Cuba.

The success of the EPLF can be measured by two criteria. First, it defeated the much larger Ethiopian army; and second, it established a state and broke an African and international consensus supporting the maintenance of post-colonial African territorial boundaries. Although the first could be explained by the disintegration of the Ethiopian regime, the persistence and military successes of the EPLF were major contributors to that disintegration. It maintained an awesome mobilization capacity for a prolonged period, despite periodic military setbacks and human loss on a large scale. Of an estimated population of 2.5 million at independence, 78,000 had been mobilized into the army, even though more than 65,000 fighters had died during the course of the war. Success in the second measure was perhaps in some degree fortuitous, since Eritrean independence occurred at the end of the Cold War, when international norms were in some disarray. Even so, had not the Ethiopian government concurred with Eritrean statehood, sovereignty and international recognition would not have been so readily forthcoming; but the EPLF's political and military strategy of alliances with Ethiopian oppositions, particularly its links to the Tigray People's Liberation Front (TPLF), played a part in shaping the position of the new Ethiopian government.

In analysing the EPLF, this chapter will focus both on its internal character and on the external military and political circumstances of which it took advantage.[1] The most important features of the former were: a cohesive and unified leadership; a rigorous internal discipline; and an organizational and institution-building capacity which enabled it to penetrate and incorporate core components of Eritrean society. In addition, the EPLF developed a seemingly contradictory combination of

[1] Much of this analysis is based on research and interviews carried out from the late 1970s onwards.

ideology and pragmatism which enabled it to utilize external developments generated by forces beyond its control. It proved highly adaptable to changing domestic and international contexts, and shifted from its original revolutionary ideological position, stressing class struggle and anti-imperialism, to a pragmatic quasi-liberalism, and from guerrilla to conventional war, and also managed the absorption of large numbers of recruits.

Whereas many liberation fronts are nurtured in a favourable environment, neither the social nor the political context from which the EPLF sprang were conducive to the creation of the most successful liberation front to fight on African soil. It seems contradictory that such a disciplined and unified movement could emerge from a society which was highly fragmented, and from a nationalist history marked by internecine conflict. Yet the EPLF's obsession with unity of nation and front emerged through a dialectical relationship with this social fragmentation and political division. It was through its political education programme, a central element of the Front's activities, that it reshaped Eritrean history.[2] We shall examine how the EPLF leadership represented political history and Eritrean society before the liberation struggle, socialized members into their *weltanschauung*, and reacted against the political and military organization of the rival ELF. All were formative of the ideology and organization of the Front. This focus provides a brief account of Eritrean society and an abridged narrative of contemporary Eritrean history.

Political Education, History and Nationalism: the EPLF Reshapes the Past

Eritrea is a heterogeneous society and, in the past, the politicization of its human diversity has been a factor in dividing Eritreans and producing a fragmented nationalist movement. The EPLF leadership deliberately shaped the Front on the basis of their conception of the causes of past nationalist failures. Central to this approach was the programme of political education which all Front members underwent during their compulsory six-month training period. It socialized fighters (as well as secret cell members, peasants, workers and Eritreans abroad) into the organization, and moulded their consciousness of society and history. Political education, supported by extensive literacy programmes, was an essential part of the EPLF strategy of penetrating and establishing organizational linkages between the Front and broader society.

There is a veiled assumption in EPLF literature that the overwhelming majority of Eritreans were nationalists and supported national independence. That Eritrea did not achieve it was then explained by a combination of external influence (British occupation, Ethiopian colonialism and American imperialism) and internal treason (Eritrean feudalists and feudo-capitalists pursuing their class interests as agents of these external forces). While explanations based on class and the nature of imperialism were part of the language of African revolutionaries and nationalists of the 1960s and 1970s, in the Eritrean case they served the purpose of unifying Eritreans and

---

[2] See Dan Connell, *Against All Odds: a Chronicle of the Eritrean Revolution* (Trenton, NJ: Red Sea Press, 1993) for a summary of the contents of General Political Education for Fighters.

portraying nationalism as having been betrayed by a small minority which duped and oppressed the masses. This approach to the past occluded social and political fragmentation based on ethnicity and sectarianism, both of which had bedevilled Eritrean nationalist movements. Ironically, divisions between Muslims and Christians, their different relations to the Christian character of the Ethiopian imperial order, and the different socio-economic levels of the regions they inhabited, had been factors which precipitated the armed struggle and initially confounded it.

Eritrea is divided between Orthodox Coptic Christians and Sunni Muslims. The former inhabit the densely populated central highlands; some are village peasants, while the rest form the bulk of the urban population. Christians have had greater access to education and modern sector employment. Highland Christians speak Tigrinya, a language they share with the population of the northern Ethiopian province of Tigray, as they share Orthodox Christianity with the Christians of Ethiopia. In addition, the highland provinces have been under the rule of historic Ethiopian empires.

The Muslim communities live in an arc around the central highlands (the western lowlands, the northern highlands, and the Red Sea coastal plain), and combine settled cultivation, pastoralism and agro-pastoralism. They speak a range of languages. Tigre is the most common, but Tigre-speakers are divided between a number of tribes and clans. These include sections of the Bani Amir of the western lowlands, the Habab of the northern highlands, and tribes of the north-eastern coastal plain and the escarpment between Asmara and Massawa. Muslims are also divided into distinct ethno-linguistic groups. In addition to the Tigre, there are the Cushitic Sahho, the Nilotic Nara, the Afar of the Dankalia Red Sea coast, and half of the Bileyn community of Keren and its surroundings. Many of the Muslim tribes trace their genealogical descent to a pious ancestor from Arabia.

Arabic is both a *lingua franca* and a written language for many Muslims, particularly the educated, and is spoken widely in the Massawa area. It has also been taken up by refugees, most of whom were Muslim, who fled to Sudan and other Arab states during the course of the liberation struggle. Many Eritrean Muslims would be somewhat familiar with Arabic as the language of the Koran, through attending a *khalwa*, an Islamic primary/pre-primary school. Paralleling the links between Orthodox Christians and Ethiopian empires, many of the areas inhabited by Muslims have been subject to a variety of Islamic empires: the Sudanic Funj, the Ottoman Empire, and its Egyptian successor. Religion and geographical contiguity do not provide an exact fit. In the highlands, the Muslim Jiberti community also speak Tigrinya; in Senheit, half of the Bileyn speakers are Christian, as are one branch of the Tigre-speaking Mensa.

The EPLF stressed nationalities rather than religious communities as the major source of cultural diversity, in reaction to the fragmented imperial history of Eritrea and as a deliberate instrument of nation-building. This approach disconnected religion from society and politics, Christian highlanders from the Christian Ethiopian empire, and Muslims from the neighbouring Arab Islamic world and its culture. The focus on nationalities, defined by language, incorporated both Muslim and Christian into the Tigrinya and Bileyn nationalities, and small groups of Christians into the Tigre. The stress on nationality languages also delinked the Arabic language from Islam.

Over and above integrating diverse peoples into a common sense of nation, the EPLF's classification of Eritrean communities on the basis of nationalities was also a reaction against the way in which the latter related to politics, particularly under the British Military Administration (BMA) of 1941–52. During this period the fate of Eritrea was decided. The former Italian colony (1889–1941), rather than following the path of decolonization to independent statehood, was federated with Ethiopia in 1952 and annexed in 1962, when it simply became a province of Ethiopia. This course was determined partly by Great Power interests and partly by the polarization of Eritrean politics. The name of the movement which backed independence during the BMA speaks volumes about its orientation and support: the Muslim League. The movement which favoured association with Ethiopia was the Unionist Party, the overwhelming support for which came from Christian highlanders. Given that the Unionists were successful in achieving their goals, Eritrean Christians became identified as the community which lost Eritrea its independence, and the Muslim community with nationalism and independence. These identifications were oversimplifications, as some Muslim chiefs supported union and some Christian political leaders supported independence. They nonetheless bore sufficient resemblance to reality to shape public opinion and political consciousness, even though Ethiopian subversion of all elements of Eritrean autonomy during the federal period drew Christians into the nationalist opposition, notably through the secular Eritrean Liberation Movement which had a Christian and Muslim membership.

This emphasis on early Eritrean history and Eritrean society, and EPLF versions of it, is intended to illuminate the basis on which the EPLF socialized its recruits into an organization which aimed to negate political divisions which were partly rooted in religious communalism. The stress on nationalities allowed the Front to elevate national political unity and diversity based solely on culture, and to integrate Tigrinya-speaking Christians as one of the diverse cultures of Eritrea like the Tigre.

The ELF and the Origins of the EPLF[3]

Nationalist disunity, however, continued after the beginnings of the armed struggle, launched by the ELF in 1961. Its leadership, the original location of the armed struggle, the social character of the early fighters, and the military organization of the ELF, were all formative influences on the founders of the EPLF, albeit as a negative reaction against their experience in the ELF.

The ELF was formed through the coalescing of leaders of the independence movement of the BMA period, who went into exile in Cairo during the federation, with Eritrean students there and a small group of nationalists in Eritrea. Communally based patron-client ties, bolstered by the external leadership's control over finance and supplies, alienated many of the fighters who were later to form the EPLF. The outbreak of armed resistance began in western Eritrea, homeland of the Bani Amir, an area of pastoralism and agro-pastoralism and one of the least

---

[3] The best published account in English is John Markakis, *National and Class Conflict in the Horn of Africa* (Cambridge: Cambridge University Press, 1987).

developed parts of Eritrea, with a society formed of tribal sections and clans.[4] Agordat, the main town, was little more than a big village. The dominant culture was Islamic: *Shari'a* (Islamic law) was the basis of tribal customary law and education took place in the Islamic *khalwas* and was provided by spiritual leaders, many of whom followed or had links to the Khatmiyya Sufi order, which had lodges and mosques across most of Muslim Eritrea and provided links to the wider Muslim world.

The very first fighters were a band of seven led by Idris Muhammad Awate. The initial insurrection brought in his kinsmen and the style of fighting resembled the hit-and-run forays of feuding pastoralists and banditry traditional in the area. The next batch of recruits came from Eritrean nationalists serving in the Sudanese army and police, and from the Eritrean police. All were Muslim. As the numbers of ELF fighters expanded, so the external leadership created a more developed military organization.

In imitation of the Algerian Front de Libération Nationale (FLN), the ELF was organized into zones, most of which recruited from particular groups of the indigenous population and reproduced within some of the zones long-standing ethnic, tribal and religious animosities, many of which derived from tensions over grazing land. Although the zonal system enabled the ELF to expand from the west to other parts of Eritrea, its many critics pointed to its divisive consequences. For example, the first zone was largely agro-pastoralist Bani Amir, traditionally in conflict with the settled Kunama and the highland zone dominated by Sahho, some of whose clans in turn were in conflict with the settled Christian farmers of eastern Akalai Guzai. The few Christians who did join had to eat separately from Muslims, as both followed religiously sanctioned ritual slaughter. As Christian highlander numbers expanded, a separate highland zone was established, the effect of which was to perpetuate the sense of religio-regional difference.

Sources of external support also deepened internal problems, and helped to bring about the later EPLF's insistence on the necessity of self-reliance. From its foundation, the ELF external leadership sought funding, military supplies and training for fighters from the Muslim Arab world, portraying the struggle in any light which would facilitate assistance. Osman Salih Sabbe was particularly adept at gaining funding from Arab states. He portrayed the struggle as linked to the Arab cause and despatched batches of new fighters for military training in Syria and Iraq.

The zonal system raised the spectre of Eritrean disunity, reinforced the patronage powers of external leaders over particular zones, and undermined the basic rationale of any armed struggle: military victories. The lack of military coordination between zones aided the Ethiopian army's offensives against the ELF, allowing the former to attack the zones separately. In addition, the Ethiopian government was able to recruit Christian Eritreans to fight against the ELF, as its leadership was based in and drew support from Arab states, and the bulk of its fighters were Muslim.

---

[4] This author's earlier analysis, contrasting the agro-pastoralist social base and context of the ELF with the peasant base of the EPLF, provided too static a formulation. See D. Pool. 'Revolutionary crisis and revolutionary vanguard: the Eritrean People's Liberation Front', *Review of African Political Economy*, 19 (1980). While maintaining the general validity of this analysis, a forthcoming full-length study will stress the symbiotic relationship between highland peasant socio-economic structures and EPLF organizational and mobilizational structures.

With ELF military setbacks viewed as a function of the zonal organization, and external links as subverting the development of national unity, dissatisfaction with the movement grew, and demands for the reform of its political and military structure escalated. These were encapsulated in the slogans: 'unity of the fighters' and 'leadership in the field'. Eventually, several dissident factions split from the ELF, two of which became the core of the EPLF. The first, and initially the largest, was a group, mainly Muslim but including some Christians, which fled to Sudan, were transported to South Yemen by Sabbe, crossed the Red Sea to Dankalia and linked up with other dissidents there. In June 1970, in Dankalia, these two groups began discussing unity, after which one group decided to march to Sahel. A further meeting in November 1971 resulted in the decision to unite, agreement on a common programme, and the election of a leadership. This east-coast group, many of whom came from the Massawa and Harqiqo area, renamed themselves the Eritrean Popular Liberation Forces (PLF). They received arms supplies from across the Red Sea through Sabbe. The connection to Sabbe, who was in dispute with other members of the external leadership and required a foothold in Eritrea, was crucial for the survival of the dissidents. Although the EPLF cut ties to Sabbe in 1975, the initial retention of links set a precedent for future pragmatism.

The second was a group of exclusively Christian highland Tigrinyans, who took refuge in the Ala plain in Akalai Guzai Province after the massacre of new Christian recruits by an ELF security commander. This group was particularly keen, however, to disavow any sectarian character. In *Our Struggle and its Goals*,[5] probably written by the future head of independent Eritrea, Issayas Afeworki, and distributed widely amongst Eritreans, the major arguments were that the ELF based its struggle on Islam and Arabism and lacked a clear revolutionary line, and that the leadership were religious fanatics who viewed highlanders in religious terms and massacred many of them. The Ala group presented their separation thus:

> Should one opt to face butchery because one was born a Christian or should one surrender to the enemy? Both are abominable ... both mean death. To make neither choice is tantamount to sitting on the edge of a sharp blade. We are the fighters who chose to sit on the edge of the sharp blade.... We are freedom fighters not preachers of the gospel.

Unifying the two groups was a protracted process, lasting from 1970 to 1972.[6] Although establishing a unified leadership elected from the fighters was not so difficult, integrating fighters and creating a joint administration for a unified military force was not so easy. Not the least of the problems was that the guerrillas originating from the east coast spoke Tigre and Arabic, while the Ala group, and subsequent highlander cohorts in it, spoke Tigrinya. In October 1972, the PLF and the Ala group united, formed a joint programme of action, and elected a leadership of 57 (21 from PLF, 25 from the Ala and 11 from Obel, a largely Bani Amir western group which subsequently opted out) and an administrative committee of seven. The latter began formalizing internal administrative structures, and its members headed newly established departments like Information and Intelligence, and Finance

    [5] Translated text in *Liberation*, published by Eritreans for Liberation in North America (Boston, March 1973).
    [6] See al-Amin Muhammad Said, *al-Thawra al-Iritiriya* [The Eritrean Revolution] (Asmara, 1992, in Arabic). The author was one of the founders of the PLF.

and Supply. The integration of the fighters into a single fighting force was initiated in September 1973.

The Civil War and Internal Crisis

The outbreak of the civil war between the ELF and the PLF in 1972, following the refusal of the ELF to accept the split, and an internal crisis within the new Front, hastened the establishment of a unified army and a centralized political leadership. The internal crisis took place simultaneously with the unification process and the civil war between the PLF and the ELF, and posed a serious threat to the military and political capacity of the new unified front *vis-à-vis* both the Ethiopian army and the ELF.

The ELF initially attacked the Obel group and the PLF. Because the Ala group were determined not to rejoin the ELF, their fate was linked to the outcome of the conflict between the ELF and the PLF, and they were inevitably drawn into the fighting alongside their fellow dissidents.

During the unification process, a dissident group emerged. In Tigrinya, it was named the *manqa*.[7] It began in the Ala group and its criticisms had some influence on PLF fighters. It originated with the influx of secondary school and university students from Asmara and Addis Ababa. They brought with them an anti-authoritarian, revolutionary confidence that challenged the leadership and the emerging political structure. Root and branch criticisms were made in a relatively public way among the fighters. They ranged from poor organization to military mistakes and the lack of democracy. One of the main targets of the criticism was Issayas Afeworki. The challenge to the new leadership was so broadly based that it caused a major retrenchment of the new Front's political and military activities: it weakened it against both the rival ELF and the Ethiopian army, as all the front-line forces left their positions and arrived in the Sahel base area in January 1974. This was a crisis on a massive scale for the new Front, and appeared to replicate the pattern of dissent which had emerged within the ELF in the late 1960s.

The *manqa* crisis was resolved through the execution of some of the dissident leaders and recantation through public self-criticism by others. This had several consequences for the development of the EPLF. It gave a much greater impetus for the establishment of a highly centralized organization and a stress on ideological conformity to the political line. The punishment for internal dissent was stern. It consolidated the joint leadership of the two forces and provided a high degree of solidarity between them, particularly as the defeat of the Ala-based *manqa* was, in part, a function of the intervention of the PLF fighters in the adjudication over the opposition criticisms. As *Our Struggle* emphasized, a clear political line was necessary for the military struggle. Debating fine points of ideology was a luxury for a guerrilla army bent on national liberation. Both the unfocused organization of the ELF and the *manqa* crisis combined to reinforce the highly centralized character of the Front. Discussion and debate, with some exceptions like the *manqa* criticisms and the refusal of the leadership to condemn Soviet support for Ethiopia, were initiated by

[7] *The Destructive Movement of 1973* (EPLF, undated, in Tigrinya).

the leadership; but once decisions were made by the latter, debate amongst the fighters ceased.

The Military Context

Although stress will be laid on ideology, organization and leadership, emphasis must also be given to the development of the EPLF's military strategy and capacity. We have stressed the way in which the negative reaction to the organization and leadership of the ELF was formative of the EPLF. Most analysts of the EPLF marginalize the overriding military focus of the leadership, which successfully adapted elements of the Maoist and Vietnamese models of protracted liberation struggle, and freely borrowed from Maoist ideology and Chinese communist practices.

From its beginning, the EPLF had established base areas in Sahel, concentrated its forces there to protect them against the ELF, and used them as a launching pad for deeper forays against the Ethiopian army. Although small mobile guerrilla units were used, the concentration of forces became a central principle of EPLF military strategy, and a means of liberating the land step by step. Developments like the Ethiopian revolution, the response of the Ethiopian government to the Fronts' attacks on Asmara, the liberation of the towns in 1977–8, and the subsequent Ethiopian reoccupation provided opportunities for the EPLF, led to a considerable increase in personnel, and enhanced its military capacities.

Although armed bands from both Fronts roamed across most of Eritrea, there were core areas where one or other of the Fronts was stronger. The resolution of the internal crisis placed the PLF in a stronger position to confront the ELF and return in numbers to the highlands, where the concentrated settled peasant population provided a rich sea for guerrilla bands and a source of recruits and supplies. The major tracks were from the northern Sahel, where the base area was established, along the eastern escarpment and Red Sea coast, and into Hamasein Province, to the northern, eastern and southern surrounds of Asmara. Until the demise of the ELF in the late 1970s, these areas were EPLF strongholds and facilitated its 'eastern strategy'. The latter involved cutting Asmara from Massawa, a strategy which failed in 1978 but was ultimately successful in 1990. The ELF was predominant in the west and southern Serai. Although the town and surrounds of Keren, the urban market centre of Senheit Province, retained traditional sympathies for the ELF, the EPLF, nevertheless, had a presence in eastern Senheit.

Military successes brought an improved quality and great quantity of arms into the military stores of the front. Ammunition, military transport and equipment, tanks and artillery facilitated the shift to mobile and subsequently fixed positional warfare. Together with the strategy of concentrating forces and defending the base areas, it enabled the EPLF to defend itself in Sahel against an Ethiopian army refurbished by the Soviet Union during 1977–8 and, in the 1980s, to push it back and go on the offensive. The scale of arms and equipment captured was an important factor in the EPLF's ability to maintain its military autonomy from external powers, and sustain a policy of self-reliance. Although it is probable that the EPLF did have access to weapon supplies other than those captured, there is little information about their sources.[8]

The 1974 Ethiopian revolution gave a great boost to both Fronts, but particularly to the EPLF. The weakening of the central empire, factional struggles both within and between military and civilian revolutionary groups, and the 1977 Somali invasion of the Ogaden provided opportunities which the Fronts took. The ending of the civil war, under popular pressure, gave an additional impetus. Between December 1974 and January 1975 both Fronts launched attacks in Asmara and the violent Ethiopian response drove thousands to them. Growth in numbers and the capture of Ethiopian weapons enabled the Fronts to take many towns in 1977 and, as a consequence of the siege of Asmara, to step up activities in highland villages.

The defeat of the Somali forces enabled the Ethiopian government, with power consolidated under Mengistu, to turn to the North. The ELF, strong along the Eritrean–Ethiopian border in western Eritrea and southern Serai, was hit badly and never fully recovered. The EPLF managed a strategic retreat and pulled with it many inhabitants of the captured cities of Decamhare, the Massawa suburbs and Keren and, particularly important, the youth of the highland villages. In 1975 and 1978, the EPLF's 'frame of steel'[9] helped swell the numbers of fighters as it left the briefly liberated areas.

The EPLF again concentrated its forces in the Sahel base area and held on to the town of Naqfa, despite a series of heavy offensives by the Ethiopian army, the most important of which was the Red Star Campaign of 1982. The damage done to the ELF by the Ethiopian forces was compounded by a renewal of civil war between the Fronts, resulting in the ELF being pushed across the Sudan border. The demise of the ELF allowed the EPLF to move into western Eritrea and succeed to the agricultural estates there, the production from which became a source of supply.

By 1975 the EPLF had established both infrastructure and organization to absorb this rapid growth and to integrate new recruits. By the early 1980s, the EPLF was the only effective force fighting the Ethiopians, and its steadfast defence of its base area provided an alternative to refugee flight. In 1988, the EPLF broke out of Naqfa in a decisive battle at Afabet, and captured large amounts of armour and heavy artillery. In 1989–90, it attacked down the eastern side of the country and captured the key port of Massawa. This victory, which brought a dreadful aerial bombardment of the town, put Ethiopian forces under siege in central Eritrea, after which they could only be supplied by air. The expansion of forces into the southern highlands put the towns of Decamhare, Asmara and Keren under siege. In 1991, the EPLF broke through on the southern front and entered Asmara, as the Ethiopian army fled toward the west. Shortly afterwards the Ethiopian Peoples' Revolutionary Democratic Front (EPRDF) entered Addis Ababa, and were assisted by EPLF forces in the final battle to overthrow the Mengistu regime and take power.

[8] At times, Egypt and China have been mentioned, but evidence about the relative amount is unavailable. The consolidation of the rule of Mengistu Haile-Mariam and Soviet support for the regime opened the door to pro-Western, anti-Soviet regional forces like Egypt and anti-Soviet states like China.

[9] See note 11.

The Leadership

The nature of the leadership of the EPLF has been a central element in the movement's longevity. At its core were the founders and leaders of the PLF and the Ala group, although different waves of recruits brought in new blood, particularly after the expansion of the Central Committee at the 1987 Congress. There was a relatively permanent group in top military and administrative positions, drawn from those who founded the EPLF and those who joined after the split, but before the Ethiopian revolution. Two key individuals were Issayas Afeworki of the Ala group and Ramadan Muhammad Nur of the PLF. Both had been trained in China and had been political commissars in the zones.

At the apex of the system was the Political Bureau elected by the Central Committee, which was elected by members of the First Congress in 1977.[10] Rules for the election of the leadership at the latter were slanted in favour of veteran fighters. Founders of the PLF elected to the Political Bureau were Ramadan Muhammad Nur, the Secretary-General, Ibrahim Afa, Ali Sayyid and Mahmoud 'Sharifo'; from the Ala group came Issayas Afeworki, Haile Woldetensae and Mesfin Hagos. In addition, there were those who came later, but before the mass influx occasioned by the Ethiopian revolution, like Petros Solomon and Sibhat Efraim. An index of the coherence and solidarity of the leadership is that many of these were in key positions at liberation.

Most of these came from urban areas (Massawa, Asmara, Mendefera and small towns like Harqiqo), from lower or middle-class backgrounds, and had left university or secondary school to join the Front. Many had links to networks of classmates at secondary school and university. The top leadership remained mixed Muslim and Christian, with a core from the Highland Tigrinya speakers and the Samhar Red Sea coast, mixed Afar and Tigre, reflecting the composition of the early fighters. Absent from the leadership were representatives of the groups associated with the early fighters of the ELF – Tigre Muslims of the west, Bani Amir and Marya, and the Bileyn – although members of these nationalities were incorporated into an expanded Central Committee at the Second Congress in 1987.

Organization

A strict democratic centralism was the core organizing principle of the Front. The leaders elected at the unification meeting between the Ala and PLF groups remained more or less intact until the First Congress of the EPLF in 1977. The two key figures in the unification process were Issayas Afeworki and Ramadan Muhammad Nur, together with fighters trained in China, Cuba and Syria. Reinforcing democratic centralism and the power of the leadership were three organizational structures within the Front: a clandestine party, the political cadres and the security organization. Members of all three were selected by the leadership and allocated

---

[10] At the Congress, the Eritrean People's Liberation Forces were renamed as the Eritrean People's Liberation Front.

positions in the Front by the leadership. The extent to which there was an exact overlapping membership between the three is unclear. That the leadership controlled recruitment and activities is beyond question.

The secret party within the EPLF, the Eritrean People's Liberation Party, was recruited from 'the most active and ideologically sound members'. It provided a further structural link between the leadership and Front members until its abolition. Its founding members were Ramadan Muhamad Nur and Issayas Afeworki, who was chairman of the party. At its core were those who had split from the ELF and joined before 1974, that is, before the Ethiopian revolution. This core then recruited amongst members who joined after 1975. Although little is known of its character and organization, it functioned along the lines of South Asian communist parties within national fronts, combining propaganda about the 'mass line' with security work and reporting to the party leadership. It seems likely that policy issues decided by the leadership were transmitted to members of the broader Front by the party members, and that elections to the Front congresses and nominations for central committee membership and the agendas of 1977 and 1987 were influenced by this party.

The graduates of the cadre school, recruits to which were chosen by the leadership, took a range of positions within the Front. Not all cadres became party members. Some were selected from the cadre school or sent to it after recruitment into the party. Selection for the cadre school was considered by many to be a political honour. In general, it was a promotion within the Front and, for clandestine cell members, a recognition of the dangers they faced. Literacy, commitment and hard work were criteria for selection. The cadre school programme was essentially an advanced form of political education and training in organizational techniques. After graduation, cadres became commissars within military units, political education officers within the growing popular organizations, organizers of clandestine cells in occupied areas, and organizers of Eritrean refugee communities.

The third organization within the Front was the internal security: *halewa sawra* (defence of the revolution). Even less information has surfaced about this organization than the others. Although its major function was to combat Ethiopian infiltration and the ELF, it combined functions of military police overseeing internal discipline with intelligence, and was a feared organization within the Front. Members were recruited from units to the *ma'askar hibu'an* (camp of the ghosts), where they had special military training. Petros Solomon was the Political Bureau member responsible.

These internal organizations were paralleled by a skein of outward-reaching ones: mass organizations of women, students and workers both within Eritrea and abroad; secret cells in villages and towns; people's militias in the villages; and people's assemblies in the liberated areas. The incorporation of Eritreans into these was again based on the compulsory political education programme.

Ideology: from Political Line to Practice

A major influence of Maoist thinking was the linking of social transformation to military liberation. Stress was laid on 'learning from the people' and 'serving, organizing and arming the masses'. Although such language might seem sloganistic, the EPLF cadres put these catchphrases into sophisticated practice when establishing Front institutions at the village level. During the short period of running the towns liberated in 1977, it followed similar practices. In this process of organizing 'the masses', the EPLF took on governmental characteristics.

In the same way that the leadership set the line on nationalities, so it did on the social formation of Eritrea, making this a central component of political education. While workers remained undifferentiated, the analysis of the peasantry was based on the Maoist categories of poor, middle and rich. Political cadres divided village society using these criteria. In practical terms, this involved providing services to the most oppressed: poor and middle peasants. It established a reciprocal process: in order to move freely through the rural areas, the population of the latter were necessary for support of the armed bands, and as a source of recruits, sustenance for armed guerrillas and intelligence.

The strategy was built on armed propaganda squads going into villages, initiating discussions, with the younger generation in particular, organizing the villagers into cells and providing basic services. Village social structure would be studied and information collated using social survey techniques. The data was used as a pre-liminary to organizing village assemblies and introducing land reform. Separate organizations were established for each stratum. Representation in village institutions was based on relative proportions of those strata which, in most villages, gave poor and middle peasants a majority voice, and simultaneously connected that majority to the EPLF cadres. The longer the EPLF had a presence in a particular village or area, the deeper the reforms. Peasant militias were established and became support units for regular fighters. The EPLF drew on traditional village institutional forms like the *baito*, the village committee, but substantially changed the dominance of village social groups within them. And although the goal was to establish the autonomous functioning of village institutions along EPLF lines, EPLF cadres remained a kind of court of appeal for disputes which could not be resolved by village institutions and for disputes between villages. The establishment of this overarching authority reinforced the governmental character of EPLF, already partially developed through the provision of rudimentary veterinary and medical services. Eritrean peasant society, riddled with disputes deriving from land scarcity, was highly amenable to the EPLF's intervention. In pastoralist areas too, the EPLF took on the characteristics of 'stateness'. In the rear base area in the 1970s, the local population of pastoralists and agro-pastoralists received both medical and basic veterinary services from armed guerrillas who roamed the countryside. In Sahel, the Ethiopian state played hardly any role at all in the provision of services. In an interview with one nomadic clan leader in 1977, the respondent referred to the EPLF as the *hukuma* (Arabic for government).

Despite this clear programme, the EPLF cadres were relatively cautious in intro-ducing reforms of traditional village social and economic structures, and pragmatic in the timing of their introduction. This was especially true in Muslim areas, where Islamic law, protective of property rights, predominated. They were somewhat less cautious in parts of Muslim Sahel where the EPLF had a long presence. The emphasis on land reform, feudalism and feudo-bourgeois society, although strange language to peasant ears, had more relevance to peasants or ex-peasant workers than it did to the agro-pastoralists of the west where, until the late 1970s, the EPLF had only a limited presence. The focus on the land question aligned the EPLF with the most homogeneous sector of Eritrean society, the concentrated highland peasantry, and with the majority within that. The EPLF's socio-economic programme, be it land reform or the provision of social services, deepened its ties to the rural population and established reciprocal bonds between this population and the Front. By 1975, with the escalation of fighting between the Fronts and the Ethiopians, the EPLF had established an alternative government and, in the base areas, a liberated sanctuary for those fleeing from Ethiopian atrocities. The organizational incorporation of both rural and urban Eritreans was akin to the Chinese practice of tying the population to a 'frame of steel'; when the frame moved, so did the people.[11]

In the towns liberated in 1977 – Naqfa and Afabet in Sahel, Keren in Senheit and Decamhare in the Highlands – the EPLF established a similar system of People's Assemblies (PA), in zones based on social classes and mass organizations of women and youth. Under the guidance of the Mass Administration, these assemblies dealt with judicial cases, collective work, some security issues, checked on price controls and collected taxes. In a town like Decamhare, where EPLF secret cells had been established, the transition to authority was relatively easy, an index of the success of EPLF's pre-liberation clandestine political work. Of the 72-member PA, nine members had attended the EPLF cadre school. Indicative of the 'frame of steel' and the EPLF's connection to urban strata, 39 members of the PA went with it when the EPLF retreated before the 1978 Ethiopian offensive, and joined the Eritrean People's Liberation Army (EPLA).[12]

The author observed similar processes in 1977 in Keren, whose population was considered more sympathetic to the ELF. PAs were set up, collective work was introduced and political education and literacy classes organized. The PA introduced price controls, reduced the highest salaries and raised the lowest wages, and reduced rents for houses nationalized by the Ethiopian government. Symbolic of stateness was the introduction of 'import and export controls' between Keren and Asmara. While this kind of radical intervention in social and economic affairs was unwelcome to trading and merchant circles, the EPLF balanced this by providing transport for merchants to import from Sudan.

The clandestine infrastructure of the EPLF was more important in the highlands than elsewhere. This area had supported the Unionist Party, and provided recruits for the Eritrean commandos. Whether under the Empire or the People's Socialist Republic, it was essential for Ethiopian governments to hold on to it at minimum. The major garrison centres were at Asmara, Decamhare and also at Keren, the bridge from the highlands to the north and the west. Secret cells in Asmara and other highland towns were a recruiting ground for *fidayin* (urban guerrillas), sources of intelligence about the enemy, and support for EPLF urban raids to capture

[11] T. Kataoka, *Resistance and Revolution in North China* (Berkeley: UCLA Press, 1974), cited in K. Hartford, 'Repression and communist success' in K. Hartford and S. Goldstein, *Single Sparks: China's Rural Revolutions* (New York: M. E. Sharpe, 1989).

[12] Research and Information Centre for Eritrea, *Creating a Popular, Economic, Political and Military Base* (Sahel, Eritrea, 1982).

supplies and equipment required in the base area. After the resolution of the *manqa* crisis and the end of the civil war, EPLF highland cadres used the villages around Asmara to coordinate the activities of the secret cells in schools, government offices and factories. According to one ELF underground Asmara leader, by the mid-1970s the EPLF's recruitment of the educated and skilled far surpassed that of the ELF.[13] The EPLF could draw on the expertise and skills of these cadres when necessary to develop the functions of the base areas and train others.

The development of the infrastructure of the Front was also a key part of the success of the EPLF. In the valleys of mountainous Sahel Province, the EPLF built workshops, repair shops, schools, a hospital and a pharmacy. It was here that new recruits underwent their six-month military training and political education. In the six months, fighters from disparate social backgrounds were moulded into a cohesive and disciplined force with a strong corporate identity. All personal property was handed over to the stores. New recruits were assigned to a team which shared domestic tasks. At the lowest level, discipline was enforced through regular sessions of criticism and self-criticism. Warnings were given to those who failed in their tasks, or were recalcitrant in performing their duties. Hard labour followed for continued indiscipline after reports from the Prison and Investigation Department were passed to the leadership. At the same time, considerable care was taken over wounded and disabled fighters, the children and orphans of fighters and displaced people. Although in its early days the socialization of fighters cut ties between them and their families and clans, after 1977 fighters were permitted to marry and there emerged 'EPLF families' married under EPLF marriage laws, and children born in the base areas, the 'Sahel babies'. From its origins in the early 1970s, the EPLF laid great stress on gender issues and equality, and recruited considerable numbers of women: 30 per cent of Front members and 13 per cent of frontline fighters.

Developments in the mid-1970s brought changes in numbers, patterns of recruitment and the quality of arms. From the mid-1970s onward, the major area of recruitment into the EPLF was the highlands. Although there are no figures on the origins of recruits, one indicator is language use. By the mid-1970s it would seem that military training was given in Tigrinya, marking a shift from the earlier use of Arabic.

The External Context

Although the EPLF received limited external support, it was placed relatively favourably to gain access to supplies through neighbouring Sudan and from the Red Sea to its 1,000 kilometre coastline. Initially, the EPLF received support from across the Red Sea through the People's Democratic Republic of Yemen (PDRY); by the 1980s, it had even developed a small fleet of its own. Sudanese–Ethiopian conflicts, during both the Haile-Selassie and Mengistu governments, resulted in relatively open access for the Fronts in Sudan. Ethiopian support for Southern Sudanese dissident movements was the main motive for the Sudanese government's provision of facilities. The refugee communities in Eastern Sudan were recruiting grounds for

[13] Interview: Zemheret Yohannes, Asmara, Spring 1993.

fighters, and supplies were imported through Port Sudan and trucked to the base area in Sahel. Despite occasional tensions and restrictions, the Sudanese border crossings were never closed. Eritrea's location and geography, the EPLF's emphasis on self-reliance, and its extensive base infrastructure, freed it from significant dependence on a host government.

Nor was it dependent on a superpower. The massive supply of Soviet arms to Ethiopia from the late 1970s, however, had the ironic consequence of making the Soviet Union a major military supplier of the EPLF through its capture of Ethiopian arms and equipment. In another ironic twist, the United States became more markedly opposed to the Mengistu regime and more sympathetic to the Eritrean cause, although without favouring secession. Indicative of EPLF pragmatism, the programmatic shift from Marxist-Leninist-Maoist policies in favour of democracy, pluralism and the market at its 1987 congress facilitated sympathetic US mediation.

In place of strong regional and international backing, the EPLF built up a considerable organizational network of support amongst Eritreans abroad, particularly in Europe and the United States. Not only did these provide funding from their own income, no matter how small, but activists among them were catalysts for mobilizing sympathetic European and American left and liberal political groupings. Overseeing these Eritrean organizations abroad were EPLF offices which functioned as quasi-diplomatic missions, many of which skilfully developed webs of contacts amongst political parties, trade unions and the media.

In addition, the Eritrean Relief Association (ERA), established by the EPLF in 1975, functioned as an arm of the Front and raised money for Eritrean refugees, as well as those displaced within Eritrea. Of equal importance was the recognition that the ERA gained from NGOs in the West; by the time of the famine of the 1980s, it operated as an internationally legitimated quasi-governmental aid organization distributing relief supplies.

Essential to EPLF success were the increasing military successes of the opposition to the Mengistu regime within Ethiopia. The links between the EPLF and the TPLF, noted earlier, had their roots in connections between Eritrean and Tigray students involved in radical university politics at Addis Ababa.[14] The TPLF's commitment to self-determination facilitated cooperation between the two Fronts. Despite a breakdown in relations in the mid-1980s, the TPLF participated in battles against the ELF, and EPLF units were enabled to fight deep into Ethiopia, and even take part in the final battles against the Mengistu regime in Addis Ababa.

Conclusion

This chapter has stressed the dynamic development of the EPLF: its internal organizational capacity, its organizational outreach and its ability to adapt to increased numbers and external military and political developments. The vision and stern

---

[14] For an account of the relations between the two Fronts, see John Young, 'The Tigray and Eritrean Peoples Liberation Fronts: a history of tensions and pragmatism', *Journal of Modern African Studies*, Vol. 34, No. 1 (1996), pp. 105–20.

determination of Issayas Afeworki and the cooperative relationship between him and Ramadan Muhamad Nur were decisive in the early survival of the Front. After early problems, the leadership developed tight organizational controls, and maintained the cohesion of leadership and Front. Over time, the Front took on many of the characteristics of a state and was able to function as an alternative government. Given the protracted process of the armed struggle, the ability to control splits and divisions and maintain a unified and centralized control was essential. The internal organization and control mechanisms of the Front, as well as their broader outreach into Eritrean society, were crucial to this process. The longer Front discipline was maintained, the more effectively the internal problems, or 'contradictions' as they were called by the EPLF, could work their disintegrative effect on the Ethiopian regime.

The adaptation of the political and military structures of South East Asian communist movements was facilitated by the character of the society from which the EPLF recruited cadres and fighters. It drew on significant numbers of educated, skilled and technically trained workers. These expanded the general levels of skill and literacy to other Front members. The peasantry was relatively skilled in utilizing a primitive technology, and had roots in an earlier working class formed during the latter part of the Italian occupation. In addition, the EPLF recruited from skilled workers, educated officials and students who had moved to Ethiopia both during and after the federation. Highland Tigrinya speakers, by the 1980s, were in a majority among the rank and file fighters.

It would be mistaken to depict the EPLF as a narrow ethnic or sectarian movement. Key military commanders, like Ali Sayyid and Ibrahim Afa, and the leader of the Front from 1977 to 1987, Ramadan Muhamad Nur, were Muslim non-Tigrinya speakers of eastern lowland origin. Nor can it be argued that the Front was *identified* as a highland movement by Eritreans, as Tigrinya highlanders continued to join the ELF during the 1970s. ELF leaders have asserted that by the end of the 1970s there was a majority of highland fighters in their organization. Rather, the organizational capacity of the leadership of the EPLF, its social base in the highland peasantry, and the multi-sectarian intelligentsia which increasingly became attracted to the Front, are the factors which account for its power. After the disintegration of the ELF, the EPLF remained the only pole of attraction in the Eritrean field.

There is also a correlation between regional levels of development and the origin of most EPLF fighters. The highlands and the environs of Massawa are the most urbanized parts of Eritrea, where school-based education is most accessible. Together with the EPLF's emphasis on literacy for its recruits, the quality of its fighters was markedly superior to the illiterate and semi-literate Ethiopian conscripts. The areas from which the core of the EPLF originated have had long-established connections to empires and were imperial centres. Massawa and Harqiqo were Ottoman and the highlands had historical connections to Ethiopian imperial administrative systems, paying tax and tribute and levies of fighters. The highlands and the east were among the few peripheries of the extensive area of Ethiopia that the modernizing Ethiopian state penetrated.

The purposeful development of its eastern and highland strategy, and the penetration of the peasantry, provided a significant source of recruits for the EPLF to reproduce its military strength. The highland peasantry's attachment to the land produced a reaction against Ethiopian violence different from that of the agro-pastoralists of the west. Highland peasants rarely left Eritrea: they would abandon their villages for periods of time, join the Front, or seek refuge in the liberated areas. The overwhelming majority of the 500,000 refugees who fled to the Sudan were from the lowlands, usually after Ethiopian attacks and loss of animals. For western Eritreans, in any case, Sudan was neither geographically nor culturally far.[15]

In the post-independence period, the organizational structures of the EPLF were transposed to Eritrean government and society. At its post-independence Third Congress in 1994, the EPLF was renamed the People's Front for Democracy and Justice and expanded into a mass party, but retained EPLF cadres at its core. Its programme, formulated as *A National Charter for Eritrea*, reiterated the EPLF's stress on national unity, and the Eritrean Constitution of 1996 reinforced that emphasis. While both gave prominence to cultural pluralism, less priority was given to political pluralism. In some respects, the spirit of the EPLF's principle of democratic centralism lived on, albeit in a new context, in a different form, and with a different political language. Given the scarce resources of Eritrea and the destructive impact of such a prolonged war, the relative ease and efficiency with which the EPLF made the transition to government was an impressive feat. It was an indication of how the development of its governmental capacity during the liberation struggle had matched that of its military. Leaders, political cadres, technicians and fighters smoothly replaced both local and Ethiopian administrators. It was symbolic of the 'stateness' of the EPLF that part of its flag was incorporated into that of the new state, which gained formal independence under EPLF rule in April 1993.

[15] See Gaim Kibreab, *Refugees and Development in Africa: the Case of Eritrea,* (Trenton, NJ: Red Sea Press, 1987), Chapter 2.

3

JOHN YOUNG
The Tigray People's Liberation Front

After years of opposition led by students, the old regime of Emperor Haile-Selassie was overthrown in 1974 by a military cabal, the Derg.[1] Unwilling to share power with civilians or accept the right of Ethiopia's nations to self-determination, the Derg was challenged from many quarters: from a reinvigorated secessionist movement in Eritrea, student radicals in the towns of Ethiopia, and a host of rural-based insurgencies. Almost unnoticed in these chaotic conditions, in 1975 a small group of university students calling themselves the Tigray People's Liberation Front (TPLF) launched an armed struggle for national autonomy from their northern province of Tigray. In spite of the TPLF's inauspicious entrance on to the revolutionary stage and the poverty of the province, the Front forced the Derg's retreat from Tigray in 1989, and went on to lead a coalition of ethnic-based movements – the Ethiopian Peoples' Revolutionary Democratic Front (EPRDF) – that assumed state power in 1991.

Contemporary approaches to the study of revolution emphasize structural factors ranging from class conflict, to the destabilizing impact of commercial agriculture on peasant societies, to changing configurations within the international state system, to explain the occurrence of revolutions. Only rarely, however, do propitious structural conditions produce insurgencies; when they do, it cannot be predicted which movement will dominate the opposition; nor can it be foreseen if the opposition will be triumphant. The link between structural conditions favouring revolution, which movement leads the opposition, and the successful outcome of the struggle, is found in the political sphere. In particular three factors appear critical in understanding the Tigrayan insurgency: first, the part played by the Derg and past regimes in fostering disaffection and influencing the form the revolt took; second, the role of Tigrayan nationalism; and last, the importance of the leadership of the TPLF.

The 1974 revolution, with the subsequent upheavals which notably included the 1975 nationalization of agricultural land, called into question the relationship between the government in Addis Ababa and Ethiopia's numerous peoples or

---

[1] 'Derg' is an Amharigna term which literally means 'committee', and refers to the group within the military which took power after the collapse of the imperial regime.

'nationalities'. For the Ethiopian military, the state was the means through which the vestiges of the old regime could be removed, development forced, and political structures strengthened. Soviet style Marxism-Leninism was adopted because it met the military's needs in a variety of ways: it was revolutionary, socialist, modernist, statist, allowed little scope for popular participation, and gained much-needed support for the beleaguered regime from the Eastern bloc. Despite its revolutionary objectives, much of the disposition, if not the form and method of rule, of the old regime became embodied in the new government. The Derg thus fought to maintain a strong central state, refused to share power with either the politically conscious middle classes or the emerging regional and ethnic elites, and ensured that the state retained its predominantly Amhara character.

Apart from the Eritrean insurgents, students led the opposition against the Derg. From its inception in the mid-1960s, the student movement had a pan-Ethiopian character, but encouraged by the insurgency in Eritrea, Amhara dominance in the state, and the cultural and employment advantages of Amhara students, the issue of national self-determination increasingly came to the fore. Generally students followed Soviet doctrine, and accepted in principle the right of Ethiopia's nationalities to self-determination, up to and including secession, but at the same time held that with the replacement of the old regime by a communist party committed to ending exploitation and respecting the rights of nations and nationalities, there would be no need for secession.[2] While Oromos and others more recently incorporated into the Ethiopian empire suffered the greatest oppression under the imperial regime, it was the Tigrinya speakers of Eritrea and Tigray who were the most ethnically conscious: Tigrayans, who inhabited the heartland of the historic Ethiopian state, were especially resentful of their subordination to an Amhara-dominated state, and Tigrayan students increasingly embraced the view that the best approach would be to engage in a national liberation struggle. Their deliberations led to the formation of the Tigray National Organization (TNO), which served as a link between militants in the university and their supporters in the towns, who were largely high school students and teachers, until the TPLF took form. The TNO also endeavoured to obtain promises of assistance for the proposed Tigrayan movement from the Eritrean Fronts. The Eritrean affiliation was natural given common cultural and linguistic traditions, geography, and the prestige of the Eritrean Liberation Front (ELF) and Eritrean People's Liberation Front (EPLF), but the particular attraction of the EPLF for Tigrayan militants derived from its Marxism, secularism, and organizational unity. After the TNO accepted the EPLF's view that Eritrea was a colony and therefore had a right to secede from Ethiopia, it was promised support.

Marxism and nationalism were the dominant ideologies among students and Maoism was also very influential, but their form and interrelationship had not solidified by the time the TPLF took form. Probably most Tigrayan activists at that time were members or supporters of the Marxist Ethiopian People's Revolutionary Party (EPRP), the largest revolutionary organization in the country, which had a centrist perspective, emphasized the primacy of class struggle, and had little sympathy for national or peasant-based movements of the type favoured by the TPLF.

[2] R. Patman, *Eritrea. Even the Stones Are Burning* (Trenton, NJ: Red Sea Press, 1990), p. 13.

Insurgency, 1975–91

In the critical period between 1975 and 1978, as disenchantment grew in Tigray with Derg policies and the authoritarian manner in which they were introduced, and before the army arrived in sufficient numbers to contain dissent, various revolutionary groups struggled for opposition ascendancy in the province. The TPLF was one of these groups, and it was officially established on 18 February 1975 at Dedebit, an isolated lowland and bandit-infested area in western Tigray, where historically government control had been limited. While one section of the TPLF learned bush skills and worked on the Front's programme, a second contingent of 17 went to Eritrea for military training with the EPLF, and a further small group began propaganda work in the towns. It would appear that the leadership of the TNO/TPLF was drawn disproportionately from the educated sons of the rich peasantry and the lower-middle local nobility. Although the early TPLF did not have a developed structure of authority, nor acknowledge the traditional basis of status in Tigrayan society, a hierarchy developed within the movement based on academic standing at university, which broadly reflected social inequities in Tigrayan society. The three men who become leaders of the TPLF were Meles Zenawi and Sebhat Nega, both sons of lower nobles, and Aregowie Berhe, son of a powerful judge. The fact that there have only been three leaders of the TPLF thus far, and that generally the transfer of power between them has been peaceful, is significant given the destructive power struggles that characterized other Ethiopian and Eritrean movements. The TPLF decided early in its history not to allow a personality cult to develop and this decision was reflected in the early practice of revolving the chairmanship between Aregowie and Sebhat. Individual leaders were constrained by a commitment to collective decision making, while their presence in the countryside and on the battlefields emphasized the movement's equality. Although the elite Marxist-Leninist League of Tigray (MLLT) was established in 1985 to ensure the ideological purity of the movement, one of the most notable features of the TPLF was its pragmatism. This pragmatism, however, was tested most severely over the always controversial issue of national self-determination, which first caused internal dissension with the 1976 publication of the Manifesto of the TPLF and its advocacy of an 'independent democratic republic of Tigray'. Although the movement subsequently distanced itself from this extreme position in favour of Tigrayan autonomy within a united Ethiopia, it was an enduring source of embarrassment. The TPLF commitment to the principle that all nations had the right to self-determination, including independence, caused less controversy in the movement, but produced strained relations with the EPLF because it recognized the right of Eritrea's nine nations to independence.[3]

In the early period, there was little contact between the TPLF and the Derg, in part because of the former's preoccupation with achieving opposition hegemony, but also because of the government's limited military presence in the province. The

[3] For a discussion of this and other differences between the TPLF and EPLF, see J. Young, 'The Tigray and Eritrean People's Liberation Fronts: a history of tensions and pragmatism', *Journal of Modern African Studies*, Vol. 34, No. 1 (1996), pp. 105–20.

Derg also largely discounted the TPLF's potential, and considered it best to simply sit back and reap the rewards of internecine warfare between the various opposition groups. In meeting with Tigrayan elders, however, Colonel Kalechristos, governor of Tigray between 1976 and 1978, learned that, in spite of the superior forces of the Ethiopian Democratic Union (EDU) and the EPRP, it was the TPLF which they considered the major political threat because it articulated genuine grievances in the community. These grievances included the demand for Tigrayan equality, eliminating discrimination in government employment and education, more schools, hospitals and other infrastructure, and an end to the imposition of the Amharic language. The governor concluded that the Maoist rhetoric of the TPLF was unlikely on its own to have much impact on the religiously devout peasants, but that the Front's effectiveness at articulating popular grievances did threaten the government in Tigray.[4] The most serious challenge to the TPLF achieving opposition hegemony in Tigray was posed by the EDU, which was led by the anti-Derg nobility headed by the province's former governor, Ras Mengesha. Its rejection of the Derg's land reform, espousal of Tigrayan nationalism, and opposition to the perceived atheism and communism of the military, enabled it to mobilize some ten thousand peasants and farm workers in western Tigray and northern parts of neighbouring Gondar Province. The EDU's conservatism also attracted the support of the Sudanese and Saudi governments, and of the CIA. Despite these advantages, the EDU suffered from the weaknesses of its feudal orientation: a leadership based on privilege, not skill, loyalty linked to the leader and not the cause, and a lack of centralized control; as a result, its army was poorly motivated and ill-disciplined. Nonetheless, the militarily inexperienced and poorly armed students of the TPLF were repeatedly defeated in skirmishes with the EDU between 1976 and 1979, and suffered many defections and considerable loss of life, including key members of its leadership.[5] Fighters were also upset that the TPLF leadership was not successful in acquiring arms from either the EPLF, which supported the EPRP at this time, or from the ELF, which assisted the EDU. Offensives across a wide expanse of territory in western Tigray and north-western Gondar nevertheless exposed the Front to large numbers of peasants whose support they tried to gain. While most peasants remained unwilling to commit themselves to armed struggle, they slowly moved from positions of neutrality to passive support for the TPLF, as the Front in an isolated number of cases was able to distribute the EDU leaders' land among peasants and in other ways make clear the class differences in the approaches of the two movements. Militarily the task was more difficult and in the first three major encounters the Front was badly defeated, but after each battle the fighters received inspirational speeches, analysed their failings, and tried to supplement their growing practical experience with readings and videos on military strategy and tactics. While the TPLF developed militarily and politically even in defeat, the weaknesses of the EDU increasingly came to the fore; by the end of 1979 it had been reduced to a rump largely operating in small pockets outside Tigray in

[4] Young, 'The Tigray and Eritrean People's Liberation Fronts'.
[5] Among the key leaders killed in this period were Ayele Gessesse (field name 'Suhul') – a non-student and older member of the lower nobility, whose decision to join the TPLF gave the movement a measure of legitimacy, particularly among the peasants of western Tigray – and Mahari Haile (field name 'Mussie'), of mixed Eritrean and Tigray descent, who was first a member of the EPLF, and thus brought valuable military and organizational experience to the fledgling TPLF.

Gondar and Sudan, where it remained until the collapse of the Derg in 1991.

Having outlasted the EDU in western Tigray, the TPLF faced the EPRP in the east. The EPRP was pre-eminently an urban-based multinational student organization which had hoped to assume state power with the collapse of the Haile-Selassie regime, but which increasingly came to appreciate that the struggle would be longer, more difficult and would involve operating in the rural areas. It established three bases of operations, one of which was in the isolated Asimba mountain area of north-eastern Tigray. Military defeats at the hands of the Derg in other parts of Ethiopia, the devastating impact of the government's urban terror campaign, and divisions within the leadership weakened the EPRP – but with considerable funds, EPLF support, and a network within the Ethiopian student diaspora, the movement continued to attract many young supporters who perceived it as providing the major opposition to the Derg. Military and financial strength did not win the EPRP peasant support, however, and peasants contrasted EPRP wealth with the poverty of TPLF fighters. They contended that if the EPRP had come as liberators they should not have to pay for food and accommodation, but should be provided for by those in whose name the struggle was being fought, that is the peasantry. In interviews peasants in north-eastern Tigray repeatedly complained of the EPRP's use of violence when they refused to cooperate with it. Nor did the rights of Ethiopia's nationalities figure highly in the EPRP's programme, which emphasized a multinational approach to revolution. This proved a major weakness in Tigray, where nationalist sentiments were deeply rooted. Political competition between the TPLF and EPRP increasingly created tensions, particularly as the peasants moved to the TPLF camp. Meanwhile, war with the EDU markedly depleted TPLF forces, and it was at this point that the EPRP broke their truce with the Front and attempt to gain a hegemonic position in the anti-Derg struggle in Tigray, based on superior numbers and resources. The TPLF, however, emerged from its victory over the EDU with superior military skills, which proved critical in the contest with the EPRP, who were quickly defeated, with many crossing the border to Eritrea. Another section of the EPRP retreated to Wollo where it eventually regrouped with TPLF support as the Ethiopian People's Democratic Movement (EPDM) and later became a member of the EPRDF. The costs to the TPLF of its victories were significant: according to government estimates, the number of TPLF fighters fell from 1,200 to 450.[6]

Victories over the EDU and EPRP placed the TPLF in a dominant position in opposition to the Derg in Tigray. At approximately the same time, the government defeated the Somali invasion and was able to redeploy its Soviet-supported forces in an attempt to overwhelm the insurgencies in Eritrea and Tigray, and carry out a programme of reform necessary to securing legitimacy in the country. The increased Derg presence in Tigray produced disaffection among the peasants, however, and this was to benefit the TPLF. The incoming military regime was viewed as another Amhara-dominated government, usurping state power that rightfully belonged to Tigray's hereditary rulers. Although the Derg was aware of Tigrayan loyalty to their native leaders, the new regime's credibility depended on fulfilling its revolutionary

---

[6] Interview: Colonel Kalechristos Abbay, Addis Ababa, 4 June 1993. The TPLF does not accept these figures, but does admit to losing about half of its members in this period.

goals and this meant eliminating the patron–client relations on which the authority of the old regime rested. In doing so, however, it undermined the Tigrayan peasantry's links with the central state, and made them more open to the appeals of the TPLF.

Derg agrarian reforms were treated with suspicion by Tigrayan peasants who feared that the elimination of their traditional system of land tenure would give the government control over their land. While in southern Ethiopia land reform was welcomed by the indigenous population, who saw it as a means of acquiring land lost to outsiders, in Tigray landlordism was limited, there were virtually no non-indigenous land holders, and there were few large concentrations of land in the highlands where most peasants lived. Domination of the peasant associations by government allies also caused bitterness. Peasant disaffection increased further when the Derg began forcibly procuring agricultural surpluses at less than market prices and restricting the employment of seasonal farm labour which many peasants depended upon for survival. New taxes were imposed because the government badly needed finances to contain the insurgencies in the north. Peasants were unhappy at the Derg's closure of most rural schools on the pretext that teachers were TPLF sympathizers. As the rural insurrection spread, the Derg resorted to conscription, convoys, ever-higher levels of taxation, and, increasingly, to terror attacks on civilians. Although it had less impact than in other parts of Ethiopia, the introduction of state and cooperative farms and villagization caused further anger.[7] In early 1978 the Derg launched a resettlement programme with the stated aims of combating drought, averting famine and increasing agricultural productivity, and by the end of 1986 half a million peasants had been moved, most of them forcibly.[8] Although, in the period before the revolution, many peasants had left the northern provinces voluntarily for the richer and less populated lands in the south, from its inception the TPLF held that the primary objective of the Derg's resettlement programme was to weaken the national insurgencies. Indeed, the former head of the Derg's Relief and Rehabilitation Commission, Dawit Wolde Giorgis, acknowledged that reducing the population in rebel areas was seen by the government as an important means of depriving guerrillas of access to their peasant followers.[9] In particular, during the famine of 1984 the government encouraged starving peasants to come to the garrisoned towns with promises of food, after which they were frequently arrested and taken to camps in southern Ethiopia. In the resettlement camps many died of malaria and sleeping sickness because of poor sanitation, lack of housing, food and water, and inadequate health care, as well as the absence of the necessary seeds and tools to support themselves.

The Derg's approach to the Orthodox Church and religion was equally ill-adapted to winning popular support. Distributing Church lands won wide approval, but atheism and attacks on Church dogma, practices, and priests were abhorred by the devout Tigrayan peasants. The Derg used its mass associations to urge people to end baptisms, grieving ceremonies, fasting, and even attending church. But indirect

---

[7] See C. Clapham, *Transformation and Continuity in Revolutionary Ethiopia* (Cambridge: Cambridge University Press, 1988) for an account of these programmes.

[8] Girma Kebbede, *The State and Development in Ethiopia* (New Jersey: Humanities Press, 1992) p. 81.

[9] Dawit Wolde Giorgis, *Red Tears: War, Famine and Revolution in Ethiopia* (Trenton, NJ: Red Sea Press, 1989), p. 277.

means of undermining the Church were not the only methods used: many rural churches were destroyed, priests killed, and their wives raped. The Derg mistakenly assumed that because Tigrayans welcomed the destruction of the Church's feudal authority, their ancient ties to Orthodox Christianity could be severed. Instead, the Derg's approach served to alienate peasants and increase the authority of rural parish priests who were subsequently mobilized by the TPLF. Peasant disaffection with the government, together with the demonstrated military competence of the TPLF as a result of its victories over the EDU and EPRP, fostered support for the Front. At the same time, Derg terror tactics against the urban population, and particularly the intelligentsia which was forced to escape from the towns, gave the Front an increasing capacity to respond to peasant demands for schools, land reforms, local administrations, and improvements in the condition of women. The TPLF saw the institutions thus created as vehicles to unite peasants and advance the armed struggle. Thus the establishment of rural schools met peasant interests in educating their children, while for the TPLF they served to deepen political and national consciousness and provide training for those who could be utilized in the struggle. Where peasant and TPLF interests clashed, for example over whether younger or older students should have priority in school placements, the Front's need for fighters and administrators prevailed and older students were selected. Although the TPLF leadership had little sympathy for religion and the Ethiopian Orthodox Church, they were extremely circumspect, knowing that any serious challenge to the Church threatened to undermine their relationship with the peasants, and thus reduce their capacity to wage war. The TPLF presented itself as the defender of religion and its message emphasized that its fighters were 'operating from Christ [and] concentrated on exposing the suffering of people and practising good as a way of appealing to the peasants' religious sentiments'.[10] Unlike the Derg, the TPLF recognized that the Ethiopian Orthodox Church was not a monolithic institution and that many rural priests were not wealthy, but frequently little better off than the peasants among whom they lived. As a result, many priests became active TPLF supporters. TPLF concern with upsetting peasant religious sensitivities, however, meant that religion and the Church continued to play a role in Tigray that was not entirely consistent with the anti-feudal objectives of the Front.

A similar pattern can be observed with respect to the TPLF's approach to women. Front efforts were designed to advance the condition of women, destroy backward values and practices, and encourage women to play an active role in the struggle. These efforts were generally successful, but had to be balanced against the carefully cultivated consensus in the rural community necessary to carry on the war against the Derg. When social reforms designed to improve the lives of women caused dissension within the paternalistic culture of rural Tigray, compromises were made, usually at the expense of women. Notable in this respect were decisions to reduce the number of women fighters and eliminate a TPLF-initiated programme to teach women how to plough.

Unlike peasants, the TPLF did not see land reform as an end in itself, but as a means first to break down feudal structures and begin the process of establishing a

---

[10] Interview: Aregesh Adane, TPLF Central Committee and Secretary Tigray Region, Mekelle, 8 April 1993.

strong rural economy, and secondly to mobilize the peasantry. While class was a factor in the TPLF's mobilization, the Front did not encourage class struggle, except against the nobility. Nor did it explicitly identify with the poor peasants. But the TPLF's land reforms did involve peasants in the process and ensured that their sensitivities were not affronted. Concerned about raising the ire of rich peasants, the Front did not redistribute capital, and instead sought to win their support by convincing them that its land reform would provide security of land tenure and corruption-free administration. In this they were largely successful, but as a result such peasants usually maintained higher standards of living than their neighbours. This approach also caused strains within the more committed Marxist wing of the TPLF, led by its Assistant General Secretary and leading ideologue, Ghidey Zera Tsion, who left the Front in the mid-1980s over this and other issues. The TPLF's economic policy also emphasized pragmatism and flowed from its experiments with market controls, concern about alienating the province's influential merchants, and resulting conclusion that pre-capitalist Tigray was not ready for a transition to socialism.[11] Between 1979 and 1983 the TPLF attempted to introduce marketing cooperatives and price controls, but this raised the ire of traders who withdrew their produce from the market, thus forcing a Front climbdown. From this experience the TPLF developed a two-stage theory of revolution, in which it was held that Tigray must first pass from a post-feudal subsistence economy to a bourgeois capitalist economy, and that only then – under the leadership of the MLLT – could it develop into a fully fledged socialist state.

Through mobilization and a willingness to allow peasants a measure of autonomy in their own affairs, the TPLF made a major contribution to rural administration and development in the province. As soon as the Front was able to establish itself in an area, it organized mass associations based on interest groups such as peasants, women, youth, merchants and workers. The task of the associations was largely restricted to raising consciousness rather than implementing policies. Administration at the local level was initially carried out by provisional administrative committees which grouped about 11 villages and usually operated for two or three years to give the people the necessary experience and confidence, after which *baitos*, or councils, were established. *Baitos* were organizationally separate from the TPLF,[12] and typically were established after the mass associations; as a result, few of them were operational in the early years of the revolution. The role of peasants in their own administration symbolized the Tigrayan revolution, and most clearly distinguished the TPLF project from the authoritarian regimes of Haile-Selassie and the Derg. The movement's primary objective, however, was to expand and deepen the war against the Derg, and the rural administration was structured to prepare peasants for that task. Another related element was *gim gima*, an institution of Marxist-Leninist origins that was designed to evaluate the performance of both collective entities and individuals through large-scale debates in open forums. Developed in the army and later introduced into the mass associations, *gim gima* proved highly successful not only in

[11] A. de Waal, 'Tigray grain markets and internal purchase', unpublished paper (Oxfam, February 1990), p. 17.
[12] Fighters and mass association members elected representatives in equal numbers to the TPLF congress, so that the mass associations influenced the TPLF and it in turn the mass associations.

increasing the effectiveness of these organizations, but also in achieving a measure of accountability of the leaders to their followers and closely binding the TPLF to the people.

In 1978, the TPLF established the Relief Society of Tigray (REST) as a humanitarian organization with a mandate to coordinate relief programmes, rehabilitation and development both in Tigray and among Tigrayan refugees, most of whom resided in neighbouring Sudan. Internally, REST operated through the social welfare committees of the *baitos*. The founding of REST reflected the TPLF's need for a specialized body to handle relief and development, and also to respond to the Derg's efforts to restrict the flow of humanitarian and economic assistance to areas of Tigray that were coming under the control of the Front.[13] Following in the footsteps of the Eritrean Relief Association of the EPLF, the establishment of REST also reflected the growing recognition by the TPLF leadership of the importance of international assistance, and the fact that NGOs and foreign governments found it politically more acceptable to deal with a designated relief agency than with a liberation movement.

Much of the TPLF's international effort in the early years was directed at gaining the support of Tigrayans living abroad, most of whom were in the Sudan. The TPLF did not operate armed camps in Sudan, and as yet there is no evidence that the Sudanese regimes of Nimeiri or Sadiq el Mahdi (or any other foreign government) supplied the Front with weapons or let its fighters carry weapons; but both governments did allow the various Ethiopian and Eritrean opposition movements to operate in the country. As a result, TPLF cadres moved freely across the Ethiopian–Sudanese border, had a virtual embassy in Khartoum, carried on a multitude of political and service activities among the largely refugee population, and through REST conducted its relief operations in Tigray. Over the years the TPLF developed an impressive number of garages, workshops, a wide variety of refugee organizations, and the means to care for seriously injured fighters who were evacuated to Sudan. The Front was generally able to maintain amicable relations with successive Sudanese governments for a number of reasons. First, it kept no armed soldiers in the country. Second, the Sudanese feared that a break in relations could lead to the country being overwhelmed by refugees. Third, the limited support given to the Ethiopian and Eritrean opposition was a response to the much more substantial support the Derg provided to the Sudan People's Liberation Movement. And last, the Sudanese government did not have the capacity to close its borders to the rebels.[14] As a result of its military successes and establishment of a set of institutions that peasants were prepared to fight to defend, in the period 1980–2 recruitment increased by a (TPLF) estimated factor of four or five, with most new

[13] REST, *Humanitarian and Socio-economic Development Activities* (Vancouver: Oxfam/Canada, 1987), p. 1.

[14] EPLF Political Bureau member Al-Amin Mohamed Said made this point clear when he said: 'Neither Sudan nor anybody else can close the border, because the border regions contain overlapping Eritrean and Sudanese tribes. Nimeiri's regime repeatedly strove in vain to close the border in the early 1970s.' See *Adulis*, Vol. 3, No. 5 (May 1986), p. 4.

[15] TPLF statistics are invariably difficult to ascertain, but in early 1980 the Front reported that it had 572 mass associations of workers, peasants, youth, students, traders, and others inside and outside Tigray, with a membership of 171,000; in addition there were 12,670 militia members. See *People's Voice*, 18 February 1980.

recruits coming from the peasantry.[15] Indeed, the numbers drawn to the beyond its capacity to absorb, and approximately 3,000 fighters were EPLF for military training. While these were undergoing their training in the Sahel region of Eritrea in 1982, the Derg launched its Red Star campaign with the intent of completely destroying the EPLF. The EPLF then appealed to the TPLF to utilize the trainees in the defence of its base area, but the TPLF refused because they did not want to expose such inexperienced fighters; subsequently, however, four brigades of battle-trained fighters were sent to the Sahel.[16] Since these fighters may have constituted half of its non-militia forces at the time, this commitment to the EPLF attests the importance assigned by the TPLF to the outcome of the defence, and to their relations with the Eritreans. Although the EPLF was pushed far to the north and lost large numbers of fighters, the Derg's failure to destroy it shifted the strategic initiative away from the regime.

This key campaign also helped to define the emerging military differences between the TPLF and EPLF. While the TPLF recognized the need to advance from guerrilla to conventional warfare, it argued that the EPLF opted for conventional warfare too early and at too great a cost. Contrary to the EPLF, the TPLF was not committed to holding territory, a position it maintained until the expulsion of the Derg from Tigray in 1989. By 1980 EPLF military leaders largely directed an army that fought a conventional war from secure bases against the Derg. For the EPLF this demonstrated their military superiority over the TPLF; for the TPLF, the EPLF's devotion to conventional warfare indicated the ascendancy of a professional military establishment within the EPLF, a development which threatened to weaken the democratic character of the war.

The failure of the Derg's Red Star campaign provided both TPLF and EPLF with an opportunity to go on the offensive, but before that was possible the region was beset with famine. The Derg's priorities in turn were directed at making arrangements for the celebration of its ten years in power in 1984. Three years of limited harvests brought on by drought and a massive Derg ground offensive led to over 800,000 Tigrayans being internally displaced and a further 200,000 trekking to Sudan.[17] As a result, much of the resources of the TPLF and REST were devoted to ameliorating starvation and moving refugees to Sudanese relief camps. Although drought precipitated major crop failures, the severity of the famine was due to the Derg's counter-insurgency strategy. Cutting employment levels, interfering with trade flows, disrupting agricultural activity and burning crops were all elements in the Derg's strategy for subduing the TPLF by weakening the peasantry upon which it depended for survival. As well as fostering famine conditions, the Derg interfered with international relief efforts by not allowing food aid to be transported across military lines, and threatening to evict aid agencies if they delivered relief into rebel-held areas from Sudan, a threat that generally proved effective. It was thus left to a handful of NGOs operating from Sudan with minuscule resources, together with REST, to meet the needs of the majority of famine victims who were in the

[16] Interview: Assefa Mamo, TPLF Representative to North America, Addis Ababa, 10 May 1996.

[17] L. Clarke, *Early Warning Case Study: the 1984-85 Influx of Tigrayans into Eastern Sudan*, Working Paper No. 2 (Washington DC: Refugee Study Group, 1986), quoted in W. de Mars, 'Tactics of pro-tection: international human rights organizations in the Ethiopian conflict, 1980-1986', in E. McCarthy-Arnold, ed., *Africa, Human Rights and the Global System* (Westport: Greenwood Press, 1994), p. 97.

liberated territories.[18] Western governments and the United Nations knew that the majority of famine victims were behind rebel lines, but chose instead to direct most of their foodstuffs through the Derg's Relief and Rehabilitation Commission.

Compounding the problems faced by the TPLF, at the height of the famine in 1985 the EPLF broke relations with the TPLF as a result of a long-simmering dispute, and relations were not resumed until 1988. The consequences of this break included ending military collaboration, terminating political contacts and closing the TPLF's radio station in Eritrea. Crucially, the EPLF also refused the TPLF passage over its main supply link through Eritrea to Kassala in Sudan, thus causing a crisis in Tigray. Some 100,000 peasants were quickly mobilized to construct a direct road link from western Tigray to Gedaref in Sudan, following a route previously surveyed as a means to reduce dependence on the EPLF. Though this task force possessed virtually no heavy equipment or outside support, the road was made operational in less than a week, preventing major loss of life; but the route chosen repeatedly crossed the Tekezze River and could only be used when water flows were low. Militarily the famine, and the Derg's response to it, led the Ethiopian army to gain a greater degree of control in Tigray than at any time since 1977.[19] In spite of the military setback that it caused, however, the 1984 famine provided the TPLF with a major opportunity to end its largely self-imposed international isolation, introduce its struggle to the world community, and through the control of relief aid distribution to strengthen its ties with the peasantry. Moreover, it was clear that the Derg did not have the capacity to defeat its northern-based opposition.

With stabilization of the rural economy resulting from better harvests and the return of some of the refugees from the Sudan, the TPLF was able to re-exert its control over the rural areas and resume the siege of the towns. By 1987, the TPLF leadership had reached the conclusion that a stalemate existed between their forces and those of the Derg, and plans were developed to break it.[20] If troop morale was not already a serious problem for the Derg, in March 1988 Derg forces suffered their biggest defeat of the war at Afabet in the southern Sahel at the hands of the EPLF. Over 15,000 government soldiers and a mechanized division were put out of action, a large number of heavy weapons were captured, and the Derg's army was forced to retreat in disarray. Within days of the Afabet defeat the TPLF went on the offensive, although the timing appears coincidental since the two Fronts did not have relations at the time.[21]

---

[18] Gebru Tereke has noted that, with the TPLF, 'the classic guerrilla–peasant relationship [is] reversed: instead of being dependents, guerrillas have become providers'. See Gebru Tereke, 'Continuity and discontinuity in peasant mobilisation: the cases of Bale and Tigray', in M. Ottaway, ed., *The Political Economy of Ethiopia* (New York: Praeger, 1990), p. 152.

[19] A. de Waal, *Evil Days: Thirty Years of War and Famine in Ethiopia* (New York: Human Rights Watch, 1991), p. 203.

[20] The TPLF has never been forthcoming about its numbers, but former Derg Colonel Asiminew Bedane, who was captured by the Front in April 1988, told me in his POW camp in Kalema in western Tigray that army intelligence at that time estimated TPLF strength to be 60,000 fighters. He thought this was a serious under-estimation, and concluded that 'the whole population of the province is armed ... everyone supports the TPLF'. Interview: Colonel Asiminew Bedane, POW Camp Kalema, Tigray, 5 May 1988.

[21] The apparent coincidence may be due to the preference of both Fronts for launching attacks in the dry season, so that the agricultural cycle on which the peasants relied would not be disrupted.

The TPLF's 1988 offensive was based on the need to break the stalemate and reduce Derg interference in the Front-controlled countryside, but it also involved a number of political considerations, one of which was a desire to re-establish relations with the EPLF. The TPLF held that the EPLF underrated its military capacity and wanted to dominate it, and believed that a major TPLF victory would convince the Eritreans that success against the Derg was not possible without unity between equal partners. Another important motive for launching the attack against the towns was concern over the extended alienation of the urban population from the rural-focused revolution of the TPLF. The focus of the campaign was the western Tigrayan town of Endaselasie which served as the army's headquarters, occupied by some 35,000 troops. The battle began with an attack on the Derg's communications centre of Mugulat in the north-east; after it was destroyed, the TPLF launched offensives against army bases at Axum and Adwa in central Tigray. Derg forces sent from Endaselasie to relieve the garrisons were attacked en route and forced to retreat. The fighting, the heaviest of the Tigrayan war, went on for two days before the army's positions were overrun. The TPLF claimed that more than ten brigades were destroyed and over 7,000 troops captured in the rout.[22] The fall of Endaselasie spread terror among Derg forces as they retreated to positions just north of the provincial capital of Mekelle in the south-east of the province.

In consequence of its losses in Eritrea and Tigray, the Derg ended its conflict with Somalia, releasing troops and materials which could be transferred to the northern war zones. Three months after its expulsion from the towns, the Derg fielded a force of over 150,000 in Tigray, the largest army ever assembled in the province, according to TPLF sources.[23] Confronted with massive Derg reinforcements, TPLF fighters retreated, resuming their pre-1988 siege of the towns. As the army re-established its garrisons it became progressively weaker, although with the recapture of Endaselasie its total strength in the province was considerably greater than before. Some of the Derg's most heinous atrocities inflicted against the Tigrayan civilian population took place in the following months. In particular, the attack on the north-eastern town of Hausien on 22 June 1988 stands out. An all-day attack by helicopter gunships and MiGs caused more than 2,000 civilian deaths, the war's worst single atrocity since the start of the ELF insurrection in 1961.[24] In a similar attack, 250 people in the southern town of Chercha were killed during a market day in 1989.[25] Although these episodes were demoralizing, while the Derg remained pinned down in towns along the main roads and the TPLF held almost complete control of the countryside, the regime no longer had the capacity to cause the civilian dislocation that was needed to weaken the Front seriously. The string of EPLF and TPLF victories changed the entire course of the war and made it essential for the two Fronts to resolve their political disagreements and begin the final campaign to defeat the Derg, a goal accomplished after a series of meetings in Khartoum in April 1988. In the event, the Derg's collapse in Tigray came more quickly than the TPLF anticipated. Once again the struggle focused around Endaselasie, where,

---

[22] *People's Voice*, May 1988, p. 7.
[23] *People's Voice*, August 1989, p. 4.
[24] De Waal, *Evil Days*, p. 258.
[25] Interview: Yemane Bere and Kebede Gebriot, Chercha, 27 March 1993.

despite the reinforcement of the government army, the TPLF's hold on the countryside was tighter than ever, and the army found itself under siege with dwindling supplies. Derg attempts to open supply lines between Endaselasie and Asmara in September and December were repulsed. This was followed by the defeat in early February 1989 of its elite Commando Division and the loss of its command centre at Selekleka, forty kilometres east of Endaselasie.[26] The end was now only a matter of time, and on 19 February 1989 the area in and around Endaselasie was captured and 12–13,000 Derg soldiers were killed or taken prisoner in a joint operation by TPLF forces and an EPLF armoured brigade. The presence of the EPLF brigade was both a tangible expression of the recent unity agreement and a sign of the TPLF's weakness in heavy artillery. The capture of copious Derg supplies in the following weeks rapidly overcame that weakness and facilitated the development of a conventional TPLF force. Defeat of the army in western Tigray sent a shock wave through the Derg's remaining forces in Tigray, and within two weeks all the garrisoned towns in the province were abandoned, usually without a fight. The military losses in Eritrea and Tigray precipitated a mutiny against Mengistu's leadership in May 1989 by his generals. Although this was put down, it made clear the rapidly declining morale of the army.[27]

In the face of growing criticism and the loss of the Red Sea port of Massawa to the EPLF in February 1990, Mengistu announced that the government-led Workers Party of Ethiopia (WPE) would be replaced and a multi-party system introduced; that private enterprise would be encouraged; and the system of collectivized agriculture dissolved. Internationally, the weakening of communism and the reforms initiated by Gorbachev facilitated an easing of Cold War tensions, which in turn led the Soviet Union to inform Mengistu that its support could no longer be relied upon, and that attempts should be made to reach a non-military solution to the rebellions in Eritrea and Tigray. Meanwhile, the TPLF and other opposition movements increasingly directed their energy to alliance building and planning for the post-Derg administration of the country, the most important element being the establishment of the EPRDF. Led by the TPLF, this initially included only the EPDM, but was later extended to the Oromo People's Democratic Organization (OPDO), largely made up of captured Oromo soldiers of the Derg.

An immediate obstacle to the EPRDF's advance arose because TPLF fighters and Tigrayans generally questioned the need to carry the war south into Oromo- and Amhara-populated lands, arguing that the indigenous peoples should free themselves. Fighters in these areas reportedly 'thought they were at the end of the world' according to one cadre, and were also surprised to be confronted by civilian opposition in the towns. In response, some 10,000 fighters spontaneously returned to Tigray, unhindered by their leaders. With the campaign effectively suspended, the TPLF organized a province-wide debate, or *gim gima*; until it was completed almost a year later there was little progress in the war. Two factors appear critical to the conclusion reached that the war must continue: first, the contention that aerial bombing would continue unless the Derg was completely destroyed; second, priests

---

[26] *People's Voice*, May/August 1989, pp. 4–5.
[27] 'Ethiopia: The politics of power and the politics of peace', *Africa Confidential*, Vol. 30, No. 12, p. 6.

forcefully argued that Tigrayans were part of the Ethiopian Orthodox Church and should not be separated from it. The result of this debate was to convince Tigrayans that peace and security could only be assured with the Derg's elimination.

Various attempts were made, particularly by former US President Jimmy Carter, to initiate peace negotiations between the warring parties, but little was accomplished. In 1989 James Cheek, US Ambassador to the Sudan, met with TPLF Chairman Meles Zenawi in Khartoum and in the same year Meles visited the UK.[28] Meles expressed admiration for Albania during that visit, but by the time he visited Washington in March 1990 he was reported to have renounced Marxism-Leninism.[29] Observers noted a marked change in TPLF rhetoric as its members adopted the language of Western-style liberal democracy.[30] With consensus in Tigray on the need to continue the war outside the province, the focus again turned to the military front. On 23 February 1991 the EPRDF announced the launch of 'Operation Tewodros' with the assistance of the EPLF, and less than a month later Derg forces were removed from Gondar and Gojjam in the west. In May 'Operation Walleligne' was launched in Wollo and made rapid progress down the eastern corridor of Ethiopia. The Derg responded by removing forces assigned to Eritrea and attacking positions in Tigray, but while temporarily delaying the EPRDF's advance, the government no longer had the capacity to stop it. The army's ineffectual defence led Mengistu to fly to Zimbabwe and exile on 21 May, after which the regime rapidly disintegrated. Collectively these developments set the stage for the US-brokered London conference of late May 1991, attended by leaders of the TPLF, the EPLF, the Oromo Liberation Front (OLF), a rump government led by General Tesfaye and Ato Tesfaye Dinka, and largely marginalized forces such as the EPRP and the EDU. With the conference deadlocked, EPLF forces marched into Asmara on 24 May. Four days later EPRDF troops entered Addis Ababa, together with mechanized units from the EPLF and fighters from other smaller liberation movements.

Conclusion

Barrington Moore concluded that the actions of the upper classes provoke peasant rebellions and define their outcome, and that was also the case in Ethiopia.[31] Struggles for power under imperial regimes largely took the form of intra-feudal and dynastic rivalries, and were dominated by nobles who pursued their goals through conspiracies and intrigue, with armies whose loyalty was based on patron–client ties. It was the petty bourgeoisie, however, using mass political mobilization, who led the Eritrean movement for independence and various other post-1974 Ethiopian liberation movements, including the TPLF. They, in turn, after 1974 confronted a

---

[28] Andargachew Tiruneh, *The Ethiopian Revolution 1974 -1987: a Transformation from an Aristocratic to a Totalitarian Autocracy* (Cambridge: Cambridge University Press, 1993), p. 362.

[29] Andargachew Tiruneh, *The Ethiopian Revolution*, p. 362.

[30] S. Vaughan, *The Addis Ababa Transitional Conference of July 1991: its Origins, History and Significance*, Occasional Papers No. 51 (Edinburgh University: Centre of African Studies, 1994), p. 31.

[31] B. Moore, *Social Origins of Dictatorship and Democracy: Lord and Peasant in the Making of the Modern World* (Boston: Beacon Press, 1966), p. 457.

military regime which also employed political mobilization, in addition to bureaucratic measures, terror, and the ideological appeals of socialism and nationalism to
establish its rule in contest with an opposition which pressed for democratic civilian
rule. Unlike Haile-Selassie's, this regime had the capacity to prohibit dissent in the
urban areas, thus forcing opposition movements to turn to the countryside and
launch peasant-based insurrections.

Unlike the urban-based revolutionary petty-bourgeois struggle for state power,
peasant discontent had its roots in the growing crisis of the rural economy. Prior to
the modern era, the nobility and peasants of Tigray regularly expressed national
grievances against efforts by successive Shoan-based Amhara regimes to weaken
political and cultural influences at the periphery. Nationalism only became a
political movement after the revolutionaries moved to the countryside, however,
and in response to Derg policies and the authoritarian means used to implement
them. Nationalism was unable to acquire a mass basis of support in Tigray until
recently, because the Ethiopian state was poorly integrated and contacts between
ethnic minorities and the state were limited.[32] Nationalism emerges in the context of
modernization: it begins with advances in communication, transport and the media
which progressively curtail cultural isolation and break down former identities. In
Tigray, most of these processes can be dated from the brief period of Italian
colonialism that began in 1935; they found partial expression in the *Woyene* revolt
by peasants and sections of the nobility in eastern Tigray against the Haile-Selassie
regime in 1943; but they only produced a nationalist movement with a province-
wide basis of support under the emerging petty bourgeoisie in the decade or so
before the upheaval of 1974. This movement had a basis in the deep pride Tigrayans
had in their heritage, and in the fact that they had long been ruled by people from
their own ethnic community. Thus, for a people aptly described as the 'cultural
aristocrats' of Ethiopia,[33] Tigray's decline, and in this century its poverty, fuelled a
sense of national grievance which readily found expression in hostility to the
Amhara elite who dominated the central state. It is thus not surprising that the TPLF
appeal was mainly based on the perception that Tigrayans suffered discrimination at
the hands of the Shoan Amhara elite; while there is evidence to support this view,
other ethnic communities and regions experienced similar or worse forms of
discrimination without seriously challenging the state. As Brass has pointed out, the
mere existence of inequality is not sufficient to produce nationalist movements, and
anti-state movements may even arise among dominant groups.[34] Although nationalists, Tigrayans have not been prepared to relinquish their links to Ethiopian
civilization and the state their ancestors created. Moreover, while the peasants' local
and culturally based nationalism underpinned the Tigrayan revolution, it did not
determine the TPLF's national objectives. The Tigrayan youth who formed the
TPLF developed their ideology in the student movement of the 1960s and 1970s,
which fought the old regime and the military dictatorship on a pan-Ethiopian basis.

[32] W. Connor, *Ethnonationalism: the Quest for Understanding* (Princeton: Princeton University Press,
1994), p. 36.
[33] D. Levine, *Wax and Gold: Tradition and Innovation in Ethiopian Culture* (Chicago: University of
Chicago Press, 1965).
[34] P. Brass, *Ethnicity and Nationalism: Theory and Comparison* (Sage Publications, 1991), pp. 41–2.

Their decision to emphasize Tigrayan nationalism did not mark a retreat into ethnic parochialism, but proved to be an accurate assessment of the revolutionary possibilities in the country at that time. And while nationalism proved critical to the success of the TPLF, it was equally important for the movement to address the social concerns and needs of the peasants.

The TPLF's commitment to the peasants' well-being flowed from an appreciation that the revolution's success depended upon it gaining their unreserved support. Contrary to assumed notions of the peasants' collective ethos and voluntarism, the revolutionary context in Tigray is best understood by Migdal's notion of the need for a 'social exchange' between peasants and revolutionaries,[35] or by Popkin's conception of the 'rational peasant'.[36] Such peasants, Popkin found, are only prepared to join the revolution after carefully considering its prospects for victory and the benefits that would be gained by joining the revolution, as against what would be lost by not joining.[37] These notions are well expressed by the TPLF Chairman of Tigray, who commented:

> Often a peasant meeting would not end until there was a resolution and an agreement to carry out some reform. In many parts of Tigray this commitment was to land reform and only after *baitos* were set up and land reform carried out were peasants prepared to defend their institutions and join the TPLF as fighters.[38]

Peasant support for the TPLF only began to develop after cadres successfully demonstrated their commitment to the peasants' welfare by living with them and sharing their deprivations. The cadres' exemplary behaviour, particularly when compared with that of members of other revolutionary parties, served to build confidence among the peasantry. In addition, the high standards of personal behaviour and commitment displayed by the TPLF leadership reinforced the loyalty of the largely youthful membership of the movement. Older Tigrayan peasants who had contact with the various revolutionary movements that competed for their support in the 1970s can usually distinguish their main ideological differences; but, significantly, it is the personal characteristics of the fighters they emphasize, thus confirming the validity of the TPLF's approach.

In the final stages of the revolution there were indications that a number of cadres and peasants were jailed for their perceived opposition to the leadership. There is, however, no evidence to corroborate Kriger's finding that in Zimbabwe coercion by revolutionaries was of central importance in winning the compliance of the population.[39] Kriger attributes the revolutionaries' use of coercion to their inability to provide utilitarian benefits to peasants in return for the costly sacrifices they demanded,[40] but this bears little resemblance to the circumstances in Tigray, where the TPLF provided a wide range of services. According to Popkin, a 'leader must,

[35] J. Migdal, *Peasants, Politics, and Revolution: Pressures towards Political and Social Change in the Third World* (Princeton: Princeton University Press, 1968), p. 263.

[36] S. Popkin, *The Rational Peasant: the Political Economy of Rural Society in Vietnam* (Berkeley: University of California Press, 1979), p. 26.

[37] Popkin, *Rational Peasant*, p. 259.

[38] Interview: Gebru Asrat, Chairman of Tigray Region, Mekelle, 6 April 1993.

[39] N. Kriger, *Zimbabwe's Guerrilla War: Peasant Voices* (Cambridge: Cambridge University Press, 1992), p. 17.

[40] Kriger, *Zimbabwe's Guerrilla War*, p. 12.

first of all, be able to use terms and symbols his targets understand' if he is to link the revolution's goals to the lives of the peasants successfully.[41] The TPLF did this by using traditional and modern cultural forms to link their revolution to past Tigrayan battles that defended or advanced the national interest. But the revolutionaries did not simply manipulate peasant values. In the case of Tigray, these same peasant values placed limits on, and gave shape to, the course of the TPLF's military campaign and its programme to transform agrarian society.

It also meant constantly evaluating the impact of TPLF reforms on the community, on one hand, against the Front's ability to wage war against the Derg, on the other. Implementing the TPLF's programme of reforms served both as an instrument with which to transform rural society, and as a means to mobilize popular support for the war. These are not always complementary goals, however, since the social tensions caused by transformation may open up divisions that undermine the consensus needed to carry on a revolutionary war. The Tigrayan revolution makes clear that a crucial function of revolutionary struggle is the provision of political leadership; that leadership, in turn, must construct an appropriate balance between the needs for reform and for social peace.

[41] Popkin, *Rational Peasant*, p. 260.

4

DOUGLAS H. JOHNSON
The Sudan People's Liberation Army
and the Problem of Factionalism

The Sudan People's Liberation Army (SPLA)[1] is difficult to classify into the categories proposed in this volume. Is it a separatist insurgency, a reform insurgency, a state-consolidating or a state-subverting insurgency? The fact that it can be described in all of the above terms is less a product of internal political confusion, than the result of the duration of what is now Africa's longest civil war. Since the Sudanese civil war began in 1983 the Cold War has come to an end, apartheid has been defeated in Southern Africa, the West has begun to abandon its old Cold War allies in the continent and to identify a new international threat in Islamist governments and movements, many of which – including the National Islamic Front (NIF) of the Sudan's Dr Hasan al-Turabi – were Cold War friends or collaborators. All of these shifts have affected the SPLA in some way, and comparisons can be made with other guerrilla armies and liberation movements which successfully concluded their struggles during this period. Along with the National Resistance Army (NRA) and the Tigray People's Liberation Front (TPLF), the SPLA has recruited teenage soldiers in its long struggle against a national government with a succession of international backers. In common with the TPLF and the EPLF, it has diverted relief supplies for military purposes, countering the national government's ability to command relief supplies on a much grander scale from compliant international agencies such as the UN. As with the South West Africa People's Organization (SWAPO) and the African National Congress (ANC) in exile, it has used repression to stifle internal dissent, sometimes relying on the security services of its host country to arrest and punish dissidents. It has responded militarily to the threat of political factionalism, much as the TPLF and EPLF did before turning their attention exclusively to the forces of the Derg, as both Young and Pool remind us in their chapters in this volume. Also in common with the TPLF/Ethiopian Peoples' Revolutionary Democratic Front (EPRDF) and the EPLF, the SPLA has adopted Marxist language in its formulation of the 'nationalities'

---

[1] Within the movement itself it is customary to refer to the Sudan People's Liberation Movement/ Sudan People's Liberation Army (SPLM/SPLA), the movement being the ostensible political wing of the army. For reasons which will become clear later on in this chapter I will use the shorthand SPLA to refer to both.

question as underlying the inequalities inherent in the Sudanese state.

Yet those who prefer their liberation movements to be ideological have often been disappointed by the lack of consistent revolutionary ideology in the SPLA. When questioned about the movement's relationship to Marxism by a prominent Southern Sudanese exile politician, John Garang replied that his main task had always been to mobilize the anger of the Southern Sudanese against the government of the Sudan, and in attempting that task he found that the Southern Sudanese had little interest in ideology.[2]

This remark is an essential key to understanding the directions the SPLA has followed during the last 15 years, and its ability to maintain a coherent fighting force with sustained links to the civilian population throughout that time, despite phases of splintering and segmentation. For what has remained constant within the fluctuations of regional and international politics, is the structural subordination of the Southern Sudan and adjacent areas within the Sudanese state. To understand the SPLA's current position, especially with regard to the factionalism which has been its greatest problem since 1991, comparisons should be made less with other regional movements and more with its immediate predecessor, the Anyanya of the first Sudanese civil war (c. 1960–72).[3] A *history* of struggle does impose a *direction* on a movement; and the Southern Sudan has one of the longest histories of struggle in post-colonial Africa. When the SPLA was founded in 1983 it was less concerned with emulating other models from around the world and within Africa, and more intent on applying lessons learnt from the mistakes of earlier Southern Sudanese guerrillas. The guerrillas of the first civil war were bedevilled by bad organization, lack of coordination between local bands, personal and local rivalry between military and political leaders, a chronic shortage of supplies, and inadequate training throughout most of the 1960s. Lacking a strong military or political organization which could enable them to achieve their objectives, they also found that their uncompromising separatist goal isolated them from potential national and regional allies who might otherwise have helped them overcome their organizational weakness.

The Old Anyanya

The Sudan is a country of about 25 million people, speaking some hundred different languages. About half of these languages are spoken by the 4–6 million people who live in the Southern Sudan's approximately a third of a million square miles. A large

---

[2] Bona Malwal, personal communication.

[3] It is common to date the beginning of the first civil war from the Torit mutiny in August 1955. The disturbances which followed the mutiny lasted only a few weeks, after which most mutineers fled to Uganda, and a few groups remained in some of the more inaccessible areas of Equatoria. The clashes between the army and the remnant mutineers affected only a very tiny portion of the Southern Sudan, and the period from late 1955 to the early 1960s must be considered a dormant insurgency rather than an active civil war. It is therefore difficult to state precisely when the insurgency fully awoke into action. Some Southern Sudanese put it as late as 1963, when the old mutineers were reinforced by a new generation of students and political leaders, forced into exile by the increased repression of Sudan's first military regime.

percentage of the remaining half of the Sudan's languages are found concentrated in the Nuba Mountains, and in the foothills along the Sudan-Ethiopian border region of the Blue Nile. The areas of the greatest linguistic diversity within the Sudan are also the areas where there has been the least educational and economic development, and it is their marginalization from the main thrust of post-independence political and economic control in the Sudan which has created the grievances leading to two periods of civil war. They are also areas with a long history not only of 'statelessness', but of opposition to the main states of the Nile Valley. Within the Southern Sudan, the majority of the population (between a half and two-thirds) belong to the Nilotic-speaking pastoralist Dinka and Nuer peoples, who themselves are segmented into numerous tribes and sections. Any political movement within the South has had to come to terms with this widely shared historical experience of political segmentation.

The first civil war was fought exclusively in the three old provinces of the Southern Sudan, but the current war has been marked by a dramatic expansion of significant military and political activity, not only beyond the boundaries of the old South, but beyond the Sudan's national borders as well. Participants in both insurgencies were united by what they opposed within the structure of the state, but divided over how and by whom the state should be governed. The linguistic, religious and cultural diversity which bedevilled the insurgency in such a small and compact country as Eritrea[4] could be described as insignificant when compared with the much greater diversity confronting insurgents in the Sudan.

When the Sudan gained independence from Egypt and Britain in 1956, economic and political power was concentrated in the central Nile Valley region. The regions of the East, West and South were largely undeveloped. The main political parties of the centre were affiliated with the two main religious sects – the Khatmia and the Ansar – and it was through sectarian politics that the Muslim peoples of the East and West first participated in national politics. The Southern Sudan, with only a small Muslim population, was conscious of a racial and religious exclusion from the mainstream of national politics. Southern parliamentarians were in the forefront of the federal movement and made tentative approaches to representatives of the East and the West (especially the Nuba Mountains of Kordofan and the Fur of Darfur) in support of a federal constitution, but this embryonic alliance was aborted by the military take-over of 1958. With parliamentary politics abandoned and the vigorous implementation of an Arabization policy in the South (and elsewhere) by the military government, the Sudan drifted into civil war.

The original 'Anyanya' guerrillas of the South emerged in the early 1960s, as a combination of old mutineers from pre-independence disturbances, and new politically conscious Southern Sudanese administrators and students who had been affected adversely by programmes of the first military government (1958–64). Though many became refugees abroad (and there was always a close link between refugee Southern Sudanese and the Anyanya), the military bands maintained largely internal bases and training centres and for many years operated under dispersed and

---

[4] See the chapter by Pool in this volume.

informal authority.[5] This meant that there were in effect many Anyanya groups, some tenuously connected with a set of political leaders based outside, but most operating largely autonomously from – and sometimes at odds with – each other. There was some circulation of soldiers between provinces from a very early stage, but by and large Anyanya recruits stayed and fought in their home areas, and coordination or reinforcement beyond the provincial level was very difficult to organize.

Throughout the 1960s there was a fractured and exiled political leadership. By 1969 there were some five known 'movements' within the South, and their leaders frequently appeared in Kampala to denounce each other and announce new mobilizations against their rivals, rather than against the forces of Khartoum. Not until the 1970s, with Israel's involvement as a military supplier (through Uganda and Ethiopia) and provider of training, did some military cohesion emerge in the field, focused around Israel's chosen client, Joseph Lagu. Lagu thus became the sole source of supply and was able to bring in the other fighters.[6] Military unity having been achieved somewhat artificially through the efforts of one patron, political gains soon followed when the military wing of the movement effectively subordinated the political wing to its leadership. It was only after this effective unification of the leadership in 1971 that negotiations with the government were possible, leading to the Addis Ababa peace agreement in 1972.

One of the old Anyanya's greatest problems throughout the 1960s was the political isolation it suffered as a result of its separatist goal. Its call for self-determination for the South[7] meant that it could not develop the tentative pro-federalist alliances which Southern politicians had begun with other regions of the Sudan prior to the military take-over of 1958; nor could it rally the support of the Sudan's neighbours, which faced their own secessionist movements. In the event, support from Ethiopia and Uganda was opportunistic and erratic. Uganda under Milton Obote, for instance, was responsible for killing one of the South's strongest secessionist leaders, Fr Saturnino Lohure, and kidnapping one Anyanya group's mercenary adviser, Rolf Steiner, and deporting him to Khartoum.

The SPLA's founding leadership (most of whom had been serving in the Anyanya at the end of the first war) drew explicit lessons from the Anyanya experience and embodied many of those lessons in the 1983 SPLA manifesto. The old-style exile parties, with their 'paper cabinets', were roundly condemned, and it was clear that the military leadership was not going to allow the politicians such free rein again.[8]

---

[5] There is no full study of the military organization of the old Anyanya, but the most detailed published account so far is by Elias Nyamlell Wakoson, 'The origin and development of the Anya-Nya Movement 1955–1972', in Mohamed Omer Beshir, ed., *Southern Sudan: Regionalism & Religion,* Graduate College Publications No. 10 (Khartoum: University of Khartoum, 1984). A short summary can be found in D. H. Johnson and G. Prunier, 'The foundation and expansion of the Sudan People's Liberation Army', in M. W. Daly and Ahmad Alawad Sikainga, eds, *Civil War in the Sudan* (London: British Academic Press, 1993), pp. 117–20.

[6] See, for instance, R. Steiner, *The Last Adventurer. From Biafra to the Sudan* (London: Weidenfeld and Nicholson, 1978), pp. 203–4.

[7] See J. Oduho and W. Deng, *The Problem of the Southern Sudan* (London: Oxford University Press for the Institute of Race Relations, 1963), p. 60.

[8] SPLM, *Manifesto,* 31 July 1993, pp. 7–8.

So, from the start, the political and military leadership was merged under the leadership of a single chairman.

The Origin of the SPLA[9]

The renewal of civil war in the Sudan in the 1980s came about in part because of the failure of the post-Addis Ababa agreement Southern Regional governments to meet expectations, but it also happened in the context of the further marginalization of large parts of the rural areas of the Northern Sudan. During the regime of Jaafar Nimeiri (1969–85), there was a dramatic expansion of rain-fed mechanized farming in a belt extending from Darfur to the Blue Nile, involving the wholesale alienation of land or rights in the use of land from small-holding farmers and pastoralists – Muslims as well as non-Muslims – and the transfer of those rights to well-capitalized merchants and government officials from the central Nile Valley. This had a catastrophic impact on those dispossessed during the drought and famine of the early 1980s. Opposition to Nimeiri was growing stronger in the Muslim areas of the North, though the hold of the old sectarian parties on their rural constituencies was by no means assured. The national political alignments at the time of the resumption of civil war in the South were thus very different from what they had been in the 1960s. The Southern guerrillas were but one (the strongest, as it turned out) of several dissident groups within the country. There were opportunities for new political (if not military) alliances to be forged, opportunities of which the emergent leadership of the SPLA was more conscious than most of the rank-and-file guerrilla soldiers. This is certainly one reason why the SPLA from the start addressed itself to the 'national' rather than the 'Southern' problem, and advocated national solutions to structural inequalities.[10] This position allowed the SPLA greater flexibility in its political strategies, but was at odds with the motivation of most of those Southern Sudanese who joined and formed (and still form) the overwhelming majority of the movement. It also meant that as long as it was committed to a united Sudan, SPLA propaganda would have difficulty building up a political sentiment of Southern unity.

Armed opposition to the Khartoum government within the South in the late 1970s and early 1980s began in much the same way as opposition began in the 1950s: through individual armed groups, many of them Anyanya mutineers who had rejected the Addis Ababa agreement and set off for the bush or to neighbouring countries. The immediate difference was that Ethiopia very soon began to give them active support, in response to the support President Nimeiri's regime gave to anti-Derg forces as early as 1976. By 1980 a more coordinated resistance began to make itself felt through attacks on police posts and market lorries in various parts of the Upper Nile and Jonglei provinces. These new armed groups soon became known as 'Anyanya II', but they did not constitute a movement, and in fact 'Anyanya II' at this stage was little more than a general term covering a series of independent groups, some of which had a political goal, while some were

[9] See Johnson and Prunier, 'The SPLA' , pp. 120–5.
[10] SPLM, *Manifesto*.

opportunistic bandits. The influence of Ethiopia, and for a short time Libya (which provided military hardware) did, however, begin to give a coherence to these disparate bands. By 1982 the Ethiopian-backed groups were beginning to impose discipline on the other independent groups in the Jonglei, Upper Nile and Lakes provinces, and used them to forward new recruits to training camps in Ethiopia.

Ex-Anyanya and other Southern soldiers in the army garrisons in the provinces also began to establish contacts with the 'Anyanya II' in 1982 and early 1983, ultimately enabling Battalions 104 and 105 to defect with all their equipment and escape through Jonglei province to Ethiopia in May 1983. The amalgamation of army defectors (who included such senior officers as Colonel John Garang, head of the Staff College in Omdurman) and the main 'Anyanya II' groups based in Ethiopia led to the formation of the SPLA by July 1983 (again with significant Ethiopian support). Ethiopia lent its weight to the formation of a single command under Garang, and while this drew opposition from some older Anyanya veterans, it was one of the organizational achievements which enabled the SPLA to establish its presence throughout much of the Southern Sudan, by contacting and incorporating other existing guerrilla groups (such as the 'Abyei Liberation Front' in Southern Kordofan) throughout 1983 and early 1984.

Unlike the pattern of the old Anyanya in the early years of the first civil war, the SPLA by and large did not allow newly incorporated groups to run autonomous operations in their own territory; nor did it leave its new recruits to get what training they could in their home areas. Rather, all new recruits were transferred to training camps inside Ethiopia, mainly in the Gambela region. There they were organized into units under a central command and sent back to the South. In the 1980s the SPLA generally followed a three-year pattern of drawing new areas into the war. Typically this involved sending small 'mobile units' or 'task forces' to an as yet unaffected area where they undertook limited military operations and political mobilization leading to recruitment. New recruits were sent back to Ethiopia where they spent the next year training in camps such as Bonga and Pagak. In the third year these recruits would return to their home areas to recruit among their kin and generation. Government retaliation against villages which earlier recruits were known to have come from generally drove more people over to the side of the SPLA.[11]

Later, when the SPLA returned in force to these areas, they came in battalion strengths of up to a thousand guerrillas.[12] In the period 1984–6, the battalions provided the structure for a new civil/military administration (see below), and became associated with specific regions, or provinces within regions. By 1986 'task forces' sent to liberate new areas (such as the 'Abyei Task Force' or the 'Nuba Mountains

[11] For the general pattern see Johnson and Prunier, 'The SPLA', pp. 131–7; for specific accounts from Bahr al-Ghazal (1984–5), Jebel Lafon (1984–8), southern Blue Nile (1986–7) and the Nuba Mountains (1986–8), see M. L. Kuol, *Administration of Justice in the (SPLA/M) Liberated Areas: Court Cases in War-Torn Southern Sudan* (Oxford: Refugee Studies Programme, February 1997), p. 10; E. Kurimoto, 'Civil war and regional conflicts: the Pari and their neighbours in south-eastern Sudan', in K. Fukui and J. Markakis, *Ethnicity and Conflict in the Horn of Africa* (London/Athens OH: James Currey/Ohio University Press, 1994), pp. 100–9; W. James, 'War and "ethnic visibility": the Uduk on the Sudan-Ethiopian border', in Fukui and Markakis, *Ethnicity and Conflict*, pp. 145–58; African Rights, *Facing Genocide: The Nuba of Sudan* (London: July 1995).

[12] Kuol, *Administration of Justice*, p. 10.

Task Force'), or to secure and control newly liberated territory (as in the 'Lafon Task Force') were themselves often of battalion strength. By the end of the 1980s whole divisions of several battalions were organized to take the war out of the Southern Sudan, with the creation of the 'New Kush' division of six battalions sent to the Nuba Mountains in 1989,[13] and the 'New Funj' division which operated in southern Blue Nile in 1988–9, participating in the brief capture of Kurmuk and Qeissan at the end of 1988.

By the late 1980s the SPLA was no longer relying solely on small mobile units to ambush, infiltrate, and harass the enemy. From the mid-1980s, it progressively confined the majority of government forces to their bases in the larger provincial towns, and interdicted relief convoys by land and river. By 1987 it began to take and hold minor garrisons from the Sudan army. In 1988 came a string of victories which, by mid-1989, placed it in control of much of the Ethiopian border, the whole of the Kenyan border, and almost all of the rural area of the Southern Sudan, and planted its forces outside the South in the Nuba Mountains and southern Blue Nile. By early 1989 the SPLA was moving units of thousands of men, rather than tens or hundreds, and had begun capturing substantial quantities of government equipment: vehicles, tanks and heavy artillery. Tactics had changed from a guerrilla war of mobile units to entrenched sieges outside major cities and towns, the most notable being Juba, the former capital of the old Southern Region.[14]

A marked departure from the old Anyanya days was the ability of the SPLA to transfer men from front to front. The Nuer soldiers who had participated in the siege and fall of Jokau and Nasir near the Ethiopian border in 1988–9 were transferred south out of Upper Nile at the end of 1990, and helped to spearhead the capture of almost the whole of Western Equatoria in November 1990 to January 1991. At the time of the Nasir split in late 1991, there were still a substantial number of Nuer stationed in SPLA garrisons throughout Western and Eastern Equatoria.[15]

Part of this ability to transfer men was facilitated by the SPLA's own zonal system. On a national level the whole of the Southern Sudan was declared 'War Zone I' (the North potentially being 'War Zone II'), but within that area there were numerous operational zones, each under a Zonal Commander. Unlike the ELF in Eritrea, these zones were not based upon specific peoples, fostering conflict along tribal lines (as often had happened in the 1960s); rather, they were organized around existing provinces or sub-provinces, each containing a number of peoples and languages. Zonal Commanders were already in place (and referred to as such in Radio SPLA broadcasts from Ethiopia) as early as 1986. Some zones, such as Lakes, coincided exactly with pre-1983 provinces. Others, such as Southern Kordofan (in reality, the

---

[13] African Rights, *Facing Genocide*, p. 66.

[14] It is some indication of the difference in scale between the two civil wars that the Sudanese army's entire southern garrison numbered about 20,000 men at the time of the Addis Ababa agreement in 1972. By 1990 the Juba garrison alone was more than 20,000. A well-informed source has estimated the government garrison in Juba by the rains of 1997 to be some 30,000, of which only about 10,000 were regular army (the rest being ill-trained Popular Defence Force units). The SPLA force surrounding the city itself is estimated at around 20,000.

[15] This was brought home to me in October 1991 when I was part of the UN Operation Lifeline Sudan annual evaluation team. A significant proportion of the 'female heads of households' I interviewed around the Gaawar Nuer village of Ayod reported that their husbands were in the army around Torit – i.e., in Garang's 'Dinka' faction rather than Riek Mashar's 'Nuer' faction.

Nuba Mountains), Northern Upper Nile, Central Equatoria, or Central South Sudan incorporated only parts of the old provinces. A number of zones would also be grouped together in an 'axis' under the command of one of the principal SPLA commanders, and supplies and equipment were allocated to different axes.[16]

Clearly, a secure base in Ethiopia and a steady source of supplies enabled Garang and his Political-Military High Command (PMHC, composed of the Zonal Commanders) to organize liberated territory without the headquarters coming under threat from government action. The fall of Nimeiri in 1985 paradoxically increased the SPLA's dependence on Mengistu; for Qadhafi immediately abandoned military support for the SPLA and switched his full support to Nimeiri's former Muslim opponents in the North (Sadiq al-Mahdi's Umma party being one of the main beneficiaries). Libya had been the sole source of the SPLA's only SAM anti-aircraft missiles. It was at this time that the SPLA became actively engaged in battle with Mengistu's opponents in Wallega Province. These being mainly drawn from the Oromo Liberation Front (OLF), whom the SPLA commanders (as former Sudan army officers) knew operated in close support with the Sudanese army (often sharing bases inside the Sudan), the SPLA could justify this as merely fighting Khartoum's Ethiopian catspaws. Some of Garang's former commanders were later to claim that they had always opposed getting involved in Ethiopian politics in this way, but the rewards were immediate in opening up Mengistu's arsenals to the SPLA. It also forged a personal tie between Garang and Mengistu, putting Mengistu's security network at Garang's service to contain internal dissent in the SPLA. It is significant of the role Ethiopia played at this time that in 1987 when Kerubino Kuanyin Bol, Garang's chief of staff, attempted to overthrow Garang, he did so by appealing to Mengistu to remove Garang from power.[17] Mengistu responded by arresting Kerubino and handing him over to Garang.

Early Strains: The Problem of the Anyanya II

The SPLA deliberately set about to avert the localism and factions which undermined the old Anyanya, and was to a large extent successful. It achieved in a very short time an integration of forces and a unity of command that far exceeded anything attributable to the old Anyanya, and this was demonstrated in the military successes in the 1980s (it should be remembered that the old Anyanya never took and held a town of any standing throughout the first civil war). Yet the SPLA's strengths were also its weaknesses. Its reliance on Ethiopia, which was supposed to keep dissent in check, produced a split in its ranks at the very outset. Its use of recruits as a 'national' force, to be sent wherever needed, created resentment among those who had joined from mainly local grievances or from the motive of protecting

[16] In 1987 Kerubino Kuanyin Bol, Garang's second-in-command, complained that the majority of supplies were being sent to Garang's own axis in Equatoria (letter from Lt Col Kerubino Kuanyin Bol to 'Comrade Mengistu Hail M', 'Memo on SPLM/SPLA Current Problems', 6 August 1987).

[17] *Ibid.* This letter was part of the Ethiopian government's security file on the SPLA handed over to Khartoum by the EPRDF after taking Addis Ababa. I was given a copy by Riek Mashar in Nasir in November 1991. Subsequent copies were distributed in the UK by a Northern Sudanese 'peace activist', T. A. Elkhazin.

their homes. The persistence of local dissatisfactions, and resentment at the suppression of leaders with personal constituencies within the army, were to combine with explosive results once the influence of Mengistu and the Derg was removed in 1991.

To a certain extent the SPLA still relied on the local standing of commanders to give a 'national' character to the movement while at the same time attracting recruits. Local Zonal and Area Commanders such as Yusuf Kuwa in the Nuba Mountains, James Wani Igga in Western Equatoria, Galario Modi and Obuto Mamur in Torit, Daniel Aweit in Bahr el-Ghazal, Daud Bollad in Darfur, and more recently Malik Agar in the Blue Nile helped to counteract the impression of 'Dinka domination' (in particular that of the Dinka of Bor and Kongor districts, including Garang himself, who were alleged to have dominated the Southern Regional governments of Abel Alier). The defection of Riek Mashar and Lam Akol of Upper Nile was to highlight the implicit problems of too much (rather than too little) local autonomy of commanders.

The insistence of the Ethiopian government on a unified military-political command, and their support for John Garang, one of the younger and better educated of the early SPLA leaders, as well as one of the most senior in the Sudanese army, for the position of commander-in-chief and chairman of the political movement, helped to precipitate the factionalism they were trying to avoid.[18] Garang was opposed by on older generation of Anyanya leaders who had held positions senior to his at the end of the first war. Once fighting within the SPLA was precipitated inside Ethiopia by the Ethiopian army, the older leaders were thrown back on their own kin groups for support. It was only through an alliance between the Nimeiri government and the Nuer remnant of the 'Anyanya II' that this group was given a military lifeline and a political presence in opposition to Garang and the SPLA. There was an inherent contradiction in the Anyanya II political platform, which was ultimately to prove deadly to it, as it was to a subsequent SPLA splinter group, SPLA-United (later the South Sudan Independence Movement, or SSIM): this was that the group operated within an active military alliance with Khartoum at the same time as it ostensibly fought for complete independence for the Southern Sudan.

Groups of Anyanya II were recruited from quite specific sections: from the Gaajak Nuer of Maiwut, the Mor Lou Nuer of Akobo, the Lak and Thiang Nuer of the Zeraf Valley, and the Bul Nuer of Western Nuer. Presented by foreign observers as a Nuer–Dinka split, in fact most Anyanya II–SPLA fighting took place with groups of Nuer on both sides. In 1987–90 the SPLA achieved a rapprochement with the majority of Anyanya II units, using mainly Nuer commanders and politicians as intermediaries.[19] Having switched allegiance, however, the reconciled Anyanya II

---

[18] Johnson and Prunier, 'The SPLA', pp. 125–7; and G. Prunier, 'The crisis of the Sudanese Peoples [sic] Liberation Army (1991–6)', updated version of a paper presented at the Third International Sudan Studies Conference, 1996, pp. 5–7.

[19] Two of the most significant intermediaries were D. K. Matthew, who as Nimeiri's governor of Upper Nile Region organized and armed the remnant Anyanya II as an anti-Garang Nuer militia; and Vincent Kuac, the leader of the 1975 Akobo mutiny and significant figure in the pre-1983 Anyanya II groups operating out of Ethiopia. Both were subsequently to join Riek Mashar, though after 1995 D. K. Matthew appears to have managed the feat of simultaneously encouraging Garang and Mashar.

units were not fully integrated into the SPLA: they were not immediately sent back to the Ethiopian bases for retraining and reassignment, but remained in their home areas. This was to prove costly in 1991 when the Anyanya II groups sided with the splinter Nasir faction of Riek Mashar. In the fighting which broke out between the Nasir faction and what became known as the Mainstream SPLA, it was the old Anyanya II troops who took the lead in attacking civilians in Kongor and Bor districts, repeating the tactics they had used when under Khartoum's direction. Targeting the civilian base of SPLA support had been the main function of the various government-supplied militias under Nimeiri and Sadiq al-Mahdi. The activities of the Anyanya II forces within the Nasir command reintroduced a state of insecurity among the civilian population which had been absent in areas securely under SPLA control, and set in motion a series of retaliatory raids which defined the direction of the factional war within the SPLA.

The Crisis of 1991 and the Return of Factionalism

By 1990 the SPLA's position was the reverse of what it had been at the beginning of the war: it was now in an extremely strong position in the field, but its rear bases in Ethiopia were vulnerable as Mengistu's regime began to crumble on all fronts.[20] In early 1991 Garang's military strategy in response to this situation was to concentrate forces around Juba in the hope that a final military push would win him this prize (and effectively win the war in the South), while at the same time diverting troops based in Ethiopia to fight alongside the Ethiopian army in a last bid to stem the EPRDF and OLF advance in the south-west. In the meantime there is some evidence that plans were being made to evacuate the civilian refugees from their Ethiopian camps after the 1991 rainy season. This seems to have been left to the Itang camp administration and the SPLA commanders based at Nasir to organize.[21] As it happened, the Derg's sudden collapse in May 1991 intervened and upset the timetable.

The sudden removal of Ethiopian supplies and Mengistu's personal support was a serious blow to the SPLA, and to Garang. It brought to the fore the discontent among some of his commanders who were now in an exposed military position, but also found that Garang's own weakened position gave them more space in which to manoeuvre. Two of the Upper Nile commanders, Riek Mashar and Lam Akol, had already voiced objections to Garang's personal rule. They complained in particular that the PMHC had scarcely ever met as a group, so that decisions about the direction of the war and diplomatic contacts abroad were effectively made by

[20] The SPLA did establish its military command headquarters inside the Southern Sudan as early as 1985/6, following its capture of Boma in April 1985. Torit became another important internal headquarters following its capture from the government in 1989.

[21] At least one large rally was organized at Itang by Lam Akol and the camp administrator, Taban Deng Gai (both of whom were later prominent in the Nasir faction) to prepare the refugees for the coming changes. Later that year, when I visited the Pibor River for the World Food Programme (WFP), I met a number of Nuer and Anuak men who had returned to their home areas earlier in the year in order to build homesteads and open up cultivations (using maize from the Itang relief rations) in anticipation of the return of their families later in the year.

Garang and a small quorum of his closest commanders, rather than through the collective agreement of the entire body.[22] The grievances were real enough, but the unspoken concern of the Upper Nile commanders was that the concentration of troops and supplies around Juba had weakened Upper Nile to reinforce Equatoria. With the loss of the Ethiopian bases the SPLA was reduced to its East African supply line, placing Upper Nile at the far end of that line and on the front line with Khartoum.

The arrival in the Nasir area of over 100,000 returnees from Itang (directed there by the Nasir commanders) altered both the relief and the supply situation.[23] Having been virtually ignored throughout the first two years of the UN-sponsored relief operation, Operation Lifeline Sudan (OLS),[24] Nasir now became the hub of concentrated relief activity. Khartoum's restrictions on flight permission, and the UN's failure to insist on guaranteed access, meant that the relief that came in was insufficient for the returnees, and nowhere near the amounts that used to come into Itang, which also helped to supply SPLA soldiers. The relief activity also brought the Nasir commanders into direct and constant contact not only with the major relief agencies, but with representatives of donor governments, such as the US, and eventually with representatives of the Khartoum government. It was through these contacts that they canvassed the idea of removing Garang from the leadership of the SPLA, and received some external encouragement, not least from Khartoum.[25] When Garang learned of their activities, they announced his overthrow and a policy of total independence for the South over the BBC World Service on 28 August 1991.

The Nasir commanders had been unable to complete their canvassing for support before announcing their 'coup',[26] but they hoped that their unequivocal advocacy of secession would isolate Garang and bring other commanders willingly over to

[22] Riek Mashar and Lam Akol, 'Why John Garang must go now', 1991.

[23] D. H. Johnson, 'Increasing the trauma of return: an assessment of the UN's emergency response to the evacuation of the Sudanese refugee camps in Ethiopia, 1991', in T. Allen, ed., *In Search of Cool Ground: Displacement and Homecoming in Northeast Africa* (London/Trenton NJ: James Currey/Africa World Press, 1996).

[24] For a survey, analysis and critique of Operation Lifeline Sudan, see A. Karim *et al.*, 'Operation Lifeline Sudan: a Review', Geneva, Department of Humanitarian Affairs, July 1996.

[25] The Nasir commanders used the nearly daily flights to Nairobi as a means of sending letters back to SPLA leaders based in Kenya. At least two US officials with an interest in removing Garang, one a consultant to the US government's Office of Foreign Disaster Assistance (OFDA), used their access to flights to visit Nasir. Direct contact between the Nasir commanders and the government in Malakal was established, ostensibly to facilitate the distribution of relief along the Sobat River by WFP barge. The charge made by the *Sudan Democratic Gazette* (October 1991, pp. 1, 5) that UN field personnel knowingly and deliberately participated in these political contacts is, to the best of my knowledge, untrue.

[26] The timing of the announcement is important. Both commanders were expected to come to Torit in August for a meeting of the entire PMHC, of the sort that they had been demanding. The commanders claimed that they had been tipped off that once in Torit they were to be dismissed and imprisoned. Since they hoped for a groundswell of support from other commanders, they had to make their announcement before the Torit meeting. Garang is reported to have been convinced that the split was intended to prevent him from taking Juba in the expected late rains/early dry season offensive around September–October. There are some reports of private statements from one of the Nasir commanders which suggest that this, too, was a factor in the calculation of the timing of the announcement. For an insider's account of the coup see P. A. Nyaba, *The Politics of Liberation in South Sudan: an Insider's View* (Kampala: Fountain Publishers, 1997), Chapters 2 and 3.

their side. They calculated that their call for independence would appeal to most Southerners, especially Equatorians, and that their denunciation of undemocratic methods of rule would be endorsed by other commanders within and outside the PMHC. In particular, they anticipated that other Zones, such as Northern Bahr al-Ghazal and the Nuba Mountains, would have similar grievances to theirs, having been marginal in the SPLA's overall military and relief strategy, receiving very few supplies of any kind. In fact both Lakes and Northern Bahr al-Ghazal had been heavy recruiting areas for the SPLA, but most of their soldiers had been sent to the Equatorian fronts, leaving their homes open to attack, especially during the 1986–8 Murhalin militia raids. It was hoped that these areas would feel just as isolated and vulnerable as Upper Nile with the loss of the Ethiopian supply bases.

The reaction was not as expected. There had been a sustained SPLA presence in the Nuba Hills only since 1989 (before then SPLA units made only seasonal appearances), but the Zonal Commander, Yusuf Kuwa, was a pre-war politician and had spent considerable time in holding rallies and engaging in political mobilization which, by 1991, was being extended to the organization of elections to chiefly offices and courts under the SPLA. Faced with the fact that the Nasir commanders' hold on Northern and Western Upper Nile effectively interdicted any possible supplies that might have come up from East Africa, the SPLA in the Nuba Mountains held a series of local meetings at which it was decided to continue the war, despite the deterioration in the local military situation.[27] The Nasir faction's advocacy of independence for the Southern Sudan was one factor in keeping the Nuba in the SPLA fold. As part of either an independent South or a truncated North, the Nuba faced continued marginalization; whereas an alliance with a strong South in a united Sudan offered far greater possibilities for political manoeuvre. For a while it looked as if Bahr al-Ghazal and Lakes were inclined to sit out the contest between Garang and his rebellious commanders (the two Equatorias were under effective SPLA occupation and in no position to declare), but fighting between the two factions in Upper Nile and Jonglei during the months of October through December, culminating in the massacre of Dinka civilians at Kongor and Bor, among other things revealed the depths of the Nasir faction's reliance on Khartoum for military support and supplies, even at this early date. The contradiction between publicly advocating Southern independence and secretly accepting military hardware from Khartoum could never be resolved, and in the end the SPLA Nasir faction (otherwise known as SPLA-United, or SSIM) became one of a number of 'spoilers' which Khartoum armed and aimed at the civilian population in SPLA controlled areas. Eventually these were to include the independent Bul Nuer Anyanya II group of Paulino Mathip (who had never joined Garang and was subsequently only loosely associated with Riek Mashar), Kerubino Kuanyin Bol's troops in Gogrial and Northern Bahr al-Ghazal, William Nyuon's mixture of Nuer and Equatorian troops based at Jebel Lafon, as well as the Lord's Resistance Army (LRA) and Juma Oris's group in northern Uganda. To the extent that the government was successful in attracting Southern dissidents, it played upon the SPLA's weaknesses: offering John Garang's personal opponents weapons and relief supplies with which to build up their own followings. But the survival of the anti-

[27] African Rights, *Facing Genocide*, p. 316.

Garang factions depended on the good will of the government, which controlled the allocation of resources, the appointments to high position and the implementation of any proposed future constitutional changes. The vast majority of Southerners (particularly those resident in the displaced camps in the North) no longer took the good will of Northern governments for granted.

The SPLA's Response: the Impact of Civil Administration

Garang's response to this factionalism has been characterized by many critics as purely military.[28] Khartoum's directing hand, however, meant the military threat was real and immediate, and the SPLA lost considerable ground in government offensives in Eastern Equatoria, Jonglei and Lakes in 1992–4, while significant numbers of SPLA troops were tied down in Northern Bahr al-Ghazal, Jonglei and Eastern Equatoria, fighting forces under the command of Riek Mashar, William Nyuon, Paulino Mathip and Kerubino Kuanyin. It was only towards the end of 1994 that government advances were halted. At the end of 1995 the SPLA began to roll the government forces back at an accelerating pace, while Riek Mashar's SSIM coalition fell apart with internal fighting and defections either to the government or the SPLA,[29] until government forces finally turned on Riek's troops along the Sobat River and the Ethiopian border. Fighting changed dramatically in 1997 with the emergence of a small, but significant, force of Northern Sudanese soldiers from the National Democratic Alliance (NDA), as well as mixed Northern and Southern troops of the Sudan Allied Forces (SAF),[30] under Garang's overall command, opening up new fronts along the Ethiopian and Eritrean borders around Kurmuk and Kassala, while the SPLA rolled up numerous government garrisons in Equatoria and Lakes, renewing the siege of Juba. In this the SPLA/NDA alliance received active support from elements of the Ugandan, Ethiopian and Eritrean armies.

The revival of SPLA military strength was not just the product of a reform in the military structures, or the advantageous network of diplomatic alliances produced, in part, by Khartoum's alienation of Eritrea, Ethiopia and Uganda after its support for Islamist and other dissident groups in those countries. All these were significant factors, but they would not have come into play had the SPLA disappeared in 1992–4, as many external commentators expected. I suggest that it is within the framework of a functioning civil administration throughout SPLA-controlled territory that one can find the answer to the overall success of the SPLA in securing and holding on to large sections of the rural civilian population (that is, maintaining a civilian base), despite the overwhelmingly military nature of the movement, and despite the political and military upheavals of the years after 1991.

Very little attention has been given to SPLA civil administration, and what little

---

[28] E.g., Prunier, 'The crisis'.
[29] The most important defection came about in April 1995, when Nuer soldiers based at Jebel Lafon refused to collaborate with the government any longer, seized a supply convoy passing through Lafon on its way to Torit, and persuaded William Nyuon Bany to rejoin the SPLA.
[30] SAF are soldiers of the national army who have either been purged by the NIF or have deserted. Perhaps surprisingly, the majority of SAF's front-line troops are Southern Sudanese.

has been written is very sceptical of its achievements.[31] It is my own observation that, whereas this scepticism is understandable in the absence of any systematic written records of administration or legal trials (a problem in the Southern Sudan not confined to this period of its history), many of the achievements of civil administration can be judged by what happened in its absence in places most affected by the 1991 split. One thing is clear: by 1989 the SPLA had been very successful in controlling local raiding in those areas under its control. Internal raiding between Dinka groups in Lakes and Bahr al-Ghazal was contained through the establishment of SPLA courts as early as 1985.[32] Raids along the Upper Nile–Lakes–Bahr al-Ghazal border had been brought under control by a string of border police posts, and by firm and coordinated action by commanders on either side of the divide (including Riek Mashar). Even Nuer, Anuak and Murle raiding had been addressed at an inter-tribal peace conference held in Akobo late in 1990. The explosion of officially sanctioned raiding following the split in Jonglei and along the borders between Western Upper Nile and Bahr al-Ghazal makes the period which preceded it look remarkable in its tranquillity. It is true that alleged 'tribal raids' became a camouflage for much larger military operations inaugurated by either the South Sudanese Independence Army (SSIA) or the SPLA (as they did with the government militias from Kordofan and Darfur). The use of troops from outside the border areas exacerbated local conflicts.

Criticisms of the lack of modern 'civil society' institutions in the Southern Sudan are true as far as they go,[33] but a focus which merely identifies the weaknesses of local churches, or the absence of trade unions and other autonomous non-governmental organizations, ignores those institutions which do exist and have continued to function throughout the civil war. The most important are the chiefs' courts. African Rights' claim that only in the Nuba Mountains, and only as late as 1989–90, did the SPLA become involved in political mobilization and organizing chiefs' courts,[34] is false. The practice of establishing a civil administration which regulated the election of chiefs and the functions of chiefs' courts began in the SPLA's major recruiting areas as early as 1984.[35] Political mobilization on the ground was supplemented by Radio SPLA (broadcasting from Ethiopia in 1984–91), which

---

[31] African Rights: 'Great expectations: the civil roles of the Churches in Southern Sudan', Discussion Paper No. 6, April 1995; *Facing Genocide*; 'Imposing empowerment? Aid and civil institutions in Southern Sudan', Discussion Paper No. 7, December 1995.

[32] Kuol, *Administration of Justice*, p. 11.

[33] T. Tvedt, 'The collapse of the state in Southern Sudan after the Addis Ababa Agreement. A study of internal causes and the role of the NGOs', in Sharif Harir and T. Tvedt, eds, *Short-Cut to Decay: The Case of the Sudan* (Uppsala: Nordiska Afrikanistitutet, 1994); African Rights, 'Great expectations' and 'Imposing empowerment'.

[34] African Rights, *Facing Genocide*, p. 315.

[35] Kuol, *Administration of Justice*, p. 10. External commentators have frequently made the charge that there is no civil administration inside the SPLA areas. Before I had a chance to revisit the Southern Sudan I, too, repeated the charge that SPLA administration was non-existent (Johnson, 'North–South issues', in P. Woodward. ed., *Sudan After Nimeiri* (London: Routledge, 1991), p. 135). In 1990, on my first return to areas I had known before the war, I was struck by the continuity of the chiefs' courts. Not only were the same courts, representing the same sections, still operating, but many of the same chiefs I had known in the 1970s (or their sons) were still in office. Ranald Boyle, former British district commissioner of Gogrial, reported to me that when he visited Bahr al-Ghazal in 1994 on behalf of SCF-UK he was greeted by chiefs he had formerly supervised in the early 1950s, and was even invited to attend a court session for old time's sake.

not only publicized the setting up of civil administration in new areas coming under SPLA control, but used vernacular broadcasts to explain the movement's policy to civilians.[36] The role of an internal judicial system in settling and containing disputes in SPLA areas prior to 1991 must be examined with greater care. The emergence of a 'civil' administration out of a 'civil/military' administration is also not without its parallels in an earlier period of colonial administration.

In the structure of 'native administration' developed during the Condominium period, which continued throughout the Southern Sudan after independence despite its abolition in the North during Nimeiri's regime, government chiefs combined judicial with executive responsibilities. Executive authority within civil administration, however, resided not with the chiefs, but with appointed members of a civil service – first British, then Northern, and finally Southern Sudanese. This administrative structure, despite many re-namings of units and offices, remained essentially the same after independence and during the brief period of the Southern Regional government (1972–83), with chiefs being supervised at the district level by local government officials, who reported to a civil administrator within the province or region, who was in turn subordinate to the provincial commissioner/ regional governor, a political appointee. The main difference was that with independence a separate set of magistrates took over the judicial duties formerly exercised by British district commissioners.

After the current war began the old structures were retained in many important respects, but, in all those rural areas which it occupied, a civil/military administration was created within the military structure of the SPLA. Thus Zonal Commanders had overall responsibility for the civil administration of their zones. Officers from within the SPLA were transferred to specific civil administrative duties as Civil/Military Administrators (CMAs) or judicial officers, while retaining their ranks within the SPLA. The CMAs were responsible for the collection of taxes from the civil population, but the judicial officers oversaw the organization of the court system within their jurisdiction. Chiefs within the SPLA-administered areas continued to perform the same duties that they had performed since the establishment of native administration under the British: those of recruitment (both labour and paramilitary), tax collection, distribution of relief, and adjudication of disputes under customary law.

The re-establishment of administration under a direct military chain of command had a militarizing effect on the level of chiefly administration. Chiefs were still elected, and powerful, well-established chiefs were still courted, but, as the supervising authority for elections, SPLA commanders were able to exert some influence on the selection process in order to secure positions for their supporters and allies (often, however, from the same families who had filled the offices in the past). Up until 1994 many SPLA commanders also contributed to the proliferation of chiefs, through the recognition of sub-sections as sub-tribes and increasing the number of elective offices.[37] Despite the retention of the elective process, chiefs were

[36] See the *BBC Summary of World Broadcasts*; W. James, 'Radio and conflict: Sudan', paper presented at a conference on 'African Broadcast Cultures: Radio and Public Life', University of London, School of African and Oriental Studies (SOAS), 12–13 June 1997.
[37] Whereas before the war executive chiefs were supposed to represent a minimum of 1,000 (adult male) taxpayers, by 1994 they could represent groups of as few as 400 (D. H. Johnson and J. MacAskill, 'Eastern Bahr el-Ghazal Evaluation', Oxford, Oxfam, May 1995, pp. 4–6).

subordinated within the military chain of command, were given paramilitary responsibilities (such as recruitment), and lost some of their previous autonomy. This, too, had precedents from previous regimes. The old structure of colonial native administration, having grown out of a military structure, was always capable of being re-militarized, as it was selectively by the British in the Second World War, and also selectively by post-independence governments during the first civil war. One justification sometimes given by the SPLA for incorporating chiefs into the military structure was that by giving them a position within the military hierarchy, they were thus in a position to discipline individual soldiers within their jurisdiction.

The application of law within the SPLA areas has been irregular, hampered as it has been by the lack of trained magistrates, and even by sufficient copies of legal ordinances, or pens and paper with which to keep records. Yet it has been important for all that, in regulating relations between the military and civilian populations. The experience of Bahr al-Ghazal is instructive. In 1983 the SPLA enacted its own Penal Code as a disciplinary code confined to the military. In 1984, the same year in which SPLA administration began to be introduced into Bahr al-Ghazal, the 1983 code was amended so that it included a disciplinary law for the army, a general penal code, and a code of procedures. The 1984 laws specifically recognized the application of customary law in each community within SPLA-controlled territory and, in addition to recognizing the customary courts, established three tiers of military courts. This structure remained highly theoretical, and in practice the military commander of Bahr al-Ghazal created a special court in 1985 to operate in Lakes Province, as a prelude to establishing a wider judicial system throughout the rest of Bahr al-Ghazal. Over the years a series of administrative and judicial committees were established both to supervise the chiefs' courts and to take appeals from them. A special act was also passed in 1984, recognizing the pre-1983 codification of Dinka customary law in Bahr al-Ghazal.[38]

There were anomalies. The only trained legal officials in the area were the judicial officers (former magistrates), whose courts were initially subject to appeal to a general court martial composed of members with no legal background. In practice the general court martial ceased to act as a court of appeal. As the judicial structure expanded, judicial officers with no firm grounding in customary law were also appointed, and they were expected to supervise the work of chiefs whose knowledge of customary law was greater than theirs. The application of the disciplinary code was also irregular and often arbitrary. The 1983 Penal Code prescribed the death penalty for a number of crimes committed by military personnel, including looting and rape. By procedure all death sentences had to be confirmed by Garang as chairman of the Sudan People's Liberation Movement (SPLM), but in practice very few case papers were sent to him. This meant that death sentences were either carried out summarily by order of the local commander, or were not imposed at all. As one magistrate working in Bahr al-Ghazal in the 1980s later remarked,

---

[38] Kuol, *Administration of Justice*, pp. 12–13. The codified Dinka customary law can be found in John Wuol Makec, *The Customary Law of the Dinka People of Sudan in Comparison with Aspects of Western and Islamic Laws* (London: Afroworld Publishing, 1988). African Rights, *Facing Genocide*, p. 326, describes a similar process, which took place later in the Nuba Mountains, of adapting SPLA legal structures to local conditions.

Despite the fact that SPLA had its own 1983 punitive laws, which largely related to the military, it was difficult to get a copy of them. The battalion commander was well aware of those laws, but did not draw our attention to them at all, and they were non-existent in practice in the region.

Instead, soldiers accused of crimes against civilians were increasingly tried according to customary law and subjected to a series of fines and compensation.[39]

The 1983 Penal Code, whenever it was applied, was controversial and caused resentment. The Nasir commanders referred to its prescription of the death penalty for a number of offences as evidence of Garang's dictatorship and a justification for their breaking away (though in fact summary execution was frequent in that faction from its inception). Yet, the humanitarian organization African Rights reports that the imposition of the penal code on SPLA soldiers in the Nuba Mountains in 1989 did reduce military abuses against civilians.[40] Whatever the sanctions of the Penal Code, there were areas where SPLA administration meted out harsh retribution against the civilian population in general. This was most common against those who supplied recruits to government militias: the Murle, some groups of Mandari, the Toposa and the Gaajak Nuer. Such campaigns might have succeeded in circumscribing the activities of militias, or even eliminating them altogether, but they also entrenched pockets of anti-SPLA feeling in various parts of the South.

Entrenching the position of customary law was one of the reforms enacted at the SPLA's first national convention at Chukudum in April 1994. A new hierarchy of customary courts from village to county level was recognized, strengthening the role of the chiefs in matters of appeal.[41] This recognition of customary law as the basis of local law is in keeping with the legal history of the Southern Sudan and conforms to established practice. Its political significance must be seen in relation to the legal changes in the centre, with successive governments in Khartoum establishing Islamic law as the source of national laws, and as the supreme law against which customary law was judged. On the surface the SPLA approach would appear to be a *de facto* recognition of 'nationalities' internal to the South, but being a long-established practice it has not had the same divisive effect that the recognition of 'nationalities' by the Eritrean Liberation Front (ELF) had in Eritrea.[42]

The legal reforms were in keeping with other administrative and political reforms enacted by the national convention, which separated the civil administration from the military and subordinated it to a new National Executive. In addition to this, the army was divided between a 'national' mobile force, used in major offences, and locally recruited defence forces. There are many who view these reforms as little more than cosmetic, leaving control still firmly in the hands of Garang and a small group of senior commanders. While this may be true in political terms, other reports

---

[39] Kuol, *Administration of Justice*, p.12. See also African Rights, *Facing Genocide*, p. 327, for a similar lack of application of the Penal Code in the Nuba Mountains.

[40] African Rights, *Facing Genocide*, p. 81.

[41] Kuol, *Administration of Justice*, pp. 14–15.

[42] The language of 'nationalities' has been notable for its absence in the vocabulary of SPLA administration within the Southern Sudan and the liberated areas. Rather, it has been confined to theoretical discussions of the relations which currently exist, or should ideally exist between the central government and the regions.

from inside the Southern Sudan indicate that there has been an overall distancing of the SPLA from local administration, and that this has led to improved relations with civilians in some areas, such as Yei, where the SPLA was initially seen as an army of occupation. It has also led to increased enlistment into local units by peoples formerly reluctant to join the SPLA.[43]

The contrast with SPLA-United/SSIM could not be greater. In a search for a coalition of anti-Garang supporters, Riek Mashar repeated the mistakes of the Anyanya leaders of the 1960s, and spent considerable time arranging 'paper cabinets' of political exiles, which were denounced by those included in them almost as soon as they were announced. Internally he also spent considerable effort on reshuffling his local commanders, leading to charges of tribal preferment and fuelling the Nuer civil war which eventually tore his movement apart. Those local commanders who were not fighting Riek and each other were organized for raids into SPLA-controlled areas. Civil administration was neglected, and suffered further from the lack of sufficiently educated or trained personnel to supervise the administrative and legal systems. The failure of SSIM to implement reforms in its own territory to correct the defects it denounced in the SPLA leads to two observations. The first is that Riek Mashar's own reputation for efficient and fair administration, first as an Area and then as a Zonal Commander prior to 1991, was gained in part because he was supported by a structure of administration kept in place by the SPLA as an organization. His ability to control raids between Western Upper Nile, Bahr al-Ghazal and Lakes was made possible because of collaboration between himself and neighbouring SPLA commanders, their recourse to a common command structure, and their use of an established customary court network. The second is that, charges of Dinka domination notwithstanding, the SPLA before 1991 (and even after) had a much wider pool of expertise to draw on when assigning administrative and judicial officers to different areas throughout the South.[44] In withdrawing into a Nuer-based and Nuer-led movement, SSIM was reduced to a much smaller manpower base, representing a far more restricted level of experience and expertise, and civil administration suffered accordingly.

Conclusion

It is perhaps natural to seek to compare the SPLA with its more successful (and more ideological) neighbours such as the TPLF, the EPLF and the NRA. The reality is that the issues over which the war in the Sudan is being fought are very different from those in Ethiopia and Uganda, and even the issue of secession has different roots and has generated different proposed solutions than in Eritrea. Of even greater importance is that, given the territory involved, the diversity of population, and the relative lack of suitable infrastructure, what is possible in Tigray, Eritrea or Uganda is considerably more difficult in the Southern Sudan. The structures of administration

[43] Abe Enosa, 'The East African revival among the Kakwa of the Sudan', paper presented at the Fourth International Sudan Studies Conference, Cairo, 13 June 1997.

[44] The CMA of Ayod, in the Gaawar Nuer area, in 1989–90 was neither a Nuer nor a Dinka, but a Boya from the Eastern Equatoria hills.

bequeathed by the British are essentially the same building blocks that all Southern political groups have tried to work with, from the old Anyanya through the Southern Regional government to the SPLA. The SPLA has been revolutionary in some of its language but not in its approach. This is because in its origin the SPLA has been defensive: it has attempted to defend the integrity of the South in the face of attempts by a succession of central governments to dismantle Southern administration and subordinate the South politically, culturally and economically. The debate within the SPLA over whether the South is best served by restructuring the whole country, or by separating from the rest of the Sudan, is still a debate about how best to defend the South.

The Nasir faction's declaration in favour of outright independence did finally bring that issue to the fore, not just for debate among Southern Sudanese, but between Southern and Northern Sudanese. At first the SPLA's response seemed equivocal, in that it proposed a number of alternative plans to secession, including federation or confederation within a united Sudan. But talks between the Nasir faction and the NIF government produced equally equivocal results, with the Nasir faction appearing to accept very vague formulations of a referendum in the indefinite future. The agreements with the government signed by Riek Mashar, Kerubino Kuanyin and others (no longer even pretending to be part of a united organization) in 1996 and 1997 committed the Southern 'secessionists' to a highly centralized form of government with very limited devolved powers (a reworking of the semi-autonomous regional government structure first introduced by the Addis Ababa agreement), to be deferred to the indefinite future. The agreement signed by the SPLA and its Northern partners in the NDA (at the urging of the Eritrean government) is altogether more specific. The right of the South (and by extension, other 'marginalized' areas) to self-determination is defined by the options that will be available: independence, confederation or federation. The process of self-determination will begin on the overthrow of the NIF government, and a referendum on those options is to be held after a specified interim period. While it is known that the main Northern parties are unhappy about the prospect of an independent South, and Southerners fully anticipate that they will attempt to back away from the implementation of this referendum, the SPLA has now achieved what it failed to achieve prior to the elections following Nimeiri's overthrow: an agreement from the Northern parties of the process by which Southern grievances will be addressed, and possibly solved. It also opens the way for the inclusion of non-Arab Muslim areas in this process. By keeping its options open about the eventual separation of the South from the rest of the Sudan, the SPLA has gone some way towards consolidating its political position among Southern Sudanese, while expanding its recruiting beyond the old South to open up new theatres of operation. Should military successes lead to the downfall of the current government, the SPLA will be in a strong position to hold its NDA partners to this agreement.

SPLA civil and military administration follows both from past experience and the defensive nature of the movement's political enterprise. Whereas other 'revolutionary' movements in the region have attacked institutions of the *ancien regime*, the SPLA has approached the 'grassroots' through the institutions of native administration and the chiefs' courts. Garang's critics have accused him of trying to impose a centralized military structure on the entire South, whereas in fact the SPLA is built up out of semi-autonomous commands, whose autonomy grows with their distance from the main seat of operations. This autonomy of commands can lead to fragmentation, as with the SPLA–United/SSIM defection, or it can lead to a reaffirmation of commitment to the struggle, as it did in the Nuba Mountains.

The restructuring of its army also enabled the SPLA to recover from military setbacks and expand into new areas. The 'mobile' force of a 'national' character (containing soldiers from all over the South, and many other areas as well) enabled the SPLA to advance in strength into new areas of operation and, once established, entrench their positions through local recruitment. This was most noticeable in southern Blue Nile, an area with a large indigenous Muslim population, where commander Malik Agar (a native of the Ingessana hills) entered the area from a base in Ethiopia with a force of some 3,000 men, many of them Dinka from Bahr al-Ghazal. Having taken Kurmuk and driven the Sudanese army (and the Northern Sudanese merchants) out of the area early in 1997, he kept the local civil administration intact and was able to recruit a large local force.[45] Here, as in the South and the Nuba Mountains, the SPLA has ultimately been able to harness local grievances by offering to liberate and preserve local custom and livelihood against the very real threat of religious, political and economic reorganization from Khartoum, not by imposing a uniform 'revolutionary' administration, based on principles drawn from other liberation movements throughout the world. If this has left it without a clear blueprint for political and economic policy in the post-war period, and at times vulnerable to the vagaries and ambitions of local commanders, it has also established the basis for a series of local alliances which not only enabled it to overcome the crisis of internal Southern factionalism, but to link up with former enemies within the nation and the region, placing it at the centre of a formidable political and military alliance pitted against the Islamist government in Khartoum. The leading role now being played by the SPLA, an essentially Southern Sudanese army, is unprecedented in post-independence Sudanese politics, and constitutes a revolution in itself.

[45] Bona Malwal, 'In Kurmuk the thoughts are all about defeating the NIF regime', *Sudan Democratic Gazette*, September 1997, pp. 8–9.

5

DANIEL COMPAGNON
Somali Armed Movements

The Interplay of Political Entrepreneurship
& Clan-Based Factions

Travellers to the region since the earliest times have attested the fragmentation of Somali society into conflicting kinship groups. This conceptualization of Somali politics, subsequently documented by social anthropologists and political scientists, was in abeyance only in the period up to the late 1980s, when it was fashionable instead to support the myth of a 'natural' Somali nationhood, based on ethnic homogeneity.[1] Consequently there has been a widespread tendency to explain everything to do with Somali affairs in terms of lineage conflict, as though clans and lineages were corporate groups with a clear identity and common will, that under any circumstances would both create a sense of unity among their own members and differentiate them from similar groupings. This tendency, compounded by an even cruder discourse in the Western press, has readily reduced the analysis of recent political conflicts to the mere reiteration of 'traditional' inter-clan feuds.

This chapter challenges the abuse of kinship categories in the analysis of Somali armed conflicts, and seeks instead to focus on the role of political entrepreneurs in the maintenance of sustained conflict, treating lineage solidarity as a resource to be marshalled by these entrepreneurs. Of course, kinship can be said to be the political grammar of Somali pastoral society, and is readily resorted to by Somali as well as outside observers to explain the often bewildering upheavals of Somali politics. A Somali proverb has it that even the Sufi saint does not go to heaven without his clan's support. But as the work of I. M. Lewis shows, boundaries between kin groups move constantly according to the level of segmental solidarity mobilized, while politics is defined as much by contract (*heer*) as by kinship (*reer*). The dynamics of recent Somali warfare turns on a complex interaction between clan-based faction-alism and the political entrepreneurship of the faction leaders.

But first, one needs to put the politics of armed factionalism into historical per-spective. Three generations of organizations can be identified in post-independence Somalia, which differ in their objectives (both political and military), their degree of

---

[1] See, for example, I. M. Lewis, *A Pastoral Democracy: a Study of Pastoralism and Politics among the Northern Somali of the Horn of Africa* (London: Oxford University Press, 1961); I. M. Lewis, ed., *Nationalism and Self-Determination in the Horn of Africa* (London: Ithaca, 1983); D. D. Laitin and S. A. Samatar, *Somalia: Nation in Search of a State* (Boulder: Westview, 1987).

institutionalization, and the role that ideology has played (or not played) in the mobilization process.

1 The first group were irredentist movements among ethnic Somalis in neighbouring states, seeking incorporation into the Somali Republic. These movements, all of which were thoroughly manipulated by successive governments of the Somali Republic, were the Northern Frontier District Liberation Front (NFDLF) in Kenya, the Western Somali Liberation Front (WSLF) in the eastern regions of Ethiopia, and less importantly the Front de Libération de la Côte des Somalis (FLCS) in Djibouti.[2]

2 The second generation consisted of movements seeking to overthrow the personal rule of Mahamed Siyaad Barre, which I have elsewhere called 'armed opposition movements'.[3] These were for various reasons clan-based, but retained some sort of political programme, though they were not sufficiently refined to warrant the label of 'reform insurgencies'. This group originally included the Somali Salvation Democratic Front (SSDF) and the Somali National Movement (SNM), and belatedly extended to the United Somali Congress (USC) of the first period (before January 1991).

3 The third generation comprises all those movements which mushroomed just before and soon after the final overthrow of Mahamed Siyaad Barre in January 1991, and which are generally perceived as the armed branches of Somali clans and sub-clans, without any political programme as such.

However, the divide between these generations is not so clear-cut, and it is necessary to take account of changes within movements over time, rather than ascribing them to any static and narrowly defined category. The question of nomenclature is also problematic. While 'guerrilla' designates simply a mode of conducting warfare, and the most natural one in the Somali pastoralist context, an 'insurgency' refers to a movement launched to overthrow a government or at least to challenge the actions of the state; it is scarcely appropriate to the situation prevailing in Somalia after 1991, where there has been no state against which to fight. The commonly used term 'warlord', apart from the connotations carried over from its origins in 1920s–30s China, has little meaning in the segmentary Somali society with its decentralized and egalitarian political system. I therefore prefer to use the more precise notion of clan-based armed factions and their leaders.

Given the necessarily limited range of this chapter, I have chosen to focus on the last generation, the two dozen or so major armed factions which have been conducting intermittent warfare since January 1991.[4] To understand better the kind of warfare in which these have been engaged, two fundamental questions need to be addressed:

[2] On this first generation, see John Markakis, *National and Class Conflict in the Horn of Africa* (Cambridge: Cambridge University Press, 1987), pp. 169–201, 222–32.

[3] Daniel Compagnon, 'The Somali opposition fronts: some comments and questions', *Horn of Africa*, Vol. 13, Nos 1–2 (1990).

[4] A brief summary of the major factions is provided in an appendix to this chapter.

1 Why did the overthrow of Siyaad Barre not lead to a take-over of state power by the armed opposition movements, some of which had been fighting the regime for a decade or so, in a process that would have resembled the EPRDF take-over in neighbouring Ethiopia?

2 To what extent do these armed factions correspond to the various segments of the Somali kinship system, rather than to political enterprises benefiting competitors for power and spoils?

Finally, I will assess briefly the external intervention in Somalia between December 1992 and March 1995, in the light of this analysis.

Explaining the Failure of the Armed Opposition to Siyaad Barre

The inability of the Somali opposition fronts to offer any viable political formula after ousting Siyaad Barre was rooted in the organization and strategy that they had adopted while fighting the regime, the underlying weaknesses of which became dramatically evident with the total collapse of the Somali state, and the subsequent disintegration of the fronts into clan-based armed factions.

The structure and strategy of the opposition movements

Organized opposition to Siyaad Barre's increasingly personal and repressive rule developed after the 1978 coup attempt, and typically followed the lines of lineage segmentation, with a core following of Daarood/Majeerteen for the SSDF and of Isaaq for the SNM, although both organizations accommodated minority sections of other clans.[5] While the urban petty bourgeoisie who led these movements, and the merchants of the diaspora who largely financed them, mobilized the grammar of kinship, they used other ideological models which ranged from Western democracy to Islamic fundamentalism. Indeed, the early history of the SSDF and SNM indicates considerable debate over constitutional structure and the political model to follow. The SSDF included a strong contingent of Marxist intellectuals, who had come from the Somali Workers Party, a leftist dissident group formed in Aden in 1980, or who had defected from Siyaad's Somali Revolutionary Socialist Party. These came from different clans, including the Dulbahante, Habar Gidir, and Isaaq. Equally, during the Ethiopian-sponsored unity negotiations between the SSDF and SNM in 1981, the issues of leadership and democracy were high on the agenda.

Nor should each movement's claim to be a nationalist alliance seeking the

---

[5] This chapter adopts a standardized system for referring to segmentary lineage groups: thus, 'Daarood/Majeerteen' refers to the Majeerteen clan of the Daarood clan family. Sub-clans are similarly indicated: 'Majeerteen/Umar Mahamuud' refers to the Umar Mahamuud sub-clan of the Majeerteen clan. The main clan families (as I. M. Lewis calls the major sub-divisions of Somali society) referred to in this chapter are the Daarood (spread throughout most of Somalia, and including the Dulbahante, Majeerteen, Marehaan, Ogadeen and Warsangeli clans), Isaaq (largely northern) and Hawiye (entirely southern, including Abgaal and Habar Gidir clans).

overthrow of Siyaad Barre, rather than a clan-based organization, be too quickly dismissed, at least during the 1980s. Both SSDF and SNM were divided between chauvinistic sections, which sought the aggrandisement of the clan forming the majority of their following and from which most of the leadership was drawn, and more nationalist groups who supported broader objectives, including the overthrow of Siyaad Barre and the establishment of a new and more democratic political regime. The latter group, for both tactical and ideological reasons, supported the opening of the organization's membership to a wide range of clans, whilst the former was not prepared to give power to minority segments. This created a lively debate for most of the 1980s, especially in the SNM, and provided opportunities for internal manipulation, as for instance by Ahmed Silanyo, SNM chairman from 1984 to 1990, who used the Hawiye against his own internal Isaaq opposition. Each of the opposition Fronts long retained a small component from other clan affiliations than the majority of the membership. For example, the last group of Hawiye/Sa'ad left the SSDF only in October 1988, and after a brief affiliation to the SNM joined the newly formed USC in January 1989. Dulbahante elders and officers were involved at various stages in the Isaaq-dominated SNM, despite the fact that Dulbahante are Daarood and have been portrayed as deadly enemies of the Isaaq by many careless observers, while the vice-president of the breakaway Somaliland Republic in 1997 was a Gadabuursi who had played a major role in the SNM fighting force almost from the beginning.

The failure of such multi-clan organizations was due in large part to manipulation by Siyaad Barre, who managed to create profound distrust between the clans which opposed him, in order to defuse opposition to his rule.[6] One of his tactics was to militarize the clans by creating clan militias, giving them weapons, and then implicating them in the repression against a targeted clan segment: the Hawiye/ Sa'ad against the Majeerteen/Umar Mahamuud, the Dulbahante against the Isaaq/Habar Ja'alo, the Gadabuursi against the Isaaq/Sa'ad Muuse, and later, the Harti of Kisimayo against the Ogadeen, and the Majeerteen against the Isaaq. Quite often, these clans herded their camels together in the bush; they had long histories of feuds, indeed, but also of marriages and alliances. Siyaad's propaganda used every opportunity to discredit the opposition fronts: for example, the fact that there was indeed a separatist current within the SNM enabled him to portray the movement as an enemy of Somali unity in the eyes of the Hawiye and Daarood. By 1987, when tensions arose in the SNM between the Hawiye minority and the Isaaq, it was clear that opposition fronts had to be based on clan families or clans. Ali Mahamed Osooble Wardhigley, a Hawiye and vice-president of the SNM until 1987, left to create the USC in Rome in January 1989; and when Colonel Umar Jees defected from the Somali army in Hargeisa in June 1989, he formed an Ogadeen front, the Somali Patriotic Movement (SPM), with the blessing of SNM commanders.

More practical considerations militated in favour of clan-based organizations. Given the lack of resources (both money and weapons), the unit size requirements

---

[6] Siyaad Barre was himself from the Reer Ugas Diini, a segment of the Daarood/Marehaan clan, and he actively used kinship as a political resource; see Daniel Compagnon, 'Ressources politiques, regulation authoritaire, et domination personnelle en Somalie: le régime de Siyaad Barre (1969– 1991)', PhD thesis, Université de Pau, 1995, pp. 172–4, 210–18, 453–84.

of guerrilla warfare, and the difficulty of giving military training to individualistic camel herders, it was more efficient to opt for a military structure based on kinship segmentation. This was particularly the case in the SNM, where each of the six major Isaaq clans had formed its own unit by 1988. The conditions of the war were then such that the support of clan elders was essential, and these were more comfortable with this kind of organization. When the SNM military wing had been formed in 1982, it created an integrated Isaaq force; but by 1988 this had been decimated, and its remnants dispersed to their own clan militias. Its attempt in 1986 to launch a classic frontal attack led to a stunning defeat, and demonstrated that a loose military coordination of clan-based units was the best way to fight the Somali army. But this meant that every unit commander retained a considerable amount of autonomy and initiative, and this was to be a problem in 1991–2 when the Somaliland president tried to restore a chain of command.[7]

This problem was compounded by the fact that, before 1988, neither the SSDF nor the SNM were able to establish sanctuaries in liberated areas and build their own administrative apparatus. They were by no means comparable to the EPLF in Eritrea and TPLF in Tigray, which had developed a sophisticated apparatus and a kind of state in miniature. The Somali fronts lacked the depth of territory required to create base areas, the terrain was unfavourable, and their training camps in Ethiopia were closely monitored by Ethiopian military security. SSDF troops were trained by Ethiopian officers, and during the invasion attempt of June–August 1982, SSDF guerrillas were integrated into the much larger Ethiopian army units. During SSDF internal squabbles in 1983 and 1984, Ethiopian security entered the camps and arrested Central Committee members, showing how little autonomy they enjoyed. The SNM had the same problem when its leadership moved to Addis Ababa in 1981, and was confined to the Ethiopian capital. Later, it managed to move its headquarters to Harer, and then to Jigjiga. The situation improved in 1988 with the creation of several refugee camps between Jigjiga and the Somali frontier, which Isaaq guerrillas could use as a sanctuary for the usual purposes, such as food supply, recruitment and medical treatment. By that time, however, the SNM had largely dissolved itself as a distinct organization, becoming part of a popular rebellion led by clan elders. This was reflected in its organization at the 1990 congress, held in the border town of Baleh Gubaadle, when the Central Committee was enlarged to include elders from all major clans, and membership raised to a highly symbolic 99 (a magic number according to the Koran). This meant that the original political cadres became a minority. The struggle had become an end in itself, and no provision was made in advance to establish an administration of the liberated areas.

The organization of rebel forces according to lineage segmentation was even more pronounced in the Hawiye-dominated USC and the Ogadeen SPM. The battle of Mogadishu which culminated in the flight of Siyaad Barre was basically a confrontation between Hawiye clan militias on one side, and Daarood elements of the Somali army and armed Daarood civilians on the other, rather than a battle between an insurgency and a state that no longer existed.

[7] On SNM organization in the field, see Gérard Prunier, 'A candid view of the Somali National Movement', *Horn of Africa*, Vol. 13, Nos 3–4 and Vol. 14, Nos 1–2; Daniel Compagnon, 'Dynamiques de mobilisation, dissidence armée et rebellion populaire: le cas du Mouvement National Somali (1981–1990)', *Africa* (Rome), Vol. 47, No. 1 (1992).

The collapse of the Somali state

By the time Siyaad Barre fled Mogadishu on the night of 27 January 1991, the Somali state had virtually disappeared. Its finances had been in shambles since 1989, and the most competent ministers, like the Minister of Agriculture, had fled abroad in the latter half of 1990. The army, the core of the regime since 1969, was affected by low morale and unpaid salaries, and offered little resistance to the insurgents until they reached Mogadishu. Upon leaving the capital for his home town of Garbaharrey, the former president plundered the central bank of what was left of the country's gold and foreign currency reserves. In the wake of his escape, the presidential palace was occupied by USC guerrillas and a following crowd, who looted the place in an act of powerless rage. The archives were dispersed or burnt, and every piece of furniture and equipment of value was taken away. Most of the ministries and public offices, including the national library, were treated in the same way. Without records, with civil servants conscripted into the guerrilla force or scared away, there was little chance of restoring even the pretence of an administration. The new power-to-be had no money to operate with, and the Hawiye businessmen who had financed the USC uprising had little left to offer, and were concerned to recoup their investment by any possible means and as quickly as possible.

The attitude of the USC leadership certainly did not help. They endorsed the witch-hunt against Daarood people, who were shot on the spot without trial, or even a minimal assessment of the role that they had personally played in the ousted regime. This is how Dr Abyan, a member of the Manifesto Group, was killed in the yard of the house where several Hawiye leaders (including Ali Mahdi, the new provisional president) were meeting, without one of them making any attempt to save their colleague's life, even though they had been struggling for democracy together less than a month earlier. Hundreds of innocent people were killed, including Isaaq, because Hawiye militia men knew that Daarood/Dolbahante claimed to be Isaaq, with whom they share a common dialect, in order to save their lives.[8] Beyond the horror of this primitive form of ethnic cleansing, the violence unleashed by victory targeted all non-Hawiye, including the wealthy Swahili merchants of the inter-river region, and provoked a mass exodus from Mogadishu. Most of the Daarood civil servants fled to the countryside, mainly towards the Kenyan border, and later regrouped around Kisimayo. From then on, the would-be USC government had no qualified personnel, apart from Hawiye, to restore the state apparatus.

The faction leaders had also neglected the major problem of demobilization. Because in pastoral society a feud would only temporarily mobilize the men of the clan for military service, after which they would resume their pastoral activities, and because the insurgent force had been mobilized in much the same fashion as a

---

[8] Although Hawiye leaders later apologized half-heartedly, claiming to have lost control over vengeful crowds, a video showing the arrest and execution by USC guerrillas of a Daarood man in civilian attire was welcomed with laughter by the Abgaal people with whom I watched it. The USC had massacred Daarood/Ogadeen refugees in November 1990, when they took control of the region between Belet Ouen and Jowhare along the Shebelle River.

traditional raiding party, it was wrongly assumed that young armed pastoralists would return to the bush after final victory. This was not to happen. The Hawiye uprising had started near Galcaio on the Ethiopian border in late 1989, and then spread south-west towards Mogadishu. As USC guerrillas seized control of vast tracts of lands in this mainly Hawiye-populated area, the various lineage segments were conscripted, and between September and December 1990 clan militias converged on Mogadishu. This process brought to the capital an enormous number of armed pastoralists from rural segments of the Hawiye clan family, especially from the Habar Gidir clan whose territory stretches from Galcaio to Belet Ouen, as well as Hawaadle from the south-west of the latter town. Abgaal clansmen, whose territory surrounds Mogadishu, were logically the last to be involved, a fact that gained some importance when the time came to settle scores among the Hawiye.

These armed militias did not return to their home areas after Siyaad Barre was ousted, however, but remained in Mogadishu.[9] This happened partly because the elders and military leaders of the clans concerned wanted to have a say in the power sharing, and did not trust the Abgaal, who had already obtained the provisional presidency in the person of Ali Mahdi Mahamed. But the young militiamen had tasted life in the big city, with almost free licence to loot, kill and rape, and had come to enjoy it. The distinction between USC combatants and bandits (mooryan) became blurred.[10] Although the inability of USC faction leaders to demobilize and control their militias was part of the problem, effective maintenance of law and order would have required a far more institutionalized political movement, and/or the continuity of the state. These conditions were met for the EPLF in Eritrea and TPLF in Ethiopia, when they won power later in 1991. In Somalia, there was no state to take over, and the fronts started to disintegrate immediately after victory.

The situation was even worse in the north, where 70 per cent of buildings in Hargeisa had been destroyed or damaged in the indiscriminate shelling of June–July 1988. During my visit in January 1993, there were large blocks still in ruins. They had not been cleared because the houses were booby-trapped with landmines by Siyaad Barre's troops before they left the town in January 1991. The so-called Somaliland government ministries lacked all essentials, from furniture to pens and paper, electricity and telephones. Everything that could be taken away had been looted during the fighting between 1988 and 1990, including corrugated iron roofing, electric and telephone wires, and wooden window and door frames. The sight of the bare and teetering walls which were all that remained of what had once been the best secondary school in the country at Sheikh was depressing. It was no wonder that, despite the best efforts of some young intellectuals, the SNM administration could not operate.

Unlike the SSDF, which had been armed and financed by Qadhafi from 1980 until 1985, the SNM had never received any substantial external aid. Even Arab League members which were sometimes said to have helped it actually supported Siyaad Barre. The major but irregular source of finance was remittances from the

[9] See Roland Marchal, 'La guerre à Mogadiscio', Politique Africaine, 46 (1992).

[10] See Roland Marchal, 'Les mooryan de Mogadiscio: formes de la violence dans un espace urbain en guerre', Cahiers d'Etudes Africaines, Vol. 33, No. 2 (1993). Banditry started to develop seriously in the Somali capital in the later 1980s, and gangs of destitute Hawiye youths engaged in partially politically motivated graft; they took a prominent part in the fighting to oust Siyaad Barre in January 1991.

worldwide Isaaq diaspora. The SNM certainly enjoyed some logistical support from the Ethiopian army from 1984 to 1988, but this was terminated soon after the 1988 peace agreement between Mengistu and Siyaad. This prompted the SNM's last-ditch offensive of late May 1988, since its leaders understood, quite correctly, that Mengistu would kill, jail or disperse them once they were no longer useful to him, as he had done with the SSDF. The strength of the SNM during the 1988–90 campaign lay in the support that it received (in both men and food) from the Isaaq clans inside Somalia and on the border with Ethiopia, but this provided no clear framework for post-war administration. Trade had been disrupted increasingly during the war, and taxes had not been levied for many years. Any incoming government, whatever its merits, would have suffered from the same shortage of resources.

The SNM, too, faced the problem of demobilization. Its fighting force was drawn largely from refugee camps in Ethiopia, where the inhabitants of Burao and Hargeisa had fled in mid-1988. The original well-trained guerrillas had been decimated in the heavy fighting of June–July, and were replaced by contingents drawn from all lineage segments. Many of these new combatants came from ravaged towns, and had lost their closest relatives in the war. Most of them had no formal education, because the school system had been disrupted since as early as 1984, and the majority had been unemployed before they became guerrillas. Warfare became a way of life, and the automatic rifle a means of living. They were fully supported by their clans during the war, but became a burden on society after liberation, when they clustered around the main towns. The government of Somaliland, which declared its formal independence on 18 May 1991, had neither the money to pay them and turn them into a trained professional army, nor the means to help them resume a civilian life. Ironically, the clans which 'lost' the 1988–91 war in the north – the Dulbahante and Warsangeli in the east, and the Gadabuursi in the west – were better off, since they did not have strong militias, whereas the Isaaq 'victors' suffered from the abuses of their own clan militias.

The disintegration of the opposition movements

From the previous analysis of the opposition fronts, it is possible to deduce the main reasons for their rapid disintegration. The USC, especially, had never been a real organization. It was a loose coalition of Hawiye clans, whose contribution to the liberation war took different forms, and was certainly unequal from one segment to another. It had been founded in Rome by Ali Wardhigley, and was dominated by his own Murusade clan. General Aidid's sub-clan, the Habar Gidir/Sa'ad, were reluctant to join, and Aidid himself, then Somali ambassador in India, was persuaded to defect by the SNM, who hoped that he would form a southern branch of the movement with the growing number of Hawiye soldiers deserting from the Somali army. Although Aidid flew to Addis Ababa in September 1989, he refused to join either the SNM or the USC, establishing instead his own USC organization at a congress in June 1990 near Mustahil, where most of the Hawiye defectors were stationed. This in turn was dominated by the Sa'ad. Overseas branches were created in London, Toronto and Washington, and a war of press releases took place between the two USCs, headquartered in Rome and London, for the rest of 1990.

Although USC-Rome lost momentum with the deaths in mid-1990 of its leader and his expected successor, it maintained close contacts with Hawiye businessmen in Mogadishu, who in turn were actively involved in the Manifesto Group, a multi-clan group (excluding only the Isaaq) which had requested Siyaad Barre in an open letter of May 1989 to step down and introduce a democratic constitution.[11] It supported the ousting of Siyaad by peaceful means and a transition process backed by foreign diplomatic missions,[12] whereas Aidid favoured guerrilla war and a close alliance with SNM. Political competition within USC had thus started well before Siyaad Barre was overthrown, and was intensified by the defection from the army of Hawiye/Abgaal officers at the beginning of the battle of Mogadishu. An Abgaal, Ali Mahdi Mahamed, was appointed as interim president on 28 January 1991, without consulting Aidid, who was still out of the capital. The election in June of Aidid as chairman of a temporarily united USC strengthened his own claim to power, and created two rival authorities – the interim president and the chairman of the party – which were poised for confrontation. Aidid saw any of Ali Mahdi's initiatives as provocations and attempts to sideline him, whilst the interim president was obsessed by Aidid's alleged plan to stage a coup, using the strength of the Habar Gidir militias. With armed clan militias on every street corner, a city where public services, employment and food supply were totally disrupted, and where political violence was for many a convenient excuse to indulge in looting, it was not surprising that a tense political climate would culminate in fighting. There was a first clash in September 1991, which was resolved by a joint committee of elders and intellec-tuals, and a sustained war from November 1991 to March 1992 that prompted the first interest of the UN Security Council in Somali affairs, before the full-fledged intervention of December 1992.

There is not enough space here to recount in detail the complex movement of reorganization which affected the Daarood clans after Siyaad Barre fled the capital in January 1991 and the country in April 1992. After a short-lived unity to face the Hawiye campaign of extermination, both the pre-war divide between pro-Siyaad and anti-Siyaad elements, and everybody's concern for their own clan interests, led to a fragmentation of the Daarood front. The Majeerteen SSDF was revived when its historic leader Abdullahi Yuusuf was released from jail in Ethiopia by the EPRDF, but soon afterwards started to collapse. Among the various factors which contributed to this outcome, three are prominent: first, the rivalry between the brutal military leader, Abdullahi Yuusuf, and Mahamed Abshir Muuse, a more urbane civilian 'elder' member of the Manifesto Group and a respected police general before the 1969 coup, a rivalry compounded by their tendency to side with opposing Hawiye factions; second, the challenge of the Islamic group Al-Ittihad, which controlled the port of Bossasso for the major part of 1992 (a situation ultimately resolved through negotiations brokered by the Majeerteen elders); and third, the failure of the successive peace and reconciliation conferences in which the SSDF took part, claiming to represent the Majeerteen. The SSDF's organization,

[11] See Compagnon, 'Ressources politiques', pp. 638–43.
[12] The Italians especially were closely involved with the Manifesto, having decisively departed from their support for Siyaad after the assassination of the Catholic archbishop by elements of the military police on 9 July 1990, and subsequent bloody repression in the capital.

which had never really recovered from Mengistu's crackdown in 1984–5, dissolved, and a regional administration of the north-east was slowly established under the auspices of the customary chief of the Majeerteen (*Boqor*) and a council of lineage elders. In sharp contrast to its attitude elsewhere, the United Nations Operation in Somalia (UNOSOM) supported this effort until the end of its mandate.

In the north, the situation was at first very different, because the SNM was the uncontested winner, and had a legitimate claim to exercise power. The leadership and the elders also avoided revenge killings, and insisted on involving the other clans in the political process. A first inter-clan conference (*shir*) was held in Berbera in February 1991, and worked successfully to resolve tensions inherited from a much longer war than in the south. There is no space here to assess the lengthy process which led to the proclamation of independence, but this decision was largely endorsed by the representatives on the spot of the minority Dulbahante, Warsangeli and Gadabuursi clans.[13] It was not forced on them, although a popular demonstration made clear the strong support for independence among the Isaaq. Many leaders, both Isaaq and others, thought at the time that the decision was provisional, pending the emergence in Mogadishu of a legitimate power with which to negotiate a new union to replace the hasty agreement of 1960.[14]

By then the SNM leadership had already lost the political initiative, however, even though its chairman, Abdirahman Ali Tuur, was appointed interim president of Somaliland for two years. The SNM central committee was divided on the issue of independence, with a majority including Tuur and his predecessor Silanyo favouring the continuation of the alliance with Aidid, and the formation of a national government in which seasoned Isaaq politicians (such as themselves) would have a place; but the guerrilla commanders, who were closer to the people, supported independence and participated actively in the debate. In the provisional government which eventually emerged, ministers were selected according to the rules of clan balance, and saw themselves as the representatives of their clans; so did the militia commanders, who looked to their own elders, rather than to the Somaliland government. Lacking public resources, the infant political system fell apart. A crisis was soon precipitated by the authoritarian behaviour of Tuur and his deputy Hasaan Iise Jaama, their misappropriation of funds,[15] and their paranoid reaction when some prominent clan figures criticized their tenure of office. The conflict over demobilization, and the integration of the various clan militias into a Somaliland army, led to a full-fledged war between coalitions of Isaaq clans between December 1991 and November 1992. The fact that the November 1992 agreement which ended the

[13] I derive this conclusion, which contradicts the claims made by absentee leaders of movements which claimed to represent these clans (SDA and USP), from interviews with Dulbahante and Gadabuursi elders in Somaliland in January 1993; see also Daniel Compagnon, 'Somaliland, un ordre politique en gestion?', *Politique Africaine*, No. 50 (1993).

[14] For the root causes of insurgency in the north-west, see Compagnon, 'Dynamiques de mobilisation', especially pp. 504–13.

[15] For example, in February 1992 Hasaan Iise forcibly emptied the banks of all available cash to finance the war in Berbera, including the account of CARE, an American NGO which ran a programme of mönetarization of food aid, supposedly with the full support of the SNM government. Other NGOs likewise suffered from this predatory behaviour. It was widely believed that the president's desire to control the port of Berbera was linked to his personal interest in the revenue from customs duties.

fighting in Berbera had to be brokered by elders from other clans, including the Dulbahante and Gadabuursi, underlined the disintegration of the SNM over a year of factional strife.

Understanding the Dynamics of Somali Factionalism

This parallel disintegration of the USC and SNM, the two movements which appeared to be in a position to inherit power in the south and north respectively, raises the question of what actually fuels Somali factionalism. Even though this appears to stem from clan rivalry, in almost every instance it has been manipulated by individuals or small cliques in order to further their own interests. To perceive the various armed factions as the mere expression of lineage segments would be simplistic and misleading. It neglects not only the important role of political entrepreneurs, who mobilize (or fail to mobilize) certain segments in order to pursue their own objectives, but also the differing origins of competing factions. Finally, it misinterprets the aim of each faction, which is as much to secure the spoils as to achieve clan or sub-clan dominance. This debate is of more than theoretical interest: the clear identification of the force behind factionalism is central to any attempt at conflict management.

Political entrepreneurs and clan-based factions

Factions are based on clans because – as a legacy of Siyaad Barre's regime, as much as a constraint of traditional pastoral society – a fighting force can be recruited only through clan affiliation. Any political entrepreneur will look first to his own lineage to build support, whether for electoral competition as in the 1960s during the parliamentary regime, or for military competition as in the 1990s. But these political entrepreneurs are not parochial clan chiefs or pastoral elders. They are ambitious modern politicians, former army officers, civil servants, members of parliament, merchants or university professors, who have quickly adapted to the new rules of the game of competition for power. Most of the factions have been created by such people, some of the smaller ones representing little more than themselves and a handful of followers. The bigger the faction, however, the more complex the politics involved: top entrepreneurs – who are not absolute monarchs, but are certainly more than chief executive officers – have to bargain with their various stakeholders, such as intellectuals, elders, financiers, militia commanders, and even women's groups. Kinship helps to form a political arena, but does not capture the essence of competition: the language of kinship, rather, provides a ready-made ideology through which combatants stigmatize the enemy (especially in oral poetry), ascribe unthinkable violence to the other side, and in turn justify their own atrocities, while claiming to uphold the social values of clan solidarity.

The rival political enterprises of Mahamed Faarah Haasan Aidid and Ali Mahdi Mahamed are better explained by their individual careers than by any 'ancestral hatred' between their Sa'ad and Abgaal clans. Aidid was already a lieutenant-colonel when the military coup took place in 1969, but was left out of the Somali Revolutionary Council junta, because Siyaad Barre feared his close relations with the

Russians; he was jailed for a few years, and then sent abroad as a military attache. He missed another opportunity in 1978, when a coup attempt in which he was to be involved collapsed. Mahamed Aidid was a power-seeker who had been made to wait far too long, and was eager for revenge. Ali Mahdi was a former member of parliament, who was jailed with other civilian politicians after 1969 and subsequently became a businessmen, making a fortune especially through his wife's connections with the office of the president in the 1980s. In 1989 he became the financier and organizer of the Manifesto Group, whose members often met in his hotel in Mogadishu, emerging as a leader of the Abgaal clan through contacts with the USC in Rome. By January 1991 he mustered some valuable political resources, including money and both domestic and external connections, and many underestimated the modest businessman whom they hoped to manipulate. Between Mahamed Aidid and Ali Mahdi there was a clash not only of ambitions but also of ethos, between the professional and authoritarian military elite and the new merchant bourgeoisie.

Lineage polarization is a product of competing enterprises, and not their cause. Clan-based political support is constantly shifting, according to the segments and the level of segmentation that the entrepreneur is able to mobilize. At the same time, the more important entrepreneurs must build larger coalitions, like the Somali National Alliance (SNA) formed by Aidid with fractions of various movements which at least on paper supported his claim to supreme power. These broader alliances are largely opportunistic, and do not conform to kinship proximity: they resemble the *gashaanbur* of pastoral society, alliances of small lineages which unite despite their lack of close kinship ties to fight a stronger lineage.

The multiplication of guerrilla factions is often explained in terms of the Somali kinship system, which is prone to endless segmentation. This is true, but does not suffice to explain the propensity of almost all Somali guerrilla organizations to split. Conflicting personal ambitions often provide a more convincing explanation. For example Usman Ato, who was once described as Aidid's most trusted lieutenant and supplied his money and weapons, broke away from Aidid in 1994 to form his own militia, and later fought fiercely against the group led by Aidid's son Huseen. This defection was ascribed to the weariness of Ato's lineage for the endless fighting prompted by Aidid; but it is more plausibly accounted for by suggesting that Ato, having observed Aidid for three years, thought that he could do better and accumulated the resources to launch his own political enterprise when the time was ripe. With the emergence of new factions and the decay of others, the interplay of clanism and political entrepreneurship remains the creative force behind factionalism.

In Somaliland, clan elders as a whole generally exercised greater control over the political process, and entrepreneurial behaviour was contained but not suppressed. A good example is the former interim president, Abdirahmaan Ali Tuur, a former senior diplomat under Siyaad Barre who defected in 1984, when he was recalled to Mogadishu as part of a crackdown against the Isaaq/Habar Yunis clan. Tuur was coopted onto the SNM executive by Ahmed Silanyo, whom he succeeded as leader in 1990. With Somaliland's declaration of independence, he became interim president, but he spent more time abroad than in Hargeisa, and was criticized for his procrastination, his secretiveness, and his endorsement of the corrupt practices of his Minister of Finance. When he was defeated in the 'presidential election' of May

1993, he left Somaliland and soon after denounced its independence, becoming a willing pawn of UNOSOM in its attempts to undermine the authority of his successor Igal. Claiming to remain the legitimate president of the SNM, Tuur participated in various 'peace conferences' sponsored by the United Nations, and eventually joined Aidid's 'provisional national government'. His associate Jaama Mahamed Ghalib Yare was also defeated in the May 1993 election, and remained in Somaliland, where he distributed money of undisclosed origin (speculation ranges from UNOSOM to Aidid) among clan militias to foment opposition to the new president, thus helping to promote the fighting in Burao and Hargeisa in the second half of 1994 and early 1995.

In short, what is often mistaken for an endless and senseless feud between rival clans can often be described in the more traditional categories of political science. In a society where no one exerts a monopoly of physical constraint, private violence is an accepted means to attain political objectives. *Condottieri* abound in Somalia.

Competition for spoils as the motive for conflict

From the outset, Somalia's factional war was associated with extensive looting, not only by the *mooryan* but by the civilian population itself. This phenomenon puzzled foreign journalists and participants in the 'Restore Hope' intervention: newly finished infrastructure handed over by foreign contingents to villagers was immediately dismantled by those who were supposed to benefit from it, including an iron bridge over the Shabelle River near Belet Ouen. This behaviour can be understood only by taking three factors into account. First, looting had started long before the fall of Siyaad Barre, and was carried out by the army and other repressive forces of the regime. Second, in the patrimonialized regime of Siyaad Barre, the distinction between public and private goods had long since vanished; any unprotected property was open to looting, and the only way to make sure of it was to act first and take it oneself, before a stronger contender came to steal it. Third, with the failure of the productive economy and the collapse of the formal job market, looting became a way of life for a large portion of the population; regardless of how honest they might have remained in another social context, the sale of booty became the only source of income.

A culture of loot has indeed developed in Somalia, and will be difficult to eradicate once effective government is re-established, but it is equally important to acknowledge the creation of a whole economy organized around this activity. Soon after goods are looted, they are sold at bargain prices to merchants who market them, either inside or outside the country.[16] Some merchants have made a fortune during the years of factional strife, and their financial support for the factions is a rational investment in a kind of controlled low-level conflict that generates a lot of profitable opportunities. Behind each faction leader, there is a group of businessmen who have invested both for long-term benefits (the hope of eventual state power), and for short-term ones (the illegal acquisition of goods at discount prices, ranging

---

[16] At one point in 1992, a whole cargo of second-hand computers, television sets and other office equipment was exported from Mogadishu to one of the Gulf states by a wealthy businessman who had systematically purchased it from looters.

from raw materials to sophisticated electronic equipment and weapons). Although it would be grossly inaccurate to describe political entrepreneurs as puppets manipulated by economic entrepreneurs, the proverbial role of money as the sinews of war still applies. Combatants could not do without money, and supplies of petrol and ammunition.[17] Some businessmen, such as Ali Mahdi and Usman Ato, crossed the boundary and became faction leaders in their own right, in the process also furthering their own economic interests.

What was called the 'informal sector' in other developing countries became the whole economy in Mogadishu, and humanitarian relief was part of it, especially in 1992 when foreign NGOs could not operate without paid protection from faction militias.[18] Most of the heavy fighting in the city occurred around the port and the airport, because control over shipments of goods, both commercial and humanitarian, provided undreamt-of opportunities for extortion. *Khat*, the mild narcotic consumed in large quantities by Somalis of all ages and walks of life (and not only by young thugs as the press often suggests) was imported daily from Kenya all through the war, and was also a very lucrative business in both parts of Mogadishu, crossing the so-called 'green line' without difficulty throughout the fighting. Initially, the factions fought for state power, or at least for the symbol of it provided by control of the capital city and the main means of communication with the outside world. But with the prolonged absence of a central government, and the loss of international interest after the departure of UNOSOM in March 1995, the expected spoils proved less attractive than the daily benefits of the criminal economy. Occupying a certain pocket of territory provided opportunities for *ad hoc* 'taxation' of individuals, markets and relief workers: indeed kidnapping became fashionable with the reduction of employment opportunities after the departure of UNOSOM, which served above all as a huge spender. This narrowing of objectives also clouded the prospects for peace and reconstruction in the south of Somalia, as factional warfare continued for the sake of the economic benefits that it provided to the 'new rich'.

The Impact of External Intervention

It is in this light that one must assess the impact of the international intervention in Somalia between December 1992 and March 1995.[19] Any thorough appraisal of operation 'Restore Hope' and UNOSOM I and II would go beyond the scope of

---

[17] At the peak of fighting in February 1992, Aidid's troops, who had made a major foray into northern Mogadishu, had to stop their offensive because their business supporters refused to pay for more petrol and ammunition.

[18] See Roland Marchal, 'La militarisation de l'humanitaire', *Cultures et Conflits*, 11 (1993); Alex de Waal and Raakiya Omar, 'Doing harm by doing good? The international relief effort in Somalia', *Current History*, 5 (1993).

[19] UNITAF was authorized to intervene by UN Security Council Resolution 794 on 3 December 1992, and ceased to exist on 4 May 1993. UNOSOM I was established with a limited mandate by Resolution 751 on 27 April 1992, and continued to function during UNITAF's mandate. UNITAF was responsible, under the code name 'Restore Hope', for the safe delivery of humanitarian relief to Somalis in need, while UNOSOM I was charged with conflict resolution. UNOSOM II was established by Resolution 814 of 26 March 1993, and took over the responsibilities of both UNOSOM I and UNITAF on 4 May 1994, its mandate being terminated on 31 March 1995 by Resolution 954 (1994).

this chapter, and there is already a considerable literature on the subject, though one of uneven value.[20] I am concerned, rather, with the impact of external intervention on the warring factions in the country. In this respect, despite Crocker's claims, everything did go wrong.[21] Not only did the operation fail to restore any lasting peace, seriously disarm the factions, or bring any decisive reconciliation or institution building; it also, most disastrously, fostered the conditions for lasting conflict by consolidating the clan-based factions.

Initially impressed by the deployment of 36,000 soldiers from 22 nations, Somali warriors soon realized that it was largely a show for Western public opinion. The original mandate of the United Task Force (UNITAF) was limited to the protection of relief convoys and, despite its overwhelming military superiority, it neither disarmed the factions nor arrested the so-called warlords whose behaviour had been used to legitimize the intervention.[22] US ambassador Oakley negotiated a safe landing for the troops with Aidid and Ali Mahdi, and, by his friendly handshake in front of the television cameras, conveyed the message to Somalis that the faction leaders were accepted as legitimate partners. Disarmament, when it was eventually implemented, was also largely a show: a few garages and weapon stores were blown up in Mogadishu at the start of the first Addis Ababa conference in January 1993, in an unavailing attempt to put pressure on Ali Mahdi and Aidid. The 'safe environment' for humanitarian agencies advertised by President Bush was a mirage, since apart from the heavily armed UNITAF convoys, the security situation was as bad as ever. In Mogadishu, NGOs had to rehire their security guards, since UNITAF soldiers turned a blind eye to security violations taking place a few metres from their checkpoints. UNITAF's attempt to stop the famine with massive food distribution, at a time when it was abating anyway, failed to address its root causes.[23] Politics was left to the United Nations, deprived of the talented Mahamed Sahnoun who was replaced as Special Representative in Somalia by the uninventive Ambassador Kittani. Pressed by the Americans to obtain quick results, the UN organized a dozen

[19] (cont.) Both UNITAF and UNOSOM operated under Chapter VII of the UN Charter, and were authorized to use military force to execute their mandate.

[20] The most complete bibliography to date on international intervention in Somalia is W. S. Clarke, *Humanitarian Intervention in Somalia* (Carlisle: US Army War College, 1995). I have attempted to summarize the causes of UN failure in Somalia in Compagnon, 'Les limites de l'ingérence "humanitaire"; l'échec politique de l'ONU en Somalie', *L'Afrique Politique 1995* (Bordeaux/Paris: CEAN/Karthala, 1995).

[21] Chester A. Crocker, 'The lessons of Somalia: not everything went wrong', *Foreign Affairs*, Vol. 4, No. 3 (1995); like much quasi-official US commentary on the intervention, this is designed to cover up the US failure in Somalia, and to counter widespread domestic hostility to US involvement in UN peace-keeping operations, such as that in Bosnia. For another example, see J. L. Hirsch and R. B. Oakley, *Somalia and Operation Restore Hope* (Washington: US Institute of Peace, 1995); Oakley served as US ambassador to Somalia in the early 1980s, and was at that time instrumental in building US support for Siyaad Barre's regime through arms deliveries.

[22] The French Foreign Legion, which had started to disarm the factions, was moved to Baidoa and Huddur, where it organized an efficient storage for heavy weapons and a system of control with individual licences for light arms – a success not broadcast on CNN.

[23] See Alex de Waal and Raakiya Omar, *Operation Restore Hope: a Preliminary Assessment* (London: African Rights, 1993); the famine in southern Somalia was due to raids and counter-raids by the armed factions, while north of Belet Ouen, in the north-east (Mijurtania) and Somaliland, there was no famine in any case.

'peace and reconciliation' conferences, with a growing number of factions,[24] escalating costs, and negligible achievements.

The operation was thus on the wrong track from the start, when the Americans were in full command, and not only from the beginning of the UNOSOM II mandate, as some American commentators have sought to argue. Although UNOSOM tried to implement a 'bottom-up' approach based on broader consultation at regional level,[25] in a vain attempt to sideline the faction leaders, it never succeeded in brokering an agreement between Aidid and Ali Mahdi. Instead, it only managed to alienate Aidid through a succession of provocations, which led to the confrontation of mid-1993 and the humiliating defeat of the Americans in October that year.[26] Having been legitimized from the first month of the UNITAF intervention, through the American embrace and the UN conference in Addis Ababa, the faction leaders and other self-appointed political entrepreneurs could not be excluded from the subsequent negotiation process by UNOSOM. Whatever results this process might produce, these leaders represented very little, and had even less capacity to get things done on the ground. Aidid was quickly perceived as hostile by the UN, and he himself rightly saw the UN strategy as a ploy to reduce his influence. By mid-1993, it was far too late to eliminate him from the game: too many Somalis had already been disappointed by the intervention, and Aidid was able to play on nationalist feelings to rally support beyond his own clan. In December 1993, Aidid was rehabilitated by the UN and the Americans, and the deadlock between his SNA and Ali Mahdi's Somalia Salvation Alliance (SSA) resumed and persisted until UNOSOM's departure from Mogadishu.

The UN's approach was even more misguided in the case of Somaliland, because Boutros Boutros-Ghali, who personally opposed secession, had as Egyptian Minister of Foreign Affairs been directly involved in support for Siyaad Barre until the very end.[27] Although there was a *sui generis* bottom-up approach to reconciliation and political reconstruction through the council of elders (*Guurti*) which met in Borama from late March to early May 1993,[28] UNOSOM not only failed to support this effort financially, but repeatedly tried to undermine the authority of the Hargeisa government. The UNOSOM regional office in Bossasso openly supported elements of the Dulbahante and Warsangeli clans who opposed incorporation into Somaliland and asked instead to join the Majeerteen-dominated north-eastern region, while money was given to Abdirahman Tuur to further divisions among the Isaaq and

[24] Seven organizations took part in the Djibouti conference of July 1991, 16 in the January 1993 Addis Ababa conference, and 24 a year later; some factions were created from scratch by UNOSOM itself, and the multiplication of factions usually ascribed to the fissiparous tendencies of the Somali lineage system was partly the product of the UNOSOM approach to political settlement.

[25] See J. P. Lederach, 'The intervention in Somalia: what should have happened', *Middle East Report*, No. 2 (1993), for a clear distinction between 'top-down' and 'bottom-up' strategies.

[26] Gérard Prunier, 'L'inconcevable aveuglement de l'ONU en Somalie', *Le Monde Diplomatique*, November 1993.

[27] The Isaaq vividly remembered in early 1993 that Hargeisa had been shelled in 1988 with Egyptian ammunition; the last consignment arrived in December 1990, a few weeks before Siyaad Barre was overthrown.

[28] See A. M. Y. Farad and I. M. Lewis, *Peace-Making Endeavours of Contemporary Lineage Leaders: a Survey of Grassroots Peace Conferences in North-West Somalia/Somaliland* (London: Action-Aid, December 1993).

sustain the fiction of SNM participation in UN-sponsored conferences. These plots, which violated the UN mandate to the total indifference of the Security Council, became so obvious that President Igal expelled UNOSOM from Somaliland.

By the time that UNOSOM eventually left its bunker in Mogadishu in March 1995, the achievements of foreign intervention were very meagre. The clan-based factions were as strong as ever, heavy weapons had been recovered from their hideouts in the bush or replaced, and the capital was as divided as it had been in 1992. The factions were both politically strengthened and financially enriched by the UNOSOM presence. A lot of money was made by the political entrepreneurs and their financial associates, and Ali Mahdi and Aidid, who had exhausted most of their resources in the intense fighting between late 1991 and early 1992, managed to recover under UN patronage. Although some factional alliances shifted and the fortunes of the two main contenders for supreme power fluctuated during the period up to Aidid's death in 1996, the structure of clan-based factionalism remained unchanged. Despite its empty rhetoric about a 'regional approach' and the need to empower civil society, UNOSOM not only failed to achieve these goals but left the country with entrenched political entrepreneurs who had little to lose from continued warfare and no format for conflict resolution. Any restoration of an effective central government remained a prospect beyond the foreseeable future.

Appendix:
Major Somali Guerrilla Movements and Armed Factions

This list should not be used to convey a false impression of stable political organizations. Over the seven years from January 1991, some of the names changed, and most of these so-called 'fronts' and 'parties' split into several factions which fought one another. In any event, most of the groups that were officially invited to the various UN-sponsored conferences were shadowy organizations, often not even present in the field, and without any real support from the people whom they claimed to represent.

The list gives the name of each movement or faction, its claimed clan or clan family base, and its region of potential or actual support.

Al-Ittihad al-Islami. All clans and some non-Somalis; Bossasso, Gode (Ethiopia), and later Lugh in upper Juba Valley

FLCS. Dir (Iise and Gadabuursi); Djibouti and Zeilah

Muki Somali African Organization. Wa Gosha of Bantu origin; lower Juba Valley

NFDLF. Mainly Daarood/Ogadeen; northern frontier district of Kenya, early 1960s

RRA. Rahanweyn; between Juba and Shebelle rivers

SDA. Dir/Gadabuursi; Borama District in northern Somalia

SDM. Digil and Rahanweyn; between Juba and Shebelle rivers

SNA. Various Hawiye and Daarood clans; coalition of factions headed by Mahamed Aidid and later his son Huseen

SNDU. Daarood/Leelkase and Awrtable; south-west of Galkaio near Ethiopian border

SNF. Daarood/Marehaan; Gedo, between Juba River and Kenya border

SNM. Mainly Isaaq; central part of northern Somalia (Somaliland)

SNU. Swahili-speakers; Mogadishu, Merka, Brava and Bajun islands

SPA. Various Hawiye and Daarood clans; coalition of factions headed by Ali Mahdi

SPM. Daarood/Ogadeen; middle Juba Valley, south of Bardera

SSA. Various Hawiye and other clans; coalition of factions headed by Ali Mahdi Mahamed, in opposition to SNA

SSDF. Daarood/Majeerteen; north-east Somalia

USC (both Aidid and Ali Mahdi factions). Hawiye, initially with some other southern clans; central Somalia, from Galkaio to Mogadishu

USF. Dir/Iise; Djibouti and Zeilah

USP. Daarood/Dulbahante and Warsangeli; eastern Somaliland between Las Anod and Las Koreh

WSLF. Mainly Daarood/Ogadeen, with elements from other clans; Ogaden region of Ethiopia

6

PASCAL NGOGA
Uganda:
The National Resistance Army

The National Resistance Army (NRA) of Uganda,[1] which captured the capital, Kampala, in January 1986, has some claim to be the first insurgent movement effectively to take over power from an incumbent African government.[2] It achieved this triumph without any significant external support, a feature of the insurgency which distinguishes it from the great majority of other African cases. Its main camps, moreover, were located no more than 20 miles away from the capital. Whereas a number of other African insurgencies splintered into rival factions, leading to internecine conflicts which culminated in the collapse of the state that they sought to take over, in Uganda the process worked the other way round: inheriting a state which had shattered under the brutal rule of Idi Amin and his successors, the NRA succeeded in re-establishing an effective central government, which at time of writing has governed Uganda without interruption for about 11 years. Although it is too early to suggest that the post-insurgency regime has provided solutions to all of the problems that had made armed insurgency inevitable, and insurgent opposition to the regime itself has continued in the north of the country, it has proved both the longest-lasting and, it could well be argued, the most stable government that Uganda has enjoyed since independence from British colonial rule in 1962. It therefore provides a particularly significant example of insurgency in Africa.

This chapter will start by examining the origins of the NRA, paying particular attention to its founder, Yoweri Museveni, and the conditions which led him to conclude that armed insurgency provided the only means through which the collapse of Ugandan statehood after independence could be reversed. It will then examine the internal organization of the NRA, drawing on extensive interviews with participants, before going on to outline the main features and phases of the five-year war which eventually brought it to power. It will close with a brief discussion of the impact of the NRA's legacy on post-1986 Uganda.

[1] The NRA was the military wing of the National Resistance Movement (NRM); for convenience, this chapter usually refers to the organization as the NRA.

[2] The first successful insurgency directed against an incumbent African government was in Chad, but this failed to establish an effective regime.

The Origins of Insurgency in Uganda

The dismal record of Uganda's first two decades of independence is very widely known.[3] The first post-independence government of Dr Milton Obote, whose Uganda People's Congress (UPC) drew its support very largely from the north of the country, lasted only until 1971. Governing at first in coalition with the Kabaka Yekka (KY), which was based on the southern kingdom of Buganda headed by the Kabaka (King), Obote broke with them in 1966, calling on the army to oust the Kabaka, until then titular president of the country, and took over as executive president himself. This left Obote dependent on the army, and especially on its commander Idi Amin, who launched his own *coup d'état* against Obote in 1971. Many of Uganda's subsequent problems can be traced to the rule of Amin, under whom the country became internationally notorious for the brutality of its dictatorship.

Amin's coup and subsequent brutality prompted many Ugandans to go into exile. One of them was Yoweri Tiburahurwa Kaguta Museveni, a young graduate from Ankole in south-western Uganda who had been working in the president's office as a politico–economic researcher. Though this association with Obote could have got him into trouble with the new regime, he claimed to have seen the coup as an opportunity 'to dismantle the colonial state and rebuild it on a proper national basis', and to have left to make external contacts for this purpose.[4]

Museveni had already developed an interest in revolutionary guerrilla warfare. He had joined the University of Dar-es-Salaam in 1967 because of his admiration for President Nyerere's progressive leadership, and because the liberation movements active in Southern Africa were based there, and had made a name for himself in radical student politics.[5] He was influenced by revolutionary thinkers including Walter Rodney, then a lecturer at the university, and Stokely Carmichael, who visited the campus in 1967. He made contact with the Frente de Libertação de Moçambique (Frelimo), then fighting an insurgent war against Portuguese colonialism, and in December 1968 organized a visit for seven students, including himself, to the liberated zones of northern Mozambique. The influence of this visit and his readings in revolutionary literature, particularly Fanon, on his attitude towards insurgent violence as a means of political liberation is attested by an early article, 'Fanon's theory on violence: its verification in liberated Mozambique'.[6]

Returning to Dar es Salaam in 1971, Museveni made contact with President Nyerere, who promised to help on condition that all opposition groups work together under Obote. The early part of 1971 was therefore spent mostly in trying to find common ground with Obote in organizing resistance to the Amin regime, but there were fundamental differences in strategy and organization. Whereas

---

[3] For historical background, see T. V. Sathyamurthy, *The Political Development of Uganda 1900–1986* (Aldershot: Gower, 1986); S. R. Karugire, *A Political History of Uganda* (Nairobi: Heinemann, 1980); and Peter M. Gukiina, *Uganda: a Case Study of African Political Development* (London: Notre Dame, 1972).

[4] Yoweri Museveni, *Sowing the Mustard Seed: The Struggle for Freedom and Democracy in Uganda* (London: Macmillan, 1997), p. 48.

[5] See John Saul, 'Radicalism and the Hill', *East African Journal* (Nairobi), Vol. 7, No. 12 (December 1970), pp. 289–90.

[6] Yoweri Museveni, 'Fanon's theory on violence: its verification in liberated Mozambique', in N. M. Shamuyarira, ed., *Studies in Political Science, No.3* (Dar es Salaam: TZ Publishing House, 1974).

Museveni and his group advocated guerrilla insurgency, Obote sought a conventional war with support from Tanzania, Sudan and Somalia. Equally, while Museveni sought a common front of all opposition groups, Obote wanted the resistance to be organized in his name as president.

This failure prompted Museveni and a few friends to form their own resistance movement, which at this time was known as the Front for National Salvation (Fronasa). In August 1971, Fronasa tried to infiltrate insurgents from Tanzania into the Mount Elgon region of eastern Uganda to establish a guerrilla base, but its poorly trained and ill-disciplined recruits were soon discovered by Amin's forces and arrested. During 1971 and 1972, Fronasa sent about 30 cadres for training under Frelimo in the liberated areas of Mozambique, and most of these were infiltrated back into Uganda. The first major attempt to overthrow Amin was in September 1972, when Ugandan exiles including Fronasa abortively invaded from Tanzania. Of the 1,340 men involved in the invasion only 887 survived; the remainder, including two of Fronasa's co-founders, Mwesigwa Black and Omongin Raila, were killed in action or captured and executed. After this failure, Museveni – who had led the survivors back to Tanzania – re-entered Uganda in December 1972 to establish resistance cells, but these were betrayed and their members publicly executed. After this disaster, Fronasa was forced to suspend its internal insurgent struggle, and not until 1986 did it again start training cadres, some of whom later became the core of the NRA.

When the Tanzanians invaded Uganda to overthrow the Amin regime in 1978–9, Fronasa was one of a number of exile movements which entered Uganda with them, gathering further recruits as the invasion force advanced through the area in which it had most support. Museveni subsequently became a minister in the short-lived provisional government of Professor Lule, which was installed by the Tanzanians but subsequently ousted in favour of a succession of short-lived regimes, until elections were held in December 1980. Museveni unsuccessfully contested these as leader of the Uganda Patriotic Movement (UPM).

Enjoying the active support of his friend President Nyerere of Tanzania, Obote was deemed to have won the elections – a result certified as 'free and fair' by a Commonwealth observer mission, but very widely believed in southern Uganda to have been rigged. The formation of the NRA followed directly from this failure. Indeed, resistance to the regime installed by the Tanzanians had been precipitated by Lule's dismissal; one of Lule's ministers, Andrew Lutakoma Kayira, had formed an urban terrorist organization called the Uganda Freedom Movement (UFM), which attacked institutions and individuals in Kampala, while Lule himself had founded the Uganda Freedom Fighters (UFF) from exile in London. Both of these organizations, however, were politically and militarily ineffectual.

The Decision for Protracted War

Following the controversial election of December 1980, Museveni convened a meeting of opponents of the new Obote regime to consider means of removing it from power. The possibility of launching a *coup d'état* or an urban insurrection was considered but rejected. For one thing, the Tanzania People's Defence Force

(TPDF), which was still stationed in Uganda, supported Obote and would suppress any attempted coup. For another, Obote's own armed forces, the Uganda National Liberation Army (UNLA), would scarcely hesitate to mow down any mass demonstration in the streets of Kampala. The strategy of protracted or insurgent warfare, on the other hand, offered both military and political advantages.

First, Museveni's main source of military support, Fronasa, had been dispersed in the aftermath of the Tanzanian invasion, and could be reassembled only gradually. Fronasa had been identified readily as a potential threat – not only for ideological reasons, but because it was drawn largely from southern and western Uganda, whereas Obote's support came mostly from the north. When the war ended, Fronasa forces, which by then numbered about 9,000, were ordered to report for 'retraining'. On arrival, only about 4,000 were accepted, the remainder being disqualified on the grounds that they were Rwandan or physically unfit. The officers were then sent either for cadet training in Tanzania or on a non-commissioned officers' course at Jinja, while the remainder were put through a punitive regime which appeared to be intended to dismantle the force rather than retrain it.[7] Whatever the intention, by the time the exercise was over, Fronasa as a force had been disbanded. Some of the officers were forced to resign, the soldiers were assigned to various UNLA units, while the remaining officers were posted to outlying districts in northern Uganda, where they were far distant both from their own home areas and from Kampala. Forces regarded as loyal to Obote were concentrated in and around the capital.

Second, it was argued that protracted war would involve the masses of the people, and thus make it possible to construct a viable political base for the resistance. This strategy would allow time to educate the people, organize them, and develop structures during the course of the struggle with which to replace the regime. In this emphasis on political rather than merely military objectives, Museveni was clearly drawing on the doctrines of people's war that he had imbibed in the course of his training in Mozambique. Political education was thus from the start an integral part of the NRA's programme, an emphasis that goes a long way to explain its relative success by contrast with many other African insurgencies.

Third, the conditions in Uganda at this time were conducive to the prosecution of a protracted people's war. The state itself was weak, economically, socially and politically. The disintegration of the socio-economic infrastructure, far advanced under Amin, had continued rather than being reversed under his successors. This caused further erosion of any mass support and loyalty that the regime might have expected to gain. Its legitimacy was undermined more deeply by the feeling that Obote had rigged his way to power, a view that was held particularly strongly in Buganda (where Obote had never been forgiven for his attack on the Kabaka in 1966), as well as in the West Nile area where the UNLA was brutalizing the population, whom it accused of supporting Amin. The UNLA itself, only recently established to replace Amin's defeated Uganda Army, was still too weak and too untrained to counter a well-organized insurgent challenge. There were, moreover, firearms readily available all over the country. Amin's soldiers had abandoned arms in the course of their retreat, while some of them had crossed over to Zaire or

---

[7] Interview, Brigadier Chefe Ali, January 1996.

Sudan, and could either sell their arms or use them against the new regime.

The Obote regime, nonetheless, presented a far from negligible challenge. As the government in place, it controlled such elements of the state structure as remained, while in particular it enjoyed the support of the international community. Most outside states were happy to see Uganda restored to the rule of an experienced nationalist leader, and were prepared to turn a blind eye both to his previous failings and to any evidence of election rigging or human rights abuse. The diplomatic conventions which aided any established government against its opponents, still at this time relatively unchallenged, also helped it. From the viewpoint of its opponents, protracted people's war would allow the contradictions in the incumbent regime to mature under the pressure of the insurgency, while the insurgents gradually developed their own strength.

The War Begins

The decision to resort to insurgent warfare was implemented almost immediately. On 6 February 1981 Museveni's force (known at this time as the Popular Resistance Army or PRA) attacked the barracks at Kabamba, with which most of them were already familiar, with only 35 men who between them mustered 27 guns. The attack narrowly failed, and the group retreated to Kiboga, where they attacked the police post on the next day. Over the next two months, the PRA undertook a number of hit-and-run operations, before suspending military operations entirely for three months from April to July, and going into total concealment.

There were several reasons for this pause. Most basically, having demonstrated its guerrilla credentials, the movement needed to establish the political network and build up the contacts with the local population which its strategy of protracted war required. As further recruits came forward, these needed to be trained and integrated into an expanding military structure. There were also tactical reasons, in addition to the need to absorb the military lessons of the very limited level of success achieved by the initial operations. The Tanzanian forces, which had remained in Uganda until after Obote's election, were due to withdraw from the country in June, and it was obviously sensible to delay further military action until the newly formed UNLA had been left on its own.

During these three months, a great deal was achieved. Recruits were raised from neighbouring villages, some former Fronasa fighters deserted the UNLA to join PRA, and a number of university students (including Mugisha Muntu, subsequently Major General and Army Commander) also joined, bringing the insurgent force to over two hundred fighters. The number of guns was brought up to 60, and in this period there was only one fatal casualty.

In June 1981, Museveni left Uganda for a six-month foreign tour to seek international support, and at this stage not a great deal could be done without his personal leadership. He visited Libya, which ironically had been instrumental in assisting the Amin regime before and during the 1978/9 war in which Museveni and Fronasa had been his enemy, and Qadhafi provided a small amount of military assistance. As Museveni put it, 'It is the 96 rifles, 100 landmines, five GPMGs, eight RPGs and a small quantity of ammunition that constitute the much-talked-about 'massive assistance' given by Libya to the NRA.'[8] This constituted the only external military assistance received by the NRA, all other arms and ammunition being captured from government forces.

Museveni visited London to present his case to the British government for the insurgent war against Obote, whose regime they were supporting at that time. He met Lord Carrington, the Foreign Secretary, and Richard Luce, Minister of State for Overseas Development, without affecting the British government's vain attempt to maintain the Obote regime. He also met Professor Lule in Nairobi, and after some negotiations the PRA merged with Lule's exiled UFF to form the NRA, a move which accorded Lule the titular leadership of the united movement, and added considerably to its political acceptability in Buganda (which as the base area, as well as the most heavily populated and centrally situated part of the country, was critical to eventual success), while making little difference to its effective leadership and organization on the ground, which remained firmly in the hands of Museveni and his core group of supporters. As Museveni explained: 'Lule really had no force to speak of, but we were prepared to be flexible and did not insist too much on maintaining our own identity. Apart from his image, Lule had no other contribution to make.'[9] By the time military operations resumed late in July, the movement was far more capable than before of sustaining a lengthy campaign.

The NRA : Organization and Leadership

The NRA's initial base area of operations, to become known as the 'Luwero triangle', was located immediately to the north-west of Kampala. The two longer sides of the triangle, each of about 160 kilometres, were formed by the roads which ran north from Kampala towards Gulu, and north-west from Kampala to Hoima; its shorter northern side was marked by the Kafu River. Falling entirely within Buganda, this area was hilly and densely populated at its southern end, fading out towards the drier and less densely inhabited Singo plains to the north. Until the opening of the 'Fort Portal front' in western Uganda in 1985, the NRA was almost entirely restricted to this area, though its mobile force attacked government barracks outside it.

Clandestine political networks were established from an early stage, with a few individuals to start with, followed by the recruitment of further sympathizers, until a village was sufficiently supportive to elect a village resistance council. These provided the base organizations for a pyramid, in which the members of village executive committees elected parish resistance councils, and so on up through the county and district levels to the National Resistance Council (NRC). Evidently owing much to Leninist principles of democratic centralism, this was a system which enabled local-level participants to gain a sense of local self-government combined with commitment to the organization, while placing little restriction on its central leadership. At local level, nonetheless, the change was revolutionary, since it displaced the government administrative system which, inherited from colonial rule,

[8] Museveni, *Sowing the Mustard Seed*, p. 142.
[9] Cited in NRM publication, *Mission to Freedom* (Kampala, 1990), p. 141.

was based on chieftaincy, and replaced it with the rule of local activists. These lower-level resistance councils concentrated on managing the affairs of their localities, while providing food and intelligence for the central command, recruiting and screening new recruits, manning road blocks and maintaining order. At times of danger, they advised people on when and where to hide, and when to reappear.

At central level, the NRC was the main political organ of the movement, with a membership drawn both from fighters and from civilians. It was nominally chaired by Professor Lule (who later died in London), but Museveni was its First Vice-Chairman and effective leader. The Second Vice-Chairman was Moses Kigongo, who had been Vice-Chairman of the PRA before the merger, and subsequently became Vice-Chairman of the NRM. At this stage, the NRC provided support for the PRA and later the NRA; when the war ended in victory, it became the basis of the council that exercised formal power until the elections of June 1996.

The most important military organs, the Army Council and High Command, were headed by Museveni, and were responsible for military policy and the planning and prosecution of the war respectively. The sub-committees of the NRC were responsible for essentially supportive tasks. These were:

1 The external sub-committee, headed by Matthew Rukikaire, which was based in Nairobi with branches in several countries, and was responsible for mobilizing Ugandans abroad and external fund raising. It achieved nothing like the effectiveness of its equivalent in organizations like the Eritrean Peoples Liberation Front, and in March 1985 Museveni complained that.

> mainly due to the weaknesses of our external workers, it has not been possible to get material assistance from outside. A number of good projects were spoilt by the so-called high ranking officials of our external committee. In spite of this, the internal wing has been able to sustain the struggle and expand it with quite a lot of unnecessary difficulties.[10]

2 The finance and supplies sub-committee, headed by Zak Kaheru, which was responsible for raising and distributing funds and supplies within Uganda. It would also coordinate with the external sub-committee on supplies required from outside, and supervise their distribution within the war zone.

3 The political and diplomatic sub-committee, headed by Eriya Kategaya (who was also second to Museveni in the NRA High Command), which was responsible for internal political education as well as keeping the international community informed about events in Uganda. It was based in the liberated zone, where it organized the resistance councils and helped them to carry out political mobilization and education.

4 The publicity and propaganda sub-committee, which was responsible for publicizing the struggle, exposing the crimes of the incumbent regime, and expounding the achievements of the NRA. For example, in conjunction with the New York branch of the external wing of the NRM, it helped to prompt a US Congressional hearing on 22 December 1982 about human rights violations in

[10] *Mission to Freedom*, p. 271.

Uganda. After the hearing, which was addressed by George Magezi, the leader of the NRM delegation, the House Foreign Relations Sub-committee on Africa 'expressed deep concern about the large scale violations of human rights committed by Obote's Government'.[11]

Recruitment and Organization

The original group of 35 who attacked the Kabamba barracks in February 1981 were drawn largely from the ranks of former Fronasa fighters who had trained under Museveni's supervision in Mozambique. They were soon joined by other Fronasa members, who deserted from their UNLA units once the war started and made their way to the Luwero triangle. A number of students from Makerere University also joined the struggle, along with some other trained professionals, for whom the closeness of the Luwero triangle to Kampala was an advantage. By far the greatest number of recruits, however, were drawn from the peasantry in the base area. Before the NRA gained effective control over the Luwero triangle, recruits were picked out by trusted individuals who had to operate clandestinely, but as NRA control expanded and village resistance committees were formed, these became responsible for recruitment.

In the words of one leading member, 'the main recruiting officer for NRA was Obote himself'.[12] In response to the NRA's initial successes, the security apparatus of the Obote regime engaged as a matter of routine in looting, rape and arresting young people suspected of sympathy with the NRA, both in the war zone and more generally in the south and west of Uganda. Many young people joined the NRA as an alternative to government repression. Similarly, the government sought to discredit Museveni by claiming falsely that he was Rwandan, and hence a foreigner meddling in Uganda's internal affairs. This association raised the tempo of UPC resentment against Kinyarwanda-speakers in Uganda, both Ugandan citizens and refugees from Rwanda. It was made worse by the fact that during the 1960s Kinyarwanda-speaking Ugandans had supported the opposition Democratic Party (DP), against Obote's UPC. UPC supporters also attacked Rwandan Tutsi refugees who were living in camps in Ankole; these could not flee to Rwanda, because of the persecution of Tutsis there, and instead joined the NRA insurgency *en masse*. By the time the NRA captured Kampala in January 1986, a quarter of its forces were of Rwandan origin.

Likewise, as the war grew in intensity and mass killings by UNLA soldiers increased, many of the resulting orphans joined the NRA for protection. This accounts for the thousands of child soldiers, known as *kadogos*, with the NRA during the war. Although they were trained in basic military tactics, only those aged sixteen and above were supposed to be fighters, the younger ones being employed as runners for officers, and the bigger ones as bodyguards.[13]

[11] *Mission to Freedom*, p. 129.

[12] Interview, Major General Mugisha Muntu, 7 February 1997.

[13] See Oliver Furley, 'Child soldiers in Africa', in Furley, ed., *Conflict in Africa* (London: I.B. Tauris, 1995), especially pp. 35–9.

Thus, by the end of 1982, counter-insurgency violence by government forces had greatly assisted in the recruitment of more insurgent forces and in the growth of the NRA. Recruits in turn were recommended either for training as local militia, or else to become part of the regular forces. Initially, they were taken on as scouts, and only after a preliminary assessment by NRA leaders were they selected for basic training. After this, the militia returned to their homes, while those assigned to the regular forces were posted to their units.

The initial training distinguished between recruits who were unfamiliar with military operations, and those who had already received their basic training in the UNLA, but were unfamiliar with the precepts and practice of protracted people's war. The first group were assigned to the Nkrumah training unit, in one of three sections of the NRA named after heroes of the African nationalist struggle: Nkrumah, Mondlane, and Nasser. (Given that Obote had been Nkrumah's most faithful lieutenant among other African heads of state, the naming after him of a unit dedicated to Obote's overthrow was particularly ironic.) Two further sections were named after Ugandan kings who had resisted British colonial rule in the nineteenth century, and another after an NRA supporter who had been executed by government soldiers for refusing to reveal the hiding place of the guerrillas.

Following their initial training, fighters were assigned to operational units for practical experience, after which some were recalled for specialized training according to their abilities, while others were selected for leadership courses and commissioned as junior officers. Recruits who already had a basic military training were taught guerrilla strategy and tactics. Throughout the training process, particular emphasis was placed on political education. This involved instructing recruits on the reasons for the war, the objectives of the NRA, the importance of Ugandan national unity and, most importantly, the need to maintain good relations between the NRA and the civilian population. As Museveni said:

> The population is the one which gives us food, shelter and intelligence information about the movements of the enemy troops. We are educating our soldiers in practical and everyday examples that it is the people who matter in this exercise.[14]

Political education, in Museveni's view, was a daily exercise carried out within the army and the civilian resistance committees, and provided the main link between the NRA and the civilian population. The NRA, like any serious insurgency, was aware that without the support of the population it would not win the war. At the same time, the population had learnt from the government's repression that, without the NRA to defend them, the UNLA would destroy their property, rape and even kill them. They each needed one another for their mutual benefit.

By May 1981, the number of insurgents had grown from the original 35 to over 200, a large number to conceal in one group. This prompted the division of the force into six units, each of which was allocated a zone of operations within the base area. The Abdel Nasser unit under Jack Muchunguzi operated along the Kampala–Gulu road; the Mondlane unit led by Fred Rwigyema operated around Kalasa and Mukurubita, about 30 kilometres north-west of Kampala and midway between the Gulu and Hoima roads; the Lutta unit commanded by Harrington Mugabi operated

---

[14] *Mission to Freedom*, p.151.

along the Kampala–Hoima road; the Kabalega unit under Elly Tumwine operated in Kapeka, about 50 kilometres north-west of Kampala in the central part of the Luwero triangle; the Mwanga unit under Matayo Kyaligonza operated in Mukono on the Jinja road, east of Kampala and outside the triangle; and the Nkrumah unit under Fred Mwesigye was based in Singo, in the northernmost part of the triangle. At this time, while the Adbel Nasser unit had about 40 rifles, the other units had no more than ten or 12 each. Further units were later established in the Ngoma and Kikyusa area, and from 1985 a second front was opened at the foot of the Ruwenzori mountains.

From 1983, three companies were combined to form the nucleus of the Mobile Brigade, a strike force which operated independently of the zonal units. While the zonal units were largely restricted to defensive operations and ambushes within their own zones, the Mobile Brigade attacked enemy detachments, and later attacked enemy barracks in search of arms. At the start, it was under the direct command of Museveni himself, but as the scale of activities increased it was placed under Museveni's younger brother, S. O. Salim Saleh. Relations between the zonal and mobile forces were coordinated, so that on occasion the zonal forces would launch diversionary attacks while the Mobile Brigade proceeded to attack a major target. The zonal forces provided a source of recruits, while the Mobile Brigade was the major source of captured arms. The zonal units also provided the sanctuary for the NRA's sick bay, general headquarters, and camps for displaced civilians.

Internal Conflicts and Contradictions

In the early months of the struggle, while the NRA was still a small force, its members lived together in the same camp for most of the time, and it was possible to hold the insurgents together by means of *ad hoc* rules and methods. Moreover, Museveni, whom everyone looked to for advice and direction at critical moments, was always close at hand. But as the NRA grew in size, and its area of operations expanded, *ad hoc* methods proved inadequate to maintain the cohesion of the force, and a number of potential areas of internal conflict started to emerge.

The first of these was ethnic. During the first years of the struggle, the majority of the trained NRA insurgents were former Fronasa members who had trained in Mozambique, and most of these, like Museveni himself, were from south-western Uganda. The fact that the operational zone was in Buganda, however, meant that the bulk of the NRA's recruits were Baganda, so that in its first years the NRA consisted of a large number of Baganda troops commanded by a small number of Banyankole-Bakiga officers. Inevitably, some recruits began to insinuate that Museveni was exploiting the Baganda, and a few dissidents even defected to the rival Baganda-dominated UFM insurgency of Andrew Kayira. This danger was exacerbated after the death of Ahmed Seeguya, a Muganda who had been trained in Mozambique in 1972 and became the first Commander of the NRA before he died of hepatitis in September 1981, while Museveni was away.

Further divisions arose between NRA recruits from different class and professional backgrounds. Those who had already served in the UNLA regarded themselves as military professionals, and as such better qualified than the civilians; the non-military recruits, on the other hand, had a tendency to regard themselves as volunteers, who should therefore not be subjected to the same rigid discipline as the regular soldiers. The 'intellectuals' who had joined the movement from Makerere University and professional posts in Kampala tended to regard themselves as the 'natural leaders' of the struggle, and to resent subordination to those whom they saw as their educational inferiors.[15]

As Museveni later commented,

> I went away in the month of June (1981) and came back in the month of December. When I came, I found some of the contradictions, and we held wide-ranging discussions within the movement, and introduced those structures which are there even today.[16]

These discussions, which extended down to the rank-and-file soldiers, resulted in two main conclusions: first, that it was a mistake to embark on a revolutionary campaign without putting in place the organizational structures that were needed to manage it; second, that it was not enough to rely on the monolithic leadership of a single individual, in the way that the NRA had relied on Museveni. On Museveni's return a general meeting at which all ranks were represented was held at Kanyanda, about 30 kilometres north-west of Kampala; as a result, the NRA underwent a major process of internal restructuring, which delayed its resumption of substantial military operations but eventually transformed it into one of the most coherently organized, effective and successful insurgencies in Africa.

At the top, a National Resistance Army Council drew together the commanders of all battalions and the heads of administrative departments. This was responsible, not for the management of specific military operations, but for devising policies for the whole army in matters of command structure and administration. Usually, it sat jointly with the National Resistance Council itself. Within each unit, a Policy and Administrative Committee was established, made up of the commanding officer (CO) of the unit with the other officers and heads of department. Its role was to help the CO to administer the unit. PACs were expected to meet twice monthly to assess the administration of the unit and its success in meeting objectives. Below the PAC, other unit committees were established to deal with such matters as food, finance, health and, most importantly, internal discipline. New roles were also established, the main one of which was the political commissar (PC) – a familiar position in revolutionary armies – who was expected to guide the army in accordance with the political line of the movement, to educate the fighters and supporters in the reason for the war, and to keep them in touch with developments. At the lowest level, there was a PC for each platoon, who was answerable to the PC of the company, who in turn was answerable to the PC of the battalion, and so on up to the NRA Chief Political Commissar, who was at that time Kahinda Otafiire, subsequently Colonel and Minister of Local Government. According to him, the PCs at every level met each month to assess their performance and to discuss new strategies, but if there was any special matter needing attention they met more frequently.[17]

---

[15] *Mission to Freedom,* p. 144.
[16] *The 6th February* (Kampala), Vol. 5, No. 2 (February 1991), p. 10.
[17] Interview, Kahinda Otafiire, February 1997.

In addition, regular meetings were adopted as a means of ensuring that the leadership remained in touch with the rank-and-file. These meetings provided an outlet for ordinary soldiers to contribute to the running of their affairs. A code of conduct was developed, discussed and approved. This was intended to serve as an instrument that would define clearly the organizational relationship between the various constituent parts of the movement, as well as between its individual members. It also provided a clear statement of the relationship between the insurgents and the civilian population. This comprehensive code of conduct was in response to some of the problems that had arisen while Museveni was away. The then Commander Magara (who took over after the death of Seeguya) had used excessive force to assert his authority over the fighters. In particular, he had ordered the execution of a boy known as Shaban Kashanku for going to Kampala without permission. This *ad hoc* decision had been disputed by most fighters and gave rise to a lot of fear and suspicion within the movement.

Under the subsequent code of conduct, the most serious offences were category 'A', which attracted the death sentence. These included: murder of a civilian; treason (acting as an enemy agent); disobedience of lawful orders resulting in loss of life; and rape. Category 'B' involved other offences, which were punishable according to their gravity and the intentions of the offender. The code emphasized that all punishments should be carried out in public, and the reasons for the punishment should be given. They covered such offences as theft of property, quest for cheap popularity (claiming collective achievements as your own), mistreating civilians, propagating tribalism, reckess destruction of military equipment, and so forth. The punishments that might be imposed included corporal punishment, suspension, demotion and imprisonment. Later, an operational code of conduct to deal with offences during operations was added. It defined the composition and powers of unit tribunals, field court-martials, general court-martials, and offences punishable under that code. The difference between this and the original code of conduct was that punishment would be instant in the case of the operational code, so that the operation could carry on. The NRA – which then became the Ugandan Peoples' Defence Force (UPDF) – continued to use this same code of conduct after the end of the war, with a few modifications.[18]

Within this structure, it was then possible to tackle the specific problems that had arisen in the movement. Care was taken to emphasize that the absence of Baganda commanders was due not to discrimination, but to the fact that the Baganda recruits did not yet have the training and experience required; increasing numbers of Baganda commanders were subsequently promoted as they gained experience. It was likewise agreed that all insurgents, regardless of their previous military or civilian background, were required to submit to the same code of discipline. Promotion, equally, was to be based on example rather than level of educational attainment; all members thus had to be subjected to the same conditions of basic training, and subsequent promotion depended solely on their capacity, commitment and contribution to the struggle.

[18] Interview, Mugisha Muntu.

The Progress of the War

Although operations were resumed in July 1981, these mainly consisted of ambushes and attacks on small targets, designed to secure the base area. The first major government offensive, Operation Bonanza, was not launched until June 1982, and proved a failure. The NRA was able to cut the UNLA supply line and attack isolated detachments. In January 1983, however, the Obote government launched a major offensive, employing about 7,000 UNLA troops in an attempt to encircle the NRA. Operating from the two roads (Kampala–Hoima and Kampala–Gulu) which defined the Luwero triangle, the UNLA by March 1983 had forced the NRA to retreat northwards from its base area towards the Singo plains, accompanied by about a million and a half refugees, fleeing from the government troops who at this time earned the second Obote regime a reputation for atrocities which exceeded even that of the Amin period. This was the most critical period of the war. The retreat was due mainly to the shortage of arms. Although the number of fighters had grown to about 4,000, they still had only 400 guns, a ratio of one to every ten insurgents. As Museveni put it, he had hoped to get some guns from outside, but because of rivalries and ideological differences within the external wing, lines of contact were disrupted and they could not get delivery of the new arms that they needed.[19] Although the NRA sought to relieve the pressure by launching attacks on UNLA positions outside the war zone, the government's encirclement strategy achieved a high level of success, especially by preventing the NRA and the civilian population from foraging for food. Eventually, a decision had to be taken to send the civilian population back into their home areas, even though these were now under UNLA control; their cattle were left behind, to support the NRA forces.

The tide turned suddenly on 2 December 1983, with the death of UNLA commander Oyite Ojok in a helicopter crash. The UNLA proved to be every bit as dependent on its own commander as the NRA was on Museveni, and for months the government army was thrown into confusion. The encirclement offensive rapidly came to a halt, while Oyite Ojok's death also started a succession dispute that divided the UNLA between its Acholi and Langi factions. From early 1984, the NRA was in a position to resume the offensive, mounting a successful attack in February on Masindi, just north of the Luwero triangle, which raised morale and resulted in the capture of large quantities of arms, including 765 rifles and ammunition. The next target was the town and barracks at Hoima, south-west of Masindi, and by the onset of 1985 the NRA was able to attack its old objective in Kabamba once more. This time they succeeded in overrunning the barracks, and captured about 600 rifles and a great deal of ammunition. In April 1985, the acting overall commander of the NRA, Fred Rwigyema, opened another sphere of operations around Fort Portal, in the foothills of the Ruwenzori mountains of western Uganda.

Conflicts within the regime eventually resulted in Obote's overthrow by a military *coup d'état* in July 1985, and his replacement by a weak and unstable military regime led by Tito Okello. The resulting confusion in the central government gave

[19] *Mission to Freedom*, p. 151.

the NRA the opportunity to extend its area of operations. The UNLA battalion stationed at Kasese in western Uganda defected *en masse* to the NRA, and the government forces at Mbabara and Masaka in the south-west were besieged. With the NRA dug in along the Katonga River, the whole of south-western Uganda was cut off from central control. From this time, other states including Kenya became involved in seeking to negotiate a peace accord. President Moi chaired peace talks between Okello's government and the NRA, but the central government was in a state of collapse, and the NRA had little interest in peace negotiations for anything but tactical purposes, when it was in any event on the brink of victory. On 26 January 1986, it captured Kampala and the war was effectively over.

Conclusion

This chapter has sought to assess some of the variables that enabled the NRA to become one of the most effective guerrilla insurgencies in Africa, and the first to defeat an incumbent regime and replace it by a successful post-insurgency government. From the viewpoint of the former senior cadres in the NRA who were interviewed in the course of research for this chapter, the success of the NRA was the result of a number of interrelated factors: the support of the people, which was precipitated by their deep-rooted hatred for Obote's regime, and fuelled by that regime's violent counter-insurgency operations; the effective organizational structures that maintained the cohesion of the movement; the politicization that clarified the course and reinforced the commitment of the insurgent forces; and the weaknesses first of the Obote and then of the Okello regimes.

But one critical variable in assessing not only the success of the NRA during the insurgent war, but also the achievements of the post-insurgent government, was the strong and visionary leadership of Yoweri Museveni, which is readily obscured by an emphasis on more general variables such as 'popular support'. Although any effective insurgency requires a combination of leadership and the support of the people, there may be considerable variation in the significance of each. In the case of Uganda, although the population's support was crucial, and from December 1981 (when it was restructured at the Kanyanda meeting) the movement had an effective organization through which to achieve its goals, Museveni remained its military and political pillar. This is no way implies that his leadership was the sole determining factor in the NRA's success, but it does suggest that it was the single most important factor. As Mugisha Muntu put it: 'His strength of character and will enabled him to impart his vision to his followers, and ensure that they adopted his vision as their own.'[20] He inspired his forces and the civilian population in the war zone to entrust him with their lives, primarily because of his competence in all situations. 'He was always there in the field with you to share the risks to which we were all exposed.'[21] Hence the role of Museveni's leadership in motivating and influencing the NRA fighters was undoubtedly crucial for success.

On the whole, the NRA political programme as conceived in the bush was

---

[20] Interview, Mugisha Muntu.
[21] Interview, Brigadier Ivan Koreta, October 1996.

translated into practice, thus confronting the main challenges that the movement faced on taking over power. Important reforms were implemented in key areas, including the constitution, the civil service, economic management, the army and local government. For example, in local government the NRM regime dismantled the institutions of chiefship, stripped the chiefs of legislative, judicial and executive power, and placed these powers in the hands of the resistance councils (RCs). Chieftaincy had been one of the long-lasting legacies of the colonial and post-colonial state, which by making the people accountable to state officials had turned upside down the democratic principle that state officials should be accountable to the populace. The NRM's introduction of RCs turned it upright by establishing a people's participatory democracy, and giving special representation to the 'historical minorities', women and youth. Most important to the population, however, was that the army became an instrument of protection, instead of the instrument of aggression and destruction that it had once been; and the successful challenge to state power by the NRA shattered the myth of people's helplessness in the face of the government's monopoly of the instruments of coercion. The NRM policy of politicization and demystification of the gun through military training and the formation of local militias reinforced their confidence and participation in looking after their own security, even though it also helped to give rise to further sectional challenges to state power, as was the case in the north of the country.

On the international scene, the success of the NRM insurgency had a tremendous impact on the neighbouring region. Although Museveni repeatedly said that the NRM revolution was not for export, a number of groups in neigh-bouring countries sought, with a considerable degree of success, to import its insurgent ideology, a process which some have suspected to have occurred by design. The successful Rwandan Patriotic Front/Army (RPF/RPA) insurgency in Rwanda had its origins in the NRA, most of its leaders having been instrumental in the Ugandan insurgency. Both Fred Rwigyema, the first political and military leader of the RPF/RPA, and his successor Paul Kagame, were among the original 35 fighters who attacked the Kabamba barracks on 6 February 1981, and had risen through the NRA's post-insurgency military structures before leading the RPF into Rwanda. Most of the senior officers in the RPF had likewise had their training in the Ugandan bush during the NRA insurgency.

Similarly, it has been admitted that Laurent Kabila, veteran of almost every up-rising against the Mobutu regime in the former Zaire (now the Democratic Republic of Congo), and political coordinator of the Alliance of Democratic Forces for the Liberation of Congo-Zaire (ADFL), which overthrew Mobutu and installed Kabila as president, had been assisted militarily by both the NRA and the RPF leadership, who sent troops to the then Zaire to help do the job for him. Most of the officers in his insurgent army were Rwandans who had taken part in the RPF insurgency in Rwanda, and many of them had previously been in the NRA struggle.

In Southern Sudan, where the SPLA fought an insurgent war against successive governments in Khartoum, culminating in the Islamist al-Bashir regime, the NRM government's material assistance probably did not amount to much, but its moral, diplomatic and tactical support was certainly substantial. Moreover, Museveni and SPLA leader John Garang had been revolutionary colleagues way back in the days of student politics at Dar es Salaam University. In retaliation, the Sudanese government sponsored the anti-NRM insurgencies of Joseph Kony's Lord's Resistance Army (LRA) and Juma Oris's West Nile Bank Front (WNBF).

In Kenya, Uganda's eastern neighbour, the main impact was one of suspicion. Kenyan president Daniel arap Moi, one of the last regional leaders of the old post-colonial school, was afraid of the potential spill-over of Museveni's insurgent ideology, and constantly accused Uganda of harbouring and training insurgents to overthrow his regime. Relations between the two governments were strained at best, and openly hostile at worst. Finally, Uganda became the fulcrum of a growing solidarity among the post-insurgent governments of the region, stretching from Eritrea and Ethiopia to Rwanda and Zaire, which presented a threat to the first generation of post-independence leaders and their foreign patrons. The revolutionary ideology and commitment to insurgent warfare which Museveni had developed ever since his student days had been destined to have an impact well beyond the confines of his own country.

There are many lessons to be drawn from the Ugandan insurgent experience. First, the victory of the NRA showed that it was possible for a small group of dedicated insurgents to launch an armed struggle which eventually led to the overthrow of an incumbent African regime. Contrary to Mao Tse Tung's assertion that it is imperative for any effective insurgency to start with political mobilization, the NRA-initiated hostilities with a *foco* of 35 combatants, only 27 of whom were armed. As Che Guevara had contended, it was mainly the government's repressive counter-insurgency operations that turned the population to support the insurgents. This is not entirely to verify Guevara's *foco* theory, however, since the NRA started intensive political mobilization as soon as hostilities began, and even suspended military operations after three months, from April to July 1981, and went into concealment while they set up a political network and mobilized the host population. Secondly, the NRA demonstrated that an African insurgency can succeed without any extensive resort to external resources, and notably without a friendly frontier across which to retreat, or to use for communications with the outside world. The NRA's military equipment came almost entirely from the government forces, and its food from the host society. Finally, it showed that an effective insurgency can offer an alternative to state decay, depending on the extent to which it represents something more than the mere interests of its leadership. The NRM has renewed the development potential of the Ugandan state, economically, socially and politically, by recreating a national political community in what had become, under Obote and Amin, a thoroughly privatized state. The post-insurgent NRM government, already the longest-serving regime in post-independence Uganda, has resuscitated the Ugandan state and provided the structures and ideology through which solutions to the endemic internal conflicts that have plagued Uganda can be found. Should the NRM prove as effective in government as it was in insurgency, it will have a fundamental significance not just for Uganda but also for other African insurgents and post-insurgent regimes which are attempting to reform their states towards constitutionalism and democratic governance.

7

HEIKE BEHREND
War in Northern Uganda

The Holy Spirit Movements of Alice Lakwena,
Severino Lukoya and Joseph Kony (1986–97)[1]

From 1986 onwards a series of religious as well as more secular movements emerged in Acholi in northern Uganda to fight the National Resistance Army (NRA) government of Yoweri Museveni, who had himself come to power by over-throwing the previous regime. Among these organizations the three Holy Spirit Movements stand out: all can be said to have 'invented' an indigenized Christian discourse and practices.[2] The original Holy Spirit Movement (HSM) was formed by a young woman, Alice Auma, from a cult of affliction centred on the healing of individual soldiers and barren women. In August 1986, in a situation of internal and external crisis, she started to organize the Holy Spirit Mobile Forces (HSMF) and to wage war against the government, against witches, and against impure soldiers. She recruited many former soldiers into her movement, and after the first military successes against the NRA, other segments of the populatioin joined her. She created a complex initiation and purification ritual, in which she freed the Holy Spirit soldiers from witchcraft and evil spirits. She promised her soldiers protection against the enemy's bullets, and invented the 'Holy Spirit Tactics', a form of warfare which combined modern military techniques and ritual practices. Under the leadership of various spirits, Alice Auma – by then called Alice Lakwena, after the leading spirit of the movement – marched towards Kampala, the Ugandan capital, with between 7 and 10,000 men and women. Near Jinja, some 30 miles from Kampala, she and her soldiers were defeated by government troops, many of them being killed or injured. Alice crossed into Kenya, where she remains to this day. After her defeat, the discourse and practices that she had produced were taken over, with variations, by her father Severino Lukoya, who fought between 1987 and 1989, and then by her cousin Joseph Kony, who is still waging war at the time of writing.

This chapter will first reconstruct the political history that led to the emergence of Alice Lakwena's original movement. It will then attempt to describe the discourse, practices, organization and internal divisions of this movement, as well as

[1] My ethnographic field research was kindly funded by the Special Research Programme of the University of Bayreuth. I am grateful for its generous support, which enabled me to work in Kampala and Gulu during various stays between 1989 and 1995.
[2] See Terence Ranger, in Eric Hobsbawm and Terence Ranger, eds, *The Invention of Tradition* (Cambridge: Cambridge University Press, 1983).

its relationships to the local population and to other movements. It will then go on to discuss the successor movements of Severino Lukoya and Joseph Kony, and compare them with Alice's HSM.

The Emergence of the Holy Spirit Movement of Alice Lakwena

In 1979, the Uganda National Liberation Army (UNLA) succeeded, with the help of Tanzanian troops, in ousting the government of Idi Amin. After an election widely alleged to have been rigged, former president Milton Obote regained power, and a brutal civil war broke out between Obote and Museveni's NRA. In this war, Acholi for the most part fought on the side of the government army, but rivalries within the UNLA led to the coup of July 1985, in which Acholi soldiers led by Bazilio Okello marched on Kampala and ousted Obote. Another Acholi, Tito Okello, became the new president, and for the first time a group of Acholi controlled state power in Uganda. They used this power, as had others before them, to gain wealth and retaliate against their enemies, who included the Langi and people from the West Nile. After this victory, the UNLA disintegrated into a number of marauding groups which divided Kampala between them. Despite a peace agreement in December 1985, the NRA marched on Kampala and ousted the Okellos on 26 January 1986, the UNLA being by then incapable of mounting effective resistance.

Thousands of Acholi soldiers fled to the north, either to their home villages or to Sudan. They hid their weapons in the villages and attempted to lead a peasant life, but only a few were successful. During the civil war, they had lived by plunder and become contemptuous of peasant existence, and their return caused disturbance and violence. They began to plunder the villages and terrorize anyone whom they didn't like; and although the elders attempted to exercise their authority over the returned soldiers, through recourse to 'Acholi traditions', they were unsuccessful.

Even after the occupation of the Acholi centres of Gulu and Kitgum by the NRA, tensions, conflicts, denunciations and acts of revenge among the Acholi continued. During the civil war, death in battle had often been interpreted in terms of witchcraft.[3] The enemy bullet that killed an Acholi was not viewed as the true cause of death; rather, a relative or neighbour with whom the deceased had been in conflict was supposed to have bewitched him, to ensure that the bullet would strike the victim and no one else. The war against the exterior enemy, the NRA, was thus turned inward, exacerbating latent conflicts and tensions among the Acholi. AIDS was also quite often interpreted by the Acholi in terms of witchcraft, and this further escalated internal conflicts. The situation was exacerbated when a new NRA battalion was stationed in Acholi, consisting of soldiers who had fought against the Acholi in Luwero during the civil war. When these soldiers took revenge on the local people through acts of looting, torture, murder and rape, some former soldiers took their weapons from hiding and joined the Uganda People's Democratic Army

---

[3] Death by witchcraft was only one of a number of alternative explanations; ancestors, the Christian god or accident could also be held responsible.

(UPDA), which had in the meantime been founded in Sudan. The NRA then ordered the general disarming of the Acholi, and carried out 'operations' in the course of which Acholi were tortured or disappeared into so-called 'politicization camps', leading more and more ex-soldiers to join the UPDA. UPDA soldiers in turn began to terrorize the civilian population. It was in this situation of extreme internal and external threat that Alice Auma became possessed by a spirit called Lakwena, who ordered her to build up the HSMF, in order to bring down the government, purify the world of sin, and build up a new world in which humans and nature would be reconciled.[4]

In summary, a number of factors thus combined to bring about the HSM's war. First, the war may be seen as an attempt to regain the state power which the Acholi had lost. Second, it may be regarded as a reaction against the abuse of power by the NRA, which conquered Acholi in March 1986 and stationed battalions in Gulu and Kitgum. Former soldiers and civilians, some of whom were tortured or never returned, were arrested and detained in military camps.[5] Acholi in senior positions were dismissed and evicted from their official residences, while property was looted, especially cars and cattle. Official propaganda on the radio and in newspapers held the people of the north, and especially the Acholi, responsible for all the sufferings that Ugandans had undergone.[6] Third, defeated soldiers who had lost their jobs, and fled as 'losers' and 'cowards' back to their homes, found themselves in a desperate situation. There, they were treated as 'internal strangers',[7] who had become unclean by killing, thus bringing *cen*, the spirits of the killed; because of their impurity, they were held responsible for the misfortune which had struck Acholi. Many of them opposed the demands of the elders that they should undergo appropriate cleansing rituals. Finally, a situation of internal terror in Acholi, which had been caused by conflicts between elders and young men, between rich and poor people, and between women and men, was actualized and reinforced by a discourse of sorcery and witchcraft. As Lonsdale remarked in relation to the comparable situation of Mau Mau in Kenya, enmities multiplied and turned parts of northern Uganda to moral panic.[8]

Discourses and Practices of the HSMF

While the government army and other resistance movements, such as the UPDA and the Uganda People's Army (UPA), all used a secularized political discourse, the HSMF was alone in responding to the crisis with a moral discourse that sought

[4] On the reconciliation of 'nature' and human beings, see H. Behrend, 'The Holy Spirit Movement and the forces of nature in the north of Uganda', in M. Twaddle and H. B. Hansen, eds, *Religion and Politics in East Africa* (London: James Currey, 1995).

[5] In addition to accounts of NRA atrocities collected in the narratives of local people, these are also attested by sources including L. Pirouet, 'Human rights issues in Museveni's Uganda', in H. B. Hansen and M. Twaddle, eds, *Changing Uganda* (London: James Currey, 1991), and M. Ocan, 'The war currently taking place in Northern Uganda' paper presented to the Sessional Committee on Defence and Internal Affairs, Parliament House, Kampala, Uganda, 1996.

[6] Ocan, 1996.

[7] See R. P. Werbner, *Ritual Passage, Sacred Journey* (Washington, DC: Smithsonian Institute Press, 1989), p. 239.

[8] See J. M. Lonsdale, 'The moral economy of Mau Mau', in B. Berman and J. M. Lonsdale, eds, *Unhappy Valley* (London: James Currey, 1992), pp. 355, 388, 441.

answers to these predicaments. In strong contrast to the UPDA, as well as to the NRA, when Alice started recruiting former UNLA and UPDA soldiers to build up the HSMF in August 1986 she stressed the moral rehabilitation of her soldiers. To the internal terror reigning in Acholi, she responded by first of all cleansing the soldiers. The rites of initiation that all the Holy Spirit soldiers had to undergo purified them from *cen*, the spirits of the killed, and from witchcraft. After the initiation, the soldiers were regarded as pure and holy – but they had to prove their purity again and again in battle. Each battle was an ordeal, in which being wounded or killed was taken as a sign of backsliding into a state of impurity and sin. After each battle, the purification ritual was repeated to render harmless the new *cen* produced by the deaths of the enemies. Thus, in the HSM's discourse, the fight was directed not only against the external enemy, the government troops, but also against sinful members within the movement itself.

Furthermore, Lakwena[9] issued the 'Holy Spirit Safety Precautions' – prohibitions against theft, looting, lying, killing, sex, smoking cigarettes, drinking alcohol and other sins – to reconstitute the moral order and to control violence. These prohibitions, with a few exceptions, were strictly obeyed, not only by the Holy Spirit soldiers but also by civilians in the 'liberated areas', particularly in Kitgum District. In contrast to the other resistance movements and the government troops, Lakwena thus succeeded, at least until the HSM reached Busoga, in disciplining the soldiers and thereby protecting the local population.[10]

The Holy Spirit Safety Precautions not only served to reconstitute the moral order, but also initiated a process which, following Delmeau and Kittsteiner, may be termed 'culpabilization'.[11] Culpabilization refers to the creation of a consciousness of guilt that no longer pushes the guilt onto another, as in the discourse of witchcraft, but instead takes it upon oneself. If a Holy Spirit soldier broke or infringed one of the Holy Spirit Safety Precautions, this made him guilty. If a bullet hit him in battle, then his wound or death would appear as a punishment of his own misdeed. No longer would another be suspected or accused. In this way, the HSM was able to keep the movement free from suspicions and accusations of withcraft: there were no witchcraft accusations among Holy Spirit soldiers.

Organization

The HSMF did not fight a guerrilla war, but a more or less conventional war; its military wing was organized according to the British colonial pattern.[12] It was the spirit Lakwena, however, who was seen as the leader and Chairman of the movement.

[9] In the perspective of the movement, it was the spirit Lakwena and not Alice herself who was acting and leading the war.

[10] It is extremely difficult to judge the amount of violence used by the Holy Spirit soldiers against local people. Alice's HSM clearly enjoyed the support and assistance of local people in many regions of northern Uganda; after her defeat, many of her soldiers claimed to have been kidnapped in order to avoid punishment, even though very often they had joined the movement voluntarily. On the other hand, there were occasions when Holy Spirit soldiers used violence.

[11] See J. Delumeau, *Le Pêche et la peur* (Paris: Fayard, 1983) and H. D. Kittsteiner 'Das Gewissen im Gewitter', *Jahrbuch für Volkskunde,* Vol. 10 (1987).

[12] John Middleton, personal communication.

Lakwena was represented by the Commander of Forces (CF), who received orders from the Chairman, and executed them accordingly.

Under the CF, there were four huge companies, named A, B, C and Headquarters company. Companies were divided into between three and 30 platoons, each headed by a platoon commander and including from 50 to 80 men. Each company was commanded by a spirit. A company was commanded by a spirit called Rankie, popularly known as Wrong Element; he was also responsible for intelligence work and for the provision of medical supplies. B company was led by Ching Poh, a spirit from China or Korea, who was responsible for the supply of weapons, trucks and other items. The commander of C company was a spirit called Franco or Mzee, who was responsible for providing food, soap, uniforms and similar items. These spirits were represented by *commandeers*, who were the equivalent of officers commanding a company.

The Headquarters company was the biggest of the four, and included various departments: the Chairman's Office; Controllers and Technicians (ritual experts, who cleansed the soldiers who had killed, and protected them during battles by praying and sprinkling holy water); the Intelligence Office; the Quartermaster Office; the Armoury, Medical and Signals Office; and in addition, Offices for the Senior Officers, Visitors, Women, and Children; the Parade Office; Nyaker's Office (Nyaker, meaning 'daughter of a chief' in Acholi, was a female spirit who worked as a nurse in the movement, and specialized in exorcising evil spirits which had taken possession of Holy Spirit soldiers); the Operation Office; and, last but not least, the Production Office.

In addition to the military wing, there were the Frontline Coordination Team (FCT) and the War Mobilization Committee (WMC), which formed part of the civilian wing of the HSMF. They were responsible for building up supportive relations with the local population. They worked together with elders, organized rallies to give moral education to the people, preached the message of the Lakwena, and provided material support, food and medicine. This highly complex organization was able at its peak to encompass between seven and ten thousand men and about a hundred women. It combined the structures of a conventional army with those of a religious cult.

Internal Domains of Conflict

Although this organization proved fairly effective, as time went by it became increasingly difficult to control the divisions which arose within the movement – between members of different ethnic groups, between intellectuals and the un-educated or less-educated, between veterans and newcomers, and between men and women. In this discussion, I will restrict myself to some comments on the domains of conflict created by ethnicity and gender.

The HSM started in Acholi. In its discourse, the appearance of Lakwena in Acholi was a planned event.

> According to the Lakwena two tribes had the most bad records in history of Uganda, namely the Acholi and the Baganda. But top on the list are the Acholi. They have been notorious for

murder, looting, raping etc. It was therefore planned by God to help the Acholi to be converted....[13]

The Acholi claim to leadership was thus founded on negative attributes: because they were the most sinful of all ethnic groups in Uganda, God sent the Lakwena to them. Their sinfulness, in a way, guaranteed their salvation. Although the HSM embodied a Christian universal discourse which attempted to transcend ethnicity, the contradiction between the Acholi claim to leadership and the negation of ethnicity in the Christian universal discourse was never solved, and led to various conflicts. Nonetheless, the 'technology of power' provided by the highly complex and flexible organization of spirit possession very often helped to reduce these tensions.[14] But while the HSM to an uncertain extent succeeded in uniting Acholi, Lango, Teso and Jopadhola as 'northerners', they could do so only in opposition to the 'Bantu' or 'southerners', thus bringing into play another ethnic/linguistic division, which they were unable to overcome. It was no accident that when the HSMF reached Busoga, a region inhabited mainly by Bantu, they lost the support of the local population.

When the movement started, the Lakwena had declared men and women as equal, thus displacing the dominant gender hierarchy in Acholi. Men as well as women went into battle, acquired ranks, cooked food and collected firewood. As has already been noted, under the Holy Spirit Safety Precautions neither men nor women were allowed to have sex. They had to stay together as brother and sister, not as man and wife. In a way, chastity guaranteed their equality, as well as their salvation. Later, however, as more and more men joined the movement, the women were asked to stop fighting, and to retreat to women's duties as these were defined in the dominant male discourse. Furthermore, while male soldiers in the movement were called *malaika*, angel, the women were named *agaba*, a parasitic creeping plant which in Acholi is also associated with sexual seduction and unlawful sex. While men as angels had in a sense already left their sinfulness behind, women in contrast were associated with evil. Women were seen to be responsible when men soiled their purity by making love. Thus, in HSM discourse, women came to be regarded as potential internal enemies. Despite the fact that it was through a woman that the spirit Lakwena expressed himself, the HSM was essentially a male venture concerned to rehabilitate and reintegrate soldiers who had become internal strangers. Thus, the HSM's later discourse could be interpreted as an attempt to discipline and control women – a point to which I will return later.

The HSMF's Relations with the Local Population and other Movements

The HSMF made considerable demands on local societies, not least for the supply of food and weapons to several thousand soldiers. Although they had a so-called Production Office, following the example of the NRA, to plant maize and millet,

[13] This quotation is taken from a document which Holy Spirit soldiers gave to some missionaries in 1987.
[14] H. Behrend, *Alice und die Geister: Krieg in Norden Ugandas* (Munchen: Trickster, 1993), pp. 157ff. (English translation to be published by James Currey, 1998).

they never succeeded in producing their own food. Instead, they relied on the offerings and gifts of the local population, and developed a more or less predatory mode of consumption. On their march towards Kampala, the support that the HSMF received varied greatly from region to region, and sometimes even from clan to clan. Often they were welcomed by an enthusiastic crowd of people who became fervent followers, while in other places they were denounced and betrayed. The local people had already suffered from the looting and plundering of government soldiers and Karimojong cattle raiders, however, and they did not have much left to supply to hungry soldiers. The various resistance movements which operated in northern Uganda all demanded the little they had, and this intensified the rivalries between the different movements. To defend its hegemonic position, the HSMF increased the violence directed against rival movements, as well as against some members of the local population.

In the course of the march on Uganda, the HSMF twice carried out 'operations' against supposedly impure and sinful soldiers. During 'Operation Coy', in July 1987, some of the bravest and most experienced soldiers were sent back to Acholi, in order to capture UNLA and UPDA soldiers who had tried to prevent the local population from donating food to the HSM. The captured soldiers were sprinkled with holy water and, if they refused to join the HSM, chopped into pieces with a panga. In September 1987, a second operation was carried out against those soldiers who had escaped the first one. These actions eventually led to actual fighting between the HSM and the other resistance movements, accelerating the cycle of violence and destruction. In addition, pagan spirit mediums, healers and diviners, known as *ajwaka* in Acholi, were persecuted by the Holy Spirit soldiers. The Lakwena held these *ajwaka*, most of whom were women, responsible for the increase in witchcraft and sorcery in Acholi. This confirmed the view held among Holy Spirit soldiers and Acholi in general that women practised witchcraft much more than men. As a result of their work as 'witchdoctors', many local women had succeeded in gaining substantial incomes and some independence from men. Their persecution can thus be seen as an attempt to bring them back under male control. They were forced to burn their charms and medicines, and then cleansed; their shrines were destroyed, and a few notorious witches were killed. While women as soldiers in the HSM were identified as potential internal enemies, the many female (and some male) *ajwaka* became the victims of male violence in the so-called liberated areas. This witch-hunting was seen by many of the local population as a positive act, however, and increased the HSM's political legitimacy.[15]

The Holy Spirit Movement of Severino Lukoya

After the defeat of Alice's HSMF in October 1987, and her flight to Kenya, many of her soldiers who had survived the last battles tried to retreat to Acholi. Some joined the UPA, a resistance movement operating in Teso, while others became members of the UPDA, which fought mainly in Acholi, or else the HSM of Joseph Kony.

[15] Cf. I. A. Niehaus, 'Witch-hunting and political legitimacy: continuity and change in Green Valley, Lebowa, 1930–91', *Africa*, Vol. 63, No. 4 (1993)

Some soldiers gave up fighting entirely, and went home to work on their farms, and others again changed sides and were recruited to the government forces against which they had been fighting. Finally, still others joined Alice's father, Severino Lukoya, who decided to continue the fight after his daughter's defeat.

Severino had already had a vision, back in 1958. He fell from the top of a roof (or according to another version, his wife beat him up), so that he became unconscious and went straight to heaven, where God told him that one of his children was the chosen child. God also filled him with a lot of spirits. When, in 1985, his daughter Alice was possessed by Lakwena and became very sick, he looked after her; his religious education as a former catechist in the Church of Uganda seems to have had a strong influence on Alice. Shortly before the spirit Lakwena took possession of Alice, however, she converted to Catholicism, thus marking a breach and a separation from her father's teachings. When Alice was already waging war and leading the HSMF, her father came and tried to participate in the movement; but at this point the spirit Lakwena immediately took possession of Alice, and explained that there was no need for Severino to become involved. He therefore took no part in his daughter's HSMF, and remained in Kitgum, in the northern part of Acholi district. Only after Alice's defeat did he succeed in gathering a following of about two thousand men and women.

While Alice had led a strongly centralized army, Severino's movement, which was called the Lord's Army, was much more decentralized. It was organized into the military, medical and religious departments, of which the military department, led by the chief of forces, operated quite independently from the other two. In contrast to Alice, Severino led a guerrilla campaign, fought mainly in Kitgum District.

Like Alice, he established ritual centres among the local population, known as *yards*, for prayer, purification and healing, and trained ritual experts known as *technicians* to work in them. He succeeded in establishing some two hundred *yards*, and people in Kitgum would leave the established churches to come and pray there. It seems that a millenarian and eschatalogical enthusiasm increased among the people of Kitgum at this time. Like Alice, Severino condemned witchcraft, and forced the *ajwakas* to leave their 'satanic' work, even killing a few of them. It seems that he was rather successful. Some people from Kitgum told me that even notorious witches burned their medicine and joined the newly established *yards*.

Severino himself did not fight, but he sent some spirits who did. He also gave his soldiers spiritual support and cleansed them, and gave them magical protection by praying for them. But although he continued the war, the healing and cleansing of people – not only soldiers but also civilians – became more important in his movement than in Alice's. This may have been a consequence of the total breakdown of health care in northern Uganda. During the war, the health centres and hospitals were destroyed, or were closed down by government forces. The spirits were therefore kept busy giving out recipes for medicines, which included various Holy Spirit drugs which could be locally produced to heal all sorts of illnesses, including AIDS.

While Alice monopolized the good, holy, Christian spirits, Severino did not. His movement was much more egalitarian in character, and everybody – not just the leader – could be possessed by a good Christian spirit. Possession by a spirit, however, was interpreted as a sign of being chosen to fight. Thus, although Severino used the power of his spirits to heal afflictions, in general spirit possession in his movement involved the duty to kill. In 1989 Severino was captured by soldiers of Joseph Kony and, although he eventually managed to escape, he was then taken prisoner by government soldiers. He was kept in prison until 1992, and returned in 1995 to Gulu, where he founded an independent Christian church. In interviews given to local newspapers, he defended his daughter Alice, but attacked Kony as nothing but 'a mere witchdoctor whose mission is to kill and bring disunity in the world'.[16]

The Lord's Resistance Army of Joseph Kony

In contrast to the movements of Alice and her father, which only lasted for a short time, the Lord's Resistance Army of Joseph Kony stayed in being from about 1987 until the time of writing in early 1997. During this time, the character of this movement changed substantially, though unfortunately only a fragmentary history can be reconstructed on the basis of currently available information.

Joseph Kony was a young school dropout from Gulu, who claimed to be the cousin of Alice. According to one account, he became a soldier in the UPDA; according to another, he joined Alice's HSMF. He then himself became possessed by the spirit Lakwena – or again, according to another account, by Juma Oris, the spirit of a former minister under Idi Amin, who was still living in Sudan and from 1993 led another movement, the West Nile Bank Front (WNBF). Following the orders of the spirit, he started to build up his own Holy Spirit Movement, which recruited its soldiers mainly from Gulu, while Alice operated in the Kitgum District and then marched towards Kampala. He offered Alice an alliance of their forces against their common enemy, but Lakwena refused, rendering Kony ridiculous. This he never forgot. To take revenge, he started cutting the food supply for Alice's forces, and killed some of her soldiers. The rivalry escalated to such an extent that the two groups started to fight against one another.

When Alice was defeated, some of her soldiers joined Kony's movement. Despite the rivalry between them, he nonetheless adopted the discourse which she had invented, establishing a complex initiation and cleansing ritual. He too issued his own Holy Spirit Safety Precautions and, like Alice, he fought witchcraft and killed the pagan spirit mediums or *ajwakas*. He likewise took over Alice's Holy Spirit Tactics, as a way of combining modern Western military techniques with ritual practices. His movement was organized into three divisions, each of which had three departments called *won*, the Father, *wod*, the Son, and *tipu maleng*, the Holy Spirit. Before a battle took place, the soldiers were ritually armoured with *malaika*, the Swahili word for angel, to protect them against the enemy's bullets. In contrast to Alice, who had led a big army and to some extent transcended ethnic boundaries, Kony was only able to fight a guerrilla war, operating in more or less independent small fighting groups in Acholi and Southern Sudan. Although he centralized power in himself by monopolizing the main spirits, other guerrilla groups were permitted to have their own peripheral spirit mediums.

---

[16] *New Vision*, 2 April 1996

In May 1988, the government signed a peace agreement with some sections of the UPDA, while the remainder of the UPDA joined Kony's movement. The leader of this section, Odong Latek, became quite influential in shaping the movement, and a process of secularization took place. The Holy Spirit Tactics were replaced by guerrilla tactics, and the name of the movement was changed to the Uganda People's Democratic Christian Army (UPDCA). The religious discourse retreated into the background, though it did not disappear completely. When Odong Latek was killed, however, Kony changed the name of his movement once again, to the Lord's Resistance Army (LRA), and the religious discourse appears to have regained prominence.

While neither Alice nor her father got much support from other countries, Kony's war after 1990 gained an international dimension, as the LRA found new allies. Kony cemented relations with the Sudanese government, which provided him with weapons and transport in retaliation for the support which the Ugandan government gave the SPLA. Kony also cooperated with the WNBF, which as already noted was led by Juma Oris, Amin's former minister who appeared as a spirit in the LRA. Idi Amin himself was also said to be closely connected with the WNBF. A further organization, the Uganda Freedom Movement (UFM), was also formed to fight the Ugandan government in the north-west of the country, and along with the WNBF appeared to get French support to assist the Sudanese government in destabilizing Uganda.[17]

Over a period of more than ten years, the war became a mode of production, and created a form of life which 'normalized' and banalized violence and brutality, and blurred the distinction between war and peace. For most of the soldiers, whether they fought on the side of the government or that of its opponents, war became a business which was more profitable than peace. They thus developed an interest in keeping the war going, and extending it to other areas, such as Rwanda[18] or Zaire. Whereas in Alice's HSMF, men and women were not allowed to have sex, in Kony's movement the spirit Silly Silindi removed the interdiction, with the result that Kony's soldiers started to kidnap hundreds of girls and boys, distributing the girls and young women as wives and carriers or porters to the soldiers. A pattern of raiding emerged which strongly recalled the slave-raiding of the nineteenth century.

With the planting of landmines from the early 1990s, the war gained an even more brutal dimension. It was, above all, the local population which was horribly maimed almost daily, and suffered most from the war. Not only did the LRA soldiers kill them and plunder their possessions, but the Ugandan army also repeatedly accused them of collaboration with Kony. As one journalist wrote, 'In the end, whether the Acholi alert the army of rebel presence or not, the Acholi end up being killed or abducted by the rebels.'[19] While, on one hand, Kony's new access to international support enabled him to access the world of the global media – he discovered the Internet, and his publicity agent in Nairobi published the LRA's *Ten Point Program* on-line – on the other hand he increasingly lost the support of the

---

[17] *Billets d'Afrique*, 44 (March 1997).
[18] Cf. Behrend and Meillassoux, 'Krieg in Ruanda: der Diskurs über Ethnizität und die Explosion des Hausses', *Lettre 26* (1994), pp. 12–15.
[19] *New Vision*, 3 March 1996.

local population. His soldiers, forming small desperate groups, lived mainly from stealing, plundering local peasants, kidnapping young girls and boys, and making attacks and laying ambushes here and there. It was only because the government soldiers behaved in an even worse manner that the LRA were tolerated in some parts of Acholi.

The government attempted by various means to destroy the linkages between the LRA and the local population. It built up militias, called the Home Guards and the Local Defence Forces, which included former 'rebels'. Local people informed me that these militias were, in contrast to the regular government forces, the only ones who were really fighting the LRA. The LRA regarded them as traitors, and killed them in the most horrible way. Thus, in contrast to the government soldiers who were much more interested in profiting from the war, these militias had an incentive to fight.

In addition, in some areas of Acholi people were forced to arm themselves for 'self-defence', and 'bow-and-arrow' groups were established. A few of them actually attempted to fight against the LRA, and were not only defeated because of their inferior weapons, but brutally treated. In an act of symbolic violence, about 50 local children, young men and women were kidnapped by LRA soldiers and marked as traitors, their noses, ears, arms and mouths being cut off. These acts of retaliation made some local people turn away from the LRA. As already noted, however, because the government soldiers behaved even worse, the government did not completely succeed in alienating the local people from the LRA. The government also alienated people by establishing so-called 'protected camps' in Acholi, purportedly to protect the people from the 'rebels'. In practice, however, these camps served to prevent people from supporting Kony's soldiers, and to punish them for alleged collaboration with the LRA. The camps lacked infra-structure, adequate food and water, and medical care. Acholi elders protested, describing them as concentration camps in which the population was terrorized. Women and men could no longer till the fields, raising the threat of famine.

As a result of these measures, the government provoked even greater resistance in Acholi. After the May 1996 elections, in which Museveni finally succeeded in legitimizing the position which he had seized by force in 1986, he announced at a press conference that he was no longer prepared to engage in peace negotiations with Kony, but would seek a military solution. He held out no prospect of peace, but instead predicted Kony's death within six months. Several thousand soldiers were remobilized. Resistance against this continuation of the war began to gather support in Acholi, and a group of Acholi elders led by Mzee Okeny Tibero sought to end the war through negotiation. Since the war by then had become a lucrative business for many officers and soldiers in the government army, however, these people warned the elders against supporting the peace process. Two elders who continued to press for political negotiations, Mzee Okot Ogoni and Mzee Olanya Lagoni, were murdered early in 1996. Acholi women formed a pressure group within the Uganda Women's Network (UWONET) to press for peace in the north. They planned humanitarian aid, and the publication and distribution of reports on the horrors that the war had inflicted on its victims.[20]

[20] *New Vision*, 20 November 1996.

Attempts to initiate peace negotiations extended to Acholi living abroad in Europe and North America. A conference held in Toronto in August 1996 passed a resolution urging peace which was sent to Museveni; after this elicited no reply, a second conference, to which LRA representatives were invited, was scheduled for London in April 1997.[21] Heated debates over the composition of the organizing committee and over issues of representation were conducted through the Internet. It appears to be through this technological innovation that Acholi living widely scattered in the diaspora were able for the first time to initiate a collective process of discussion that would bring them together. No end to the war, nonetheless, could be expected in the immediate future.[22]

[21] *New Vision*, 20 November 1996.

[22] For example, negotiations mediated by Iran between Sudan and Museveni achieved no success.

8

GÉRARD PRUNIER
The Rwandan Patriotic Front

The Rwandan Patriotic Front (RPF) is an oddity among guerrilla movements for many different reasons. It was created outside the country where it intended to operate, its members were initially recruited among the armed forces of a foreign power, most of its combatants had never set foot in the land where they were going to fight, and they never managed to get any support from the masses of the population in whose name they were struggling. It nonetheless achieved power, but only after most of its civilian supporters had been annihilated in a perversely popular genocide by another segment of the population it later had to rule over. Thus, if one were to take Mao Tse Tung's rules of guerrilla warfare as a guideline, one would have to question whether the RPF could be called a guerrilla movement at all. The key to understanding the RPF paradox lies, of course, in the very peculiar nature of the Rwandan people and of its history since the end of colonial rule.

The 1959 'Revolution' and the Roots of the Refugee Problem

We cannot go into details here about the different theories of Tutsi and Hutu identities.[1] This would take us beyond the scope of a chapter which should focus on the understanding of the RPF phenomenon. But one has to understand at least how these identities, in their recomposed mythical forms, had become operational factors in the historical development of Rwanda in the 1950s, as the colonial days came to a close. By that time there were two sharply diverging views of Tutsi and Hutu identities.[2] The

[1] For a 'classical' view of Tutsi superiority see J. J. Maquet, *Le système des relations sociales dans le Rwanda ancien* (Tervuren: MRC, 1954); for a pro–Hutu reconstruction see Donat Murego, *La Révolution Rwandaise (1959–1962)* (Louvain: Institut des Sciences Politiques et Sociales, 1975); for more nuanced analysis see J. P. Chrétien, 'Hutu et Tutsi au Rwanda et au Burundi', in J. L. Amselle and E. M'Bokolo, eds, *Au Coeur de l'ethnie* (Paris: La Découverte, 1985), and C. Vidal, *Sociologie des passions* (Paris: Karthala, 1991).

[2] We should always bear it in mind, of course, that these mythical identities were 'ideal types' in the Weberian sense. Very few people really fitted them and there were many who did not believe in them. But they constituted the subliminal basis for political action, the treasure trove of clichés for lazy journalists, the belief system which forced itself on the decisions even of those who did not really agree with it.

Tutsi tended to downplay the weight of pre-colonial social inequalities between the two social categories and to emphasize the various institutions which reinforced social cohesion and cut across the group divide (plurality of chiefly systems, *kubandawa*,[3] *kunywana*,[4] and so on). They insisted on the nefarious role played by Belgian colonial ideology in reinforcing 'racial' stereotypes, and glossed over their own role as agents of the colonial power. Finally, they denied any need for political and social redress, and touted a conservative view of social cohesion and harmony which tended to serve well their class/segmentary interests, since their better-educated group was likely to take the reins of the country at independence if no social change occurred.

On the opposite side, the growing Hutu ideology strongly emphasized the 'racial' heterogeneity of the Tutsi, practically describing them as 'foreigners' who had 'conquered' the 'genuine' (Hutu) Rwandan nation, and exaggerated the degree and manifestations of pre-colonial Tutsi domination. It denied that the old pre-colonial society had had any redeeming cohesive features. The Hutu also insisted on their poor position in Belgian colonial society and demanded a radical change, fearing that a 'smooth' transition of power would mean continued domination by the Tutsi. The clash came partly because of the Cold War polarization of the late 1950s. Better-educated, the Tutsi community had been exposed earlier and more thoroughly than the Hutu to anti-colonial ideas. The small Hutu neo-elite, created in reaction to the long-dominant Tutsi elite, was practically a pure Catholic Church product, and as such extremely hostile to anything vaguely smelling of 'atheistic marxism'. This did not predispose it to open itself to the anti-colonial discourse of the time, which carried strong 'progressive' overtones.[5] Thus Tutsi intellectuals who were highly conservative socially became, in the language then in use, 'pro-communists', while the Hutu neo-elite, which was hoping for radical social change, became 'moderate' (that is, pro-West).

As a result of this paradoxical situation, the Belgian colonial authorities, which traditionally had favoured the Tutsi, began to switch their support to the Hutu around 1956–7. The more they threw their weight behind the emerging neo-elite, the more the now worried Tutsi aristocracy tried to play for the sympathy of the UN, which was a guarantor of the Belgian Mandate.[6] This led to a considerable tension between Belgium and the United Nations, Brussels playing the 'majority' card and New York that of the 'established authority', the Tutsi monarchy.[7] By 1959, these tensions became intertwined with the decolonization conflict then

[3] A spirit possession cult: see Luc de Heusch, 'Mythe et société féodale : le culte *kubandwa* dans le Rwanda traditionnel', *Archives de sociologie des religions*, 18 (1964), pp. 133–46; and C. Taylor, *Milk, Honey and Money: Changing Concepts in Rwandan Healings* (Washington, DC: Smithsonian Institute Press, 1992).

[4] Literally, 'to drink each other', a form of blood brotherhood which cut across the lines of social categorization.

[5] See Ian Linden, *Church and Revolution in Rwanda* (Manchester: Manchester University Press, 1977); and René Lemarchand, *Rwanda and Burundi* (New York: Praeger, 1970). For an understanding of the virtuous Christian climate in which the new Hutu elite was bred, see B. Paternostre de la Mairieu, *Vie de Grégoire Kayibanda, premier président du Rwanda* (Paris: Pierre Téqui, 1994).

[6] Rwanda was a former German colony. It had been given as a Mandate Territory to Belgium after the First World War, and the UN had inherited the Trust after 1945.

[7] For a picture of this conflict between Belgium and the UN see the memoirs of Ruanda-Urundi's last governor, J. P. Harroy, *Rwanda, du féodalisme à la démocratie (1955–1962)* (Brussels: Hayez, 1984).

growing in the neighbouring territory of the Belgian Congo, and a number of local civilian and military administrators took it upon themselves to push things all the way to an open confrontation between the 'good' pro-Western Hutu and the 'bad' Tutsi communistic aristocrats. The immediate result of this confrontation, the 1959 Rwandan 'revolution', is relatively well known, even if its interpretation is highly contested.[8] What is less well known is the aftermath. The Hutu elite took power and proclaimed itself to be 'democratic', even as it proceeded to crush any sign of democratic life in the country, for the simple reason that being Hutu it 'represented' the majority of the population. Since the vanquished Tutsi had not accepted their political elimination and kept attacking Rwanda from outside for several years (the so-called *inyenzi* raids),[9] the perpetual state of emergency caused by the continued military threat was used by the new Hutu administration to confiscate political life and build a single-party system on the typical pattern of first-generation post-colonial African states.

As a result, the Tutsi population was thoroughly marginalized, often threatened and harassed, and at times killed. By 1963, when the *Inyenzi* raids petered out and the new regime began to feel a measure of security, the *rubanda nyamwinshi* (majority people) ideology had enshrined the worst prejudices of the Hutu world view encapsulated above, and the Tutsi remaining in Rwanda had settled into a form of second-class citizenship,[10] except that large numbers had chosen to go into exile instead.[11] Like the Palestinians, these refugees were neither integrated locally nor allowed back home. And like the Palestinians, they remained a recurrent political problem which eventually extended to the whole region.

The Rwandan Refugees in Uganda up to 1982

Uganda was one of the countries where the fleeing Tutsi had sought refuge in the early 1960s. According to the 1964 UNHCR census of Banyarwanda refugees, there were 78,000 Tutsi in Uganda. This was only a fraction of the 200,000 or so who had

---

[8] There are no good objective histories of the 1959 revolution in Rwanda. For an overall view the best work remains René Lemarchand, *op. cit.*, while J. R. Hubert, *La Toussaint Rwandaise et sa répression* (Brussels: ARSOM, 1965) gives the official point of view. Interesting documents can be found in F. Nkundabagenzi, *Le Rwanda politique (1958–1960)* (Brussels: CRISP, 1963). For a first-hand narrative of the events by a militant actor on the Belgian side, see Colonel Logiest, *Mission au Rwanda: un blanc dans la bagarre Tutsi–Hutu* (Brussels: Didier Hatier, 1988). For a diametrically opposed Tutsi view, see P. Tabara, *Afrique, la face cachée* (Paris: La Pensée Universelle, 1992).

[9] *Inyenzi* means cockroach. It was a derogatory term applied to the Tutsi guerrillas coming from the Congo or from Burundi, partly because, like cockroaches, they came out at night.

[10] Their employment in the public sector was limited; they were forbidden to join the Army; Army officers were forbidden to marry Tutsi wives; and Tutsis generally had to respect a 9 per cent quota in any given professional branch. Their non-participation in politics was a tacit understanding. But apart from crisis periods, the ordinary Tutsi peasants were pretty much left alone as long as they did not have to deal with the administration. The better-educated Tutsi often chose the professions, business and the Church because these occupations allowed them to escape government harassment.

[11] Their numbers are hard to compute. They were probably around 400,000, a figure which had probably grown to around 800–900,000 by 1990 if one takes children born in exile into account. The best global study of the problem is André Guichaoua, *Le Problème des réfugiés rwandais et des populations Banyarwanda dans la région des Grands Lacs Africains* (Geneva: UNHCR, 1992).

gone south to Burundi, and at first Burundi was the main base for the *inyenzi* attacks against the new Hutu regime in Rwanda.[12] By contrast, the Uganda-based Tutsi refugee community mostly wanted to be left alone, and did not get involved in politics. Nevertheless they were on bad terms with Milton Obote and his ruling Uganda People's Congress (UPC). The reason was local politics in western Uganda where most of the refugees had settled. Western Uganda is largely populated by the Banyankole people, who are divided between a 'high' group (the Bahima, similar to the Tutsi among the Banyarwanda) and a 'low' group (the Bairu, similar to the Bahutu of Rwanda). The Bahima, in an attempt to retain their traditional aristocratic authority, had played on the Protestant/Catholic divide among the Bairu (who were about evenly split between the two denominations), but nonetheless progressively lost ground throughout the 1960s.[13] A radical UPC/Protestant/Bairu group had taken the leadership of the province of Ankole. But because of cultural proximity, the Tutsi Banyarwanda refugees had been close to the opposing Bahima/Catholic coalition, and thus on the wrong side of the power divide during the late 1960s. As a result, they were among those segments of the population in Uganda who welcomed General Idi Amin's coup in January 1971. But given the extremely volatile character of Amin's regime, their situation did not really improve with his arrival. In September 1972, when tensions developed between Amin and Kigali, the Rwandan refugees in Uganda were persecuted.[14] Later, after General Juvenal Habyarimana took power in Rwanda, Amin completely changed tack and recruited a number of exiles into the State Research Bureau, the main secret service of the dictatorship. Although these recruits were few, they became notorious for their violence and earned the enmity of many Ugandans, who generalized it towards their whole community. As a result, when Amin was overthrown by the Tanzanian Army in April 1979, the Rwandan refugees were roughed up again, in spite of the fact that several of their number had taken part in the anti-Amin struggle.[15] During the last part of 1979, they viewed the growing influence of the pro-Obote camp within the Uganda National Liberation Front (UNLF)[16] with apprehension, since they remembered Obote's hostility to them during his first mandate. Their fears were increased when, upon his return from exile in May 1980, Obote chose to hold his first large political meeting in Bushenyi, in Ankole, rather than in Kampala. This meant that in Obote's mind Bushenyi and its Bairu-UPC networks were a key element in his strategy for the reconquest of power. This was quite an ominous development for the

[12] This was a logical choice. At the time Burundi had a solidly Tutsi-dominated government while Uganda was ruled by ethnic aliens, a mixture of Baganda and members of the northern Nilotic tribes, who had no special sympathy for the Tutsi.

[13] For a good description of these western Uganda political struggles, see Martin Doornbos, *Not All the King's Men: Inequality as Political Instrument in Ankole* (The Hague: Mouton, 1978), pp. 117–31 and 146–57.

[14] The cause was the attempted return by force of former President Milton Obote, who had attacked Uganda from Tanzania with a small exile army. The attempt failed but Amin seemed to believe that the Kigali authorities were in some way accomplices in the attack. In a completely illogical move, he made the Tutsi refugees living on Ugandan soil responsible for this alleged complicity.

[15] Among those were Fred Rwigyema and Paul Kagame, who later became RPF leaders.

[16] The UNLF was an umbrella organization made up of many small Ugandan exile organizations who had got together to fight Idi Amin. It was sponsored by the Tanzanian government. But within that rather confused conglomerate, President Nyerere systematically favoured his friend Milton Obote, eventually helping him back into power in December 1980.

Rwandan refugees, since those UPC circles were their direct enemies in Ankole, where they clashed over land control, grazing rights and commercial ventures. The pressure built up steadily after Obote returned to power through dubious 'elections' in December 1980. Many of the men he then promoted to the core of his new security apparatus, such as Cris Rwakasisi and Edward Rurangaranga, were Banyankole Bairu who had been active in the local UPC western networks. Given the growing insecurity brought by the civil war which had started in February 1981, the political weight of these secret apparatus men grew steadily, and they began to claim an increasing share of the politico-economic pie. Locally in the west, this brought them into a direct collision course with the Rwandan refugees. The members of the so-called Bushenyi Mafia were at the heart of the propaganda campaign aiming at portraying National Resistance Army (NRA) leader Yoweri Museveni as a Rwandan refugee.[17] This clever propaganda ploy enabled the men of the Bushenyi Mafia to kill two birds with one stone: it partly delegitimized Museveni, who could be denounced as a 'foreigner' intruding into Ugandan politics, and it prepared the ground for the persecution of the Rwandan refugees in western Uganda, who could be pilloried as 'accomplices' of Museveni in a 'foreign-engineered plot' aiming at destabilizing Uganda and victimizing good, genuine, native-born Ugandans. The final crunch took place in October 1982.

The Refugees, the NRA and the Rwandan Diaspora

The October 1982 persecution of the Rwandan refugees in western Uganda was a massive affair, much worse than the previous difficulties they had known in the late 1960s and in 1979. UPC youth-wingers, reinforced by a unit of Colonel William Omaria's Special Forces, swept through the area where the refugees had been settled for the last 20 years, beating up people, at times killing them, raping, stealing and looting cattle. In their wake, 35,000 head of cattle were herded away (this being one of the main purposes of the operation), and over 80,000 people started to move, some to the relative safety of the old refugee camp settlements, some pushing towards the border. A few managed to slip inside Rwanda to escape the thugs chasing them, but the rest were soon stopped by the Rwandan Border Guards. As a result, about 10,000 people were caught in a narrow strip of land barely two kilometres wide between the two countries, where they soon started to die from malnutrition and infectious diseases.[18] The Rwandan government reluctantly and inefficiently helped some of the refugees who had managed to get inside the country and who had been forcibly settled in camps, while the international community, equally reluctantly and inefficiently, helped those who were stuck at the border. But nobody gave any help to those – the majority – who had remained inside Uganda.

---

[17] Museveni is a Munyankole belonging to a 'small' Hima family. One of his grandmothers seems to have been a Munyarwanda Tutsi, but it would be anachronistic to call her a 'Rwandan' since this predates the birth of modern Rwanda and she is unlikely to have been a subject of the old pre-European kingdom.

[18] The only study of these events, apart from press clippings of the time, can be found in Catherine Watson, *Exile from Rwanda: Background to an Invasion* (Washington, DC: US Committee for Refugees, 1991).

For the young Tutsi men who were especially targeted by UPC thugs, running away to the bush and joining Museveni's growing NRA guerrilla movement began to look like an attractive alternative to remaining the powerless civilian victims of violence. In fact, those who went soon discovered that their chances of survival were better as guerrilla fighters than as ordinary people. Several managed to move their families into areas where they could receive military protection from the NRA. The 'Rwandan' Museveni was finally getting the Rwandans with him. But if the majority of those joining the NRA in the bush were doing so for practical survival reasons, this was not the case with every new recruit .

The Rwandan diaspora was far from shapeless. In their 20 years of exile, the Tutsi had spread all over the world. Of course 90 per cent of them lived in Africa, mostly in Burundi, Uganda, Zaire and Tanzania. But some had migrated further afield, many to Belgium, the former colonial centre, but also to France, the USA or Canada. These exiles organized themselves, mostly for purposes of social and economic mutual support, for the pleasure of talking about their former country, and to keep informed about the small world of the emigration. They structured themselves around a number of local associations and irregularly published bulletins and magazines.[19] If the majority of the exiles still lived lives of general poverty, many managed to pull themselves up to a reasonable level of economic prosperity in their countries of asylum, and a few, looked upon as the beacons of their community, even became rich. Through travel, marriages and studies the various strands of the emigration kept loose connections alive. The social and cultural nuances changed. The monarchist/aristocratic ethos which had been typical of the old *inyenzi* circles broadened into more open views. Some of the educated members of the younger generation even flirted with the left-wing ideas which were common in the late 1960s and throughout the 1970s.

Given the agitated circumstances of the exiles' community life in Uganda, it had to keep on its toes politically. In June 1979, in an attempt to help the victims of the anti-Rwandan persecutions following the fall of Idi Amin, the Tutsi community in Uganda had created the Rwandan Refugees Welfare Association (RRWF). The RRWF was soon turned into the Rwandan Alliance for National Unity (RANU), which published a bulletin called *The Alliancer*. The change in names was not fortuitous. While the RRWF had stressed mutual help for refugees at a practical level, RANU was already, by its very name which stressed a key element of Tutsi ideology ('unity', as opposed to the 'divisive politics' of the Hutu movement), an organization which was looking beyond the simple welfare of the Rwandan refugees in Uganda. For a number of the young exiles, Uganda and its stormy political climate might provide what the political tempests of post-independence Congo had failed to give their elders: weapons, military training and a rear base from which to attack Rwanda and its hated regime.[20] Among the main contenders for power in Uganda

[19] Such as *Impuruza* (The Mobilizer) in Sacramento, California; *Muhabura* (The Beacon) and *Huguka* (Be Ready) in Bujumbura, *Congo-Nil* in Kinshasa or *Ukoloni Mambo Leo* (Emigration News) in Dar-es-Salaam.

[20] In a book of memoirs about fighting with Che Guevara in eastern Zaire (then Congo), Pablo Ignacio Taiban *et al., L'Année où nous n'étions nulle part* (Paris: Métalié, 1997), the Cuban authors write about the role of the Tutsi exiles in the anti-Mobutu war. They obviously had no real interest in the fate of Zaire or in the revolutionary politics of their Cuban allies. They were there to try to get the means of forcing their way back home.

during 1979–80, Museveni was the only one who had some of the necessary qualifications for being their champion.[21] One might doubt that such an extrovert and happy-go-lucky personality as Fred Rwigyema had calculated that far when he followed Museveni into Tanzania after Amin's coup, but the introverted and secretive Paul Kagame almost certainly was thinking in the long term. Kagame had joined the Front for National Salvation (Fronasa), Museveni's tiny exile organization created in Tanzania in 1978, which had lined up a few militants to fight alongside the advancing Tanzanian Army the following year. Kagame had remained faithful to his former leader when he became Minister of Defence in the interim government, and later an unsuccessful candidate in the December 1980 national election. On 6 February 1981, when Museveni with 34 adventurous companions attacked the Police Military School at Kabamba to snatch a few guns, Kagame and Rwigyema were the only two Rwandans in the small band of rebels, and for a long time they had very few fellow-countrymen at their side. RANU had migrated to Nairobi as soon as the war had begun,[22] knowing that the new regime would be hostile to the Rwandans. What really triggered the massive arrival of the Rwandan refugees' sons in Museveni's guerrilla army was the October 1982 operation.[23] But although spontaneous and caused by reasons quite outside the control of the militant RANU nucleus, which was supporting Museveni, their arrival changed things radically for those who had longer-term views about Rwanda. Although the Rwandan exiles always remained a minority in the NRA, they played a key role in the fighting, especially in early 1984 when pressure from government troops forced the guerrillas to leave their Luwero stronghold and move westwards.[24] In January 1986, when the Museveni rebels stormed Kampala and took power, there were at least 3–4,000 Tutsi fighters, sons of the exiles who had left Rwanda 25 years earlier, in their ranks. The majority Baganda population of the Capital Area was duly thankful but not overly welcoming. Soon after 'the victory', RANU packed up in Nairobi and moved back to Uganda. In December 1987, it held its seventh congress in Kampala and decided to change its name to the much more militant appellation of Rwandan Patriotic Front.[25] A new period had begun.

---

[21] Obote, who was hostile to them, was out of the question; the so-called 'Gang of Four' was not solid enough, and the various strands of Baganda conservatism (Democratic Party, monarchist remnants) were too exclusively ethnic to encourage serious thought of collaboration.

[22] The organization's congresses for the next few years were all held in Kenya.

[23] Although the worst took place in October 1982 there were still sporadic persecutions of the Rwandan refugees in western Uganda until mid-1984.

[24] Contrary to the myths propagated by many journalists after 1994, the Rwandans never 'put Museveni in power in Uganda'. They represented between 20 and 30 per cent of NRA strength, the majority being Baganda and then Banyankole and other western groups such as the Bakiga and the Banyoro. See Ngoga's account in Chapter 6 of this volume.

[25] The name is interesting from two points of view: first, it showed that now the hard-core militants felt that the time was ripe for an activist organization, half political party and half paramilitary group; second, the use of an English name (the French *Front Patriotique Rwandais* began to be used only several months later and only in very limited ways, since practically nobody in the RPF knew any French) shows how far the militants in Uganda were from the reality of contemporary Rwanda. See Wm Cyrus Reed, 'Exile, reform, and the rise of the Rwandan Patriotic Front', *The Journal of Modern African Studies*, Vol. 34, No. 3 (1996), pp. 479–501.

The Rwandan Exiles and Political Power in Uganda

For some Tutsi hotheads, as soon as Kampala was taken the time had come to rush back to Rwanda and overthrow the Habyarimana regime. Some of the young NRA officers, mostly uneducated, who held such ideas had organized a quick conspiracy in the spring of 1986. They wanted to use certain NRA units where the Rwandans were a majority to go and attack Rwanda. The plot was poorly organized, and they were all rounded up by Ugandan Military Security and disciplined. But the Alice Lakwena insurrection in northern Uganda was by then requiring immediate military attention, and most of the hapless conspirators were quickly moved northwards rather than southwards as they had hoped.[26]

For the hard-core RANU militants, this was a boon rather than a setback. The last thing they needed were hotheads who would jump the gun and spoil everything, before the situation was really ripe and the necessary preparations had been made. The Museveni victory had given a strong psychological boost to the exile community and many were only too ready for action.[27] Socially and economically too, Rwandan Tutsi from all over the diaspora were now saying that 'Uganda is ours'. In their eyes, this actually had little or nothing to do with an eventual return to Rwanda. On the contrary, some were saying that 'Kayibanda (the first Hutu President of Rwanda) took our country, but Museveni gave us another one.' Many started to come to Uganda from all over the world; inevitably, their arrival created tensions. As time went on and the business and administrative presence of the Rwandans around Museveni became heavier and heavier, the various Ugandan tribes who had fought in the NRA during the anti-Obote struggle – and among them especially the strong and economically active Baganda – became increasingly concerned about the President's toleration of these 'foreigners' in important and lucrative positions. On the opposite side, the northern and eastern rebels who had been fighting the new regime since 1986 refused to negotiate with Museveni as long as he did not 'remove those foreigners from the Ugandan Armed Forces'.[28] Thus the Rwandans in the NRA were both an asset and a problem for Museveni. They were a definite asset from the military point of view. Many of the top military commanders with the best combat experience were Rwandan. Also, given their ethnic alienness, they could not but be absolutely loyal to Museveni. With the Rwandan soldiers, there could be no problem of betrayal or fear of a coup. But from the political point of view they were a liability: they irritated everybody in Uganda, friends and foes alike; they were brash and boastful about their new good fortune;

---

[26] On the Alice Lakwena revolt, see Gérard Prunier, 'Le mouvement d'Alice Lakwena: un prophétisme politique en Ouganda', in J. P. Chrétien and G. Prunier, eds, *L'Invention religieuse en Afrique: histoire et religion en Afrique Noire* (Paris: Karthala, 1993); Heike Behrend, *Alice und die Geister: Krieg im norden Ugandas* (Munich: Trickster, 1993); and Behrend, Chapter 7 in this volume.

[27] It was at that time that this author began to meet RPF militants and sympathizers, both in Kampala and in Nairobi. Many were so outspoken about their 'secret' plans, especially after they had had a few drinks, that it was hard to take them seriously. But in a way their boasting acted as a kind of cover for the much more serious work the hard-core leadership was doing within the new Ugandan power structure, especially at the military level.

[28] This was, for example, the position of Otema Allimadi, Obote's former Prime Minister, who eventually made peace with the new regime and came back to Uganda after the Rwandans had left.

they were capable, rapacious and often quite experienced – and thus, in a word, dangerous. So after all, if they were absolutely set on going back to Rwanda, maybe this could be a solution.

In the early days after the Museveni victory, things were still undecided. The small RPF nucleus was dead set on 'returning' to a Rwanda they had never seen, but they were a minority. For many of the exiles, although they were not opposed to the idea in principle, the task appeared too dangerous and difficult, and Uganda provided a welcoming middle ground between total exile and one's own home in Africa. What progressively swung the mood of the Tutsi community in Uganda towards supporting a return war was the growing sense of alienation between its members and the local population. Of course, since they had amply contributed to the 'anti-Obote struggle', it was out of the question to treat them in the way they had been treated in the past. But by 1988 the Ugandan resentment was palpable and it began to be turned into action. This was felt by the Rwandan exiles to be very ungrateful, and this ingratitude was even perceived as coming from Museveni himself. After the war he had promised to give Ugandan citizenship to any refugees who applied, but he was now procrastinating and finding excuses not to keep his word. In November 1989 Fred Rwigyema, Museveni's long time friend and associate, the Fronasa and Kabamba veteran, the chief architect of the war in the north between 1986 and 1988, by then a Major-General and Army Chief of Staff, was suddenly removed from his position by President Museveni. All precautions were taken to make the removal as painless as possible, but for many Rwandans in Uganda this was a turning point. If Rwigyema, after his great services to the country, and in spite of his personal friendship with the President, could not simply be a Ugandan like any other, then the path of integration was in fact a dream. For many of the Tutsi exiles, including Rwigyema who had always considered himself to be a Ugandan, things had to be reconsidered. The result of these changes occurring at the top was that many people lower down decided to turn to the RPF and its radical project of reconquest.

This was taking place at a time when the refugee question had become more and more of a problem both for Rwanda and for Rwandan–Ugandan relations. A special Rwandan–Ugandan Joint Committee on the Refugee Question had been created in February 1988 to discuss the question, in collaboration with UNHCR. The Kigali Secret Service had infiltrated the RPF and knew that it was busy organizing for an invasion of Rwanda. But, misreading the clues, the Habyarimana regime had taken Rwigyema's firing from his Chief of Staff position to be a goodwill gesture on the part of Museveni, indicating that he would somehow prevent the exiles from going all the way to an actual military attack. Not only was this a misreading of Museveni's feelings about the subject,[29] it was also a failure to realize what a boost to the RPF Rwigyema's sudden availability represented. Up to then the legendary 'Commander Fred' had remained sympathetic to the Front but

---

[29] They were easy to misread since they were somewhat contradictory. Museveni had declared several times in public that he 'refused to be the Rwandan refugees' jail keeper', which implied that they had his authorization to attack Rwanda. On the other hand he was much more careful in his dealings with Kigali through the Refugees' Joint Committe and UNHCR. But Museveni is both a cold calculator and a hot-blooded man of impulse: his dislike of Habyarimana, both personal and political, was visceral and this detestation influenced his actions.

aloof. His shabby treatment at the hands of the President after years of faithful service embittered him, and he decided to throw in his lot with the RPF. Given his charisma, his military experience and his connections, he was an invaluable recruit for the plotters.

The dynamics of their movement were by then gathering momentum. Many Tutsi businessmen in exile began to give money. Endorsements came from the old *inyenzi* monarchist circles and new militants from the exiled left-wing intellectuals in Europe and North America. For the previous two years, the plotters had worked steadily at infiltrating the key points of the military system they belonged to: Commander Musitu, a Rwandan exile, had managed to be appointed Head of Training – a position from which he could dispatch his friends to various strategic postings. Paul Kagame was Acting Head of Military Security, the brand new Army Computer Service was practically a pure Rwandan preserve, Commander Sam Kanyemera had been made Head of the Military Police, Dr Peter Banyingana ran the Army Health Services, and, finally, in spite of his being fired from his COS position, 'Commander Fred' Rwigyema still did exactly what he wanted, where he wanted and when he wanted, within the NRA.

The RPF and the Political Situation in Rwanda in 1990

Paradoxically, while everything went as well as possible for the arrangements within Uganda, the weakest point of the RPF plot was its contact with Rwanda itself. The situation inside Rwanda was by then changing rapidly, and the exiles did not always understand those changes very well. Rwanda in 1990 was in a state of crisis.[30] In April of that year, President Habyarimana had gone to France and attended the Franco-African summit at La Baule, where François Mitterrand gave his famous 'democratization' speech. The fact that this speech went way beyond his views on the question later caused many problems,[31] notably in Togo, where French policy on the ground virtually contradicted the 'theoretical' La Baule position. In the short run, however, several of the francophone African presidents decided, with varying degrees of sincerity, to play the democratic game. President Habyarimana was among those who chose to open up his country's political life relatively wide, at least formally.[32] His main problem was of course not the Tutsi, who had been politically disenfranchised for thirty years and who, with few exceptions, were extremely wary of meddling in politics, but rather the southern

[30] For a view of the way the Habyarimana regime had been slipping into progressively greater difficulties since 1988, see Filip Reyntjens, *L'Afrique des Grands Lacs en crise: Rwanda et Burundi (1988–1994)* (Paris: Karthala, 1994); and Gérard Prunier, *The Rwanda Crisis: History of a Genocide* (London: Hurst, 1995), pp. 84–90.

[31] It had been written by the novelist Erik Orsenna, then a presidential aide. Although only luke-warm about its content, Mitterrand had gone along with the theme of linking development aid to political democratization (personal communication to the author, May 1990).

[32] Whether Habyarimana really intended to fully democratize the Rwandan political system is highly doubtful. From his behaviour between November 1990 and his death in April 1994, he seems to have attempted to build a democratic facade while retaining strong central control. But he was among those francophone African heads of state who seemed to believe that their control over the political life of their country was strong enough to allow them a wide margin of apparent democracy.

Hutu who had supported Grégoire Kayibanda's First Republic and who had been progressively marginalized through the Habyarimana years. Opposition could even extend to some of the President's own northern brothers who of late had also been somewhat ill-treated.[33]

Returning from France, President Habyarimana soon proclaimed his newly acquired faith in democracy and a multi-party system in July 1990. But his pronouncement rang hollow, and he did not seem eager to act upon it, which led to the Manifesto of the Thirty-Three Intellectuals in August, demanding immediate measures of democratization. President Habyarimana answered them in a speech in November 1990, in which he tried to please everybody: he promised multi-party politics to the discontented Hutu, praised the Structural Adjustment Programme to please the foreigners, and swore that the mention of ethnicity would be removed from identity cards, something which the Tutsi had long hoped for.[34] But people were still extremely careful, and the first oppositon party – the Mouvement Démocratique Républicain or MDR – appeared only in April 1991. Several other parties were then created (Parti Social-Démocrate, Parti Libéral), with a variety of political styles and regional and/or ethnic clienteles.[35] The RPF either did not really understand what was happening or, if it did understand, did not want to take it seriously. There were good and bad reasons for this. Understandably, for example, the RPF might conclude that the opposition (especially the MDR, the largest of the new parties) was often far from liberal on the ethnic question. Their fight was against Habyarimana and the political monopoly of his *Abashiru* friends, not against the *Rubanda Nyamwinshi* ideology of Hutu predominance or in favour of full civic rights for the Tutsi minority. The opposition conceived of democracy as a Hutu preserve, just like the rest of politics.

More questionably, the RPF did not like these developments because they threatened one of their best-selling arguments for their own clientele, and to a degree for their foreign friends: the claim that they would be fighting against an oppressive dictatorship. The Habyarimana regime had never been very liberal, but as African regimes went in the 1970s it was not really among the worst ones. Its democratization, even if partial and imperfect, might earn it a place on the new 'good guys' lists which the international organizations were in the process of drawing up, as outright shooting dictatorships of the Idi Amin variety lost their international acceptability in the new post-Cold War climate. More directly, the Rwandan–Ugandan Joint Committee on the Refugee Question had decided in July 1990 that the Kigali government would discuss the issue directly with representatives of the refugee community, in order to prepare lists of people for repatriation. If this went through in the new climate of democratization, at least partial repatriation could take place without fighting and without any change in the political status quo. This is probably what President Habyarimana had in mind: controlled repatriation to pacify and divide the Tutsi refugee community; and

---

[33] As the economic vice tightened during the late 1980s, the ever-smaller fragmentation of regionalist politics had ended up dividing even the northerners, who were now struggling among themselves.

[34] The measure was of course never implemented and the mention of ethnicity on ID papers was to cost many thousands of lives during the 1994 genocide.

[35] For this, see G. Prunier, *The Rwanda Crisis*, pp. 121–6.

controlled democratization to open up the Hutu power system, but without substantially changing it. Habyarimana's failure to achieve the first of these two aims led to his failure to achieve the second, and to the eventual explosion of a whole society.

The RPF as a Fighting Organization

When it invaded Rwanda on 1 October 1990, the RPF had about 2,000 men. Most of them were NRA soldiers, although there was a small civilian contingent. They deserted their posts in Uganda and attacked Rwanda, taking advantage of a time when President Museveni was out of the country.[36] Their operational leader was Major-General Fred Rwigyema, the former Chief of Staff of the Ugandan Army.[37] Although their military equipment was quite sufficient (it had been taken from the NRA), their first days in operation were disastrous. They had hoped for a quick dash to Kigali, persuaded that the Habyarimana regime was so undermined by its internal contradictions that the slightest push from outside would make it fall, and that they would be welcomed as liberators.[38] Their whole thinking rested on a parallel with the Ugandan situation with which they were familiar, and in which the equations RPF = NRA and Habyarimana = Obote summed up their vision and seemed to promise them victory.[39] But the regime did not collapse and the population, well primed by the government propaganda machine, was afraid rather than sympathetic to the attackers. In addition, Major-General Rwigyema was killed in battle on the second day of the fighting. As a result the first days of combat proved extremely hard. Rather than using guerrilla tactics, the RPF forces were fighting a conventional war, a questionable strategy because, although the small (5,200 men) Forces Armées Rwandaises (FAR) did not have any combat experience, they were reasonably well trained and equipped, and knew the terrain better than their nearly 'foreign' adversary. Within a month the RPF was in total disarray, and its interim commanders, Peter Banyingana and Chris Bunyenyezi, had both been killed. This

---

[36] He was in New York for a UN conference, and so was President Habyarimana. Since Museveni was very probably aware that the Tutsi were about to strike, it is likely that there had been an agreement between him and the RPF leadership so that both sides could disclaim prior understanding with some credibility.

[37] Because of his popularity, he was still obeyed when he gave orders to army units. He had been moving his fellow Banyarwanda in and out of NRA units to assemble his force, and pretended that these movements had to do with the military parade due to take place for the Independence Day celebrations (9 October).

[38] This misjudgement had been reinforced by the interested reports of a number of minor politicians and businessmen from inside the country (Valens Kajeguhakwa, Jean Barahinyura, Pasteur Bizimungu, Silas Majyembere) who had fallen out with Habyarimana and who were looking for a new political deal from which they could benefit. Some left the RPF when they realized they could not steer it the way they wanted, but some others learned to ride the tiger. The Hutu Bizimungu ended up as President of the Republic, albeit with limited power, and the Tutsi Kajeguhakwa became one of the big businessmen of the new regime.

[39] Soon after, a third equation (Kagame=Museveni) was added to that simplified analysis.

[40] He was there as a Ugandan officer on a military training course. He left without completing it in order to come to Rwanda and take over the command of the RPF. His presence in the US at that time, although brief and inconsequential, led to the myth of 'Kagame, America's man in the Great Lakes'.

led to the recall of Major Paul Kagame from the United States in November 1990.[40] He immediately decided to change tactics and avoided direct battle with the FAR. He also tried to regroup his men, who had fled in various directions, and to take them into an area where the regular army was unlikely to follow. The only choice was to climb up into the Virunga, the high volcanic mountain range in north-west Rwanda, which was virtually empty of population. In spite of the hardships (poorly clothed for the high altitude, cold and underfed, several fighters froze to death), the Front survived the next few months and bided its time. In January 1991, its sudden attack on the northern *Préfecture* of Ruhengeri caused a national upheaval. The RPF quickly withdrew after this victory, and started operating in the Byumba area in true hit-and-run guerrilla style. The fighting was on a limited scale, but the Front fighters managed to cut the road to Uganda, forcing all the imports and exports of land-locked Rwanda to use a longer route through Tanzania. Slowly, the RPF 'liberated' a certain area in the north of the country, especially after the beginning of 1992 when it started to score tactical points against the FAR, inspite of the support they were receiving from France.[41] This 'liberation' was ambiguous, in that everybody ran away from the Front fighters, even the Tutsi. Government propaganda des-cribing the 'invaders' as quasi-monsters was obsessive and efficient, and people fled from the advancing RPF, usually in well-ordered groups which were already in the style of the quasi-military mass exodus of July/August 1994. The result of this movement was that massive displaced persons' camps had to be opened directly north of Kigali,[42] while the RPF ruled over an eerily empty landscape.

There were two interesting aspects of RPF functioning during these years: resupply and recruitment. Both had strong political implications. The original nucleus of the RPF had carried with it enough ammunition and equipment to last for a few days, possibly weeks, of fighting. But when the conflict turned into a protracted war, the Front had to establish channels of supply. Some equipment could be bought on the international market with the money collected (very efficiently) worldwide among the Tutsi diaspora. But the Front finances were limited and Paul Kagame and his men regularly had to beg from the Ugandans. Thoughout the war Museveni tried to maintain at least a pretence of neutrality. So his army commanders would slip ammunition to the hard-pressed RPF but ask them not to cross the border. Front fighters who went back into Uganda for unauthorized rest and recovery were severely punished and in some cases shot if they deserted. Since France had pushed for a Commission of Enquiry which was patrolling the border, the risk would have been too great for Kampala if RPF soldiers had been caught on its territory. Disci-pline was also very much a concern, and the RPF was run as an extremely tight ship where soldiers stood at attention, saluted their officers, and strictly obeyed orders.

As for the ammunition, there were many small paths where it could be carried

---

[41] France had sent a force to Rwanda in support of the Habyarimana government as early as October 1990. French troops were not involved in direct ground fighting, although they took part in the war in a variety of technical positions such as flying and maintaining helicopters, directing artillery fire, or helping communications. They also ran a rather ineffectual section of military intelligence.

[42] By the end of the war there were over 300,000 people in these camps.

[43] Many of the RPF field officers were ex-NRA men and they had retained personal contacts with their former colleagues. Ugandan aid tended to happen more through this decentralized network, which allowed President Museveni and his government to claim ignorance of the whole process.

through the heavily forested and hilly terrain, far from prying eyes.[43] Recruitment could not of course operate in the 'classical' guerilla fashion, by attracting young men from the local population, since everybody had fled and the countryside was absolutely empty. But many young people came and joined all the same, from a variety of foreign countries. From all over the Rwandan diaspora, young Tutsi exiles came to fight in the country they had never seen. The recruitment came (in roughly that order of importance) from Burundi, Uganda, Zaire, Tanzania and the rest of the world. The RPF was trying to keep pace with the FAR, which were growing at an exponential rate: from about 5,000 men in October 1990 to 15,000 by mid-1991, and twice that number by the end of the same year. By 1994 the FAR would be 50,000 men strong. The RPF could never keep pace, of course. But it also grew quite fast, reaching 5,000 men by early 1991 and about 12,000 by late 1992. Then came a big change: around that time the Front started to recruit heavily from the Tutsi population *inside* Rwanda, something which caused strong fears in government circles.

Since this chapter provides a short evaluation of the origins and development of the RPF, rather than a global study of the Rwandan crisis, which I have published elsewhere,[44] it will not go into details about the political situation which developed in Rwanda after the RPF attack, and which eventually led to the genocide. But there were constant interactions between the military developments and the political ones; one of these, not obvious at first, was the change brought about by the 'native Tutsi' recruitment to the Front. For the Habyarimana regime, and especially for the extremist elements in its ranks, this meant that the Front was now a *direct* agent in internal Rwandan politics, and that the whole Tutsi population inside the country could be viewed as potential 'fifth columnists'. It was around this time, in March 1992, that the notorious Coalition pour la Défense de la République (CDR) extremist party was born.

This does not mean that there had been no violations of human rights and killings of civilians before that time. In fact, violence against the civilian population had started right at the beginning of the war, with the massive wave of arrests in October 1990. But the internal recruitment of the RPF changed the extremists' views of the conflict. Killing civilians was promoted from the status of scare and intimidation tactics to the role of a major strategic concept. It was from that time on that the idea of the genocide ('in the air' ever since the 1959 killings), progressively began to be considered as a 'rational' political project. Guerrilla war by then was leading to something entirely different, implacably ethnicized politics following the failure of progressive internal democratization.

How can we assess the place of the RPF among other African guerrilla movements? Obviously it is an oddity, because of its peculiar origins and recruitment, and because of the bizarre political framework in which it operated. On the ground, it was closer to a (good) classical jungle army than to a guerrilla force, and it fought a mostly conventional war. It never had to face all the problems of relations with the local population which are the daily fare of practically all guerrilla movements. It always operated in a vacuum, both physically and intellectually. It took the political

[44] See Prunier, *The Rwanda Crisis*.

notions directly inherited from its Ugandan experience to Rwanda, and never had any occasion to question them through experience, since it never had any interaction with the population.

Thus its position was extremely paradoxical. During the long negotiations at Arusha about the creation of a broad-based democratic government as a condition for bringing the hostilities to an end, the diplomatic attitude of the RPF was almost that of a government, of an organized power dealing directly with the Rwandan government as another organized power. The Front kept appearing not as an insurgent group from *within* (which it was not) but as a 'foreign' army trying to *get in*. Everything from its army-like discipline to its ignorance of daily life in Rwanda gave it the odd flavour of an alien body. This was of course understandable, since its members had all been born or at least raised outside Rwanda, and since the most significant and formative experience in the lives of many of them had been their years in the Ugandan NRA. But it did not augur well for their capacity to participate in the government of a mostly hostile, mostly Hutu country after negotiating a power-sharing agreement. The subsequent genocide of the Tutsi population in Rwanda, and the ensuing RPF military victory which gave them undisputed dominance over the government,[45] did not make it any easier. Pain, anger and a hard-to-control desire for revenge were the common feelings of the Front's soldiers, while the reaction of their mostly Hutu 'fellow citizens' was to look upon them as an army of occupation. Time will tell whether political moderation will prevail and transform the minority rule which is now the *de facto* reality of Rwanda into a more open system. But the post genocide alienation of the Tutsi, and the sullen and largely unrepentant feelings of the majority of the Hutu,[46] do not augur well for the future.

[45] In spite of formal power sharing with other parties in the present cabinet, the RPF has been in a hegemonic position since the August 1995 elimination of the few moderate Hutu ministers who were men of independent political weight.

[46] Whether killed in the genocide by Hutu Power supporters, or later politically marginalized by the RPF, the moderate Hutu have been the great losers of the civil war.

9

WM CYRUS REED
Guerrillas in the Midst

The Former Government of Rwanda (FGOR)
& the Alliance of Democratic Forces
for the Liberation of Congo-Zaire (ADFL)
in Eastern Zaire[1]

In April 1994 the then President of Rwanda, Juvenal Habyarimana, was killed in a plane crash in Kigali. Within hours, a carefully framed policy of genocide was implemented which first sought to eliminate the leaders of all the newly formed internal opposition parties, the majority of whom came from the dominant Hutu community, as well as the supporters of the Rwandan Patriotic Front (RPF). Because the RPF was perceived as being supported by the entire Tutsi community, the genocide sought to eliminate as many Tutsi as possible.[2] With frightening efficiency and primitive technology, nearly one million people were killed in just over eight weeks.[3] As the killing intensified, the RPF mobilized its forces, advanced on Kigali, and the government of Rwanda fled to Zaire. Largely intact, the now Former Government of Rwanda (FGOR)[4] quickly re-established administrative control over the 800,000 or more Rwandans who had become refugees in Zaire.[5] For two years, the FGOR ruled over significant parts of eastern Zaire and pursued an active insurgency inside Rwanda. In spite of repeated calls by nearly all members of the international community to dislodge them, no concrete policies were undertaken to accomplish this until October 1996, when a hitherto unknown movement called the Alliance of Democratic Forces for the Liberation of Congo-Zaire (ADFL) mobilized and attacked the camps in which the FGOR was located.

[1] This study is based on fieldwork conducted in Rwanda and Uganda in 1994, 1995 and 1996, and was supported by a Research Grant from the Office of the Provost, the American University in Cairo.

[2] Gérard Prunier, *The Rwanda Crisis: History of a Genocide* (London and Kampala: Hurst and Fountain, 1995).

[3] African Rights, *Rwanda: Death, Despair, and Defiance* (London: 1995).

[4] This group has also been referred to as the former Armed Forces of Rwanda (EXFAR) and the Interahamwe, the militia which spearheaded the 1994 genocide in Rwanda. Because both the EXFAR and the Interahamwe are distinct (though overlapping), and both are agents of the former government, this study will use the term FGOR to refer to the overlapping political and military structures which fled Rwanda in 1994 and controlled the refugee camps in eastern Zaire until 1996.

[5] Estimates of the number of refugees in eastern Zaire range from 800,000 to 1.2 million. More than half a million Rwandans also fled to Tanzania. Because Tanzania maintained some authority over the refugee camps, the FGOR was less active there than in Zaire, where the government had neither the ability nor the desire to assert its authority over the refugees. This chapter will limit its analysis to events in eastern Zaire.

Almost as fast as they had established their authority in the region, the FGOR disappeared and the Rwandan refugees returned home.

This chapter seeks to analyse the dynamics which enabled the FGOR to establish itself in the first place, and which also led to its downfall. It will argue that alliances and policies which the FGOR pursued in the international arena both ensured its survival and, together with the policy of ethnic cleansing it pursued in eastern Zaire, mobilized a countervailing set of regional interests which were the means of its own demise. It will then examine the rise of the ADFL, and the circumstances which enabled it not only to defeat the FGOR, but to go on and seize state power in Congo/Zaire as a whole. This case study thus demonstrates the inextricable links between national and international politics, particularly at the regional level, and the rise and fall of guerrilla movements.

International Politics and National Liberation Movements: Reversing a Paradigm

The state has long been thought of as the central actor in African development. Controlling the state means, to a great extent, controlling the process of accumulation. In spite of its tremendous influence, some analysts have argued that the African state is suspended in mid-air above African societies,[6] tethered in place by an international system which, since the end of the Second World War, has recognized sovereign statehood as a right, rather than an achievement.[7] Because of this, entities such as liberation movements, which seek to topple states, often supplement a domestic armed struggle with a diplomatic one. Here, they seek to limit both the recognition and patterns of cooperation which the state against which they are fighting – the contested state – can maintain.[8] Liberation movements also seek to expand their own patterns of international alliances, and to achieve formal recognition for themselves, in order to acquire state-like characteristics. Regional and international organizations have long been the venues from which such movements in Africa obtained official status, while neighbouring states and sympathetic international partners were often the sources of de facto recognition, as they were the ones which provided training facilities and diplomatic support, and access to the battlefront.

In the case of eastern Zaire, the above scenario was turned on its head. Rather than a liberation movement seeking to enhance its status by supplementing a domestic struggle at the international level, a former state sought to use international relations to recreate its own statehood. This took several forms. First, the FGOR utilized its former status as a government to bring resources with it to Zaire, and employed these resources in turn to pursue a guerrilla-based insurgency in Rwanda. In the process, its pursuit of an insurgency became one of the principal international

[6] Goran Hyden, *No Shortcuts to Progress* (Berkeley: University of California Press, 1983), pp. 7–8.
[7] See Carl Rosberg and Robert Jackson, 'Why Africa's weak states persist', *World Politics*, Vol. 35, No. 1 (1982), pp. 1–24.
[8] Wm Cyrus Reed, 'International politics and national liberation: ZANU and the politics of contested sovereignty in Zimbabwe', *African Studies Review*, Vol. 36, No. 2 (1993), pp. 31–59.

resources for the FGOR and its allies. It also used its *de facto* status as the agency in control of the refugee camps to extract resources from the international humanitarian agencies.

The FGOR also used external relations to carve out a territorial base. Unlike traditional liberation movements, which undertake to carve out sovereign space for themselves within the territorial boundaries of the contested state, the FGOR turned to the international arena and built upon the close ties which it had maintained with the government of Zaire to secure access to territory. The FGOR also developed its alliances with regional power brokers in eastern Zaire, and helped them to pursue a policy of ethnic cleansing, whose principal, though by no means sole, victims were the indigenous Tutsi population. By so doing, the FGOR sought to establish a permanent territorial base within which its followers could settle, from which they could continue to operate, and over which they would be able to establish effective control – all well beyond the reach of the governments of Zaire or Rwanda, or that of the international community and the International Criminal Tribunal for Rwanda, based in Tanzania.

This strategy ultimately backfired. Rather than securing the future of the FGOR, it mobilized a set of regional interests which were directly threatened by its activities. While the international community remained unable to act, governments in the Great Lakes region repeatedly expressed their concern over the destabilizing influence of the FGOR, and regional opposition to it dovetailed with domestic opposition within Zaire. Here, opponents of the FGOR were able to use opposition to it and its policy of ethnic cleansing to revitalize regional opposition to the central government in Zaire. Again, international ties, both individual and organizational, played an important role. Some of the soldiers who fought with the ADFL are reported to have fought with the RPF earlier, and many of the Tutsi who fled the fighting in eastern Zaire fled to Rwanda. While the nature of the links between the ADFL and neighbouring governments of Rwanda and Uganda remains uncertain, both have a history of ambiguous involvement in guerrilla warfare in neighbouring countries. The RPF operated inside, through, and some would say from Ugandan territory until its victory over the FGOR. Uganda had also long turned a blind eye to the activities of the Sudan Peoples Liberation Movement, which was fighting against the Khartoum government. Moreover, the activities of the ADFL served the strategic interests of both Kigali and Kampala, by limiting access by domestic rebel movements to their home territory.

From Government to Guerrilla: The FGOR

The flight into exile of the FGOR was the culmination of a long series of attempts by a narrow clique of individuals who headed the political apparatus in Rwanda to preserve their own political and economic ,hegemony. Since the late 1980s, domestic and international pressures had been mounting on Rwanda to abandon its one-party status and follow a path of democratic reform; a path down which Rwanda's former President, Juvenal Habyarimana, was reluctant to walk. It was only following the invasion by the RPF in 1990, its initial defeat and subsequent advances, that Habyarimana's government agreed to a series of internationally

backed negotiations which ultimately led to the Arusha Peace Accords. If implemented, these accords would have instituted a political system based upon
competitive, multi-party elections, and an independent judiciary which would have
had the power to hold officials accountable to the rule of law. Under such a system,
many members of the ruling elite, which had long abused public authority for
private gain, would have found themselves either out of power, or behind bars.

Throughout the process, Rwanda retained close contacts with France and Zaire.
Following the initial invasion by the RPF, both Zaire and France sent troops to help
bolster Habyarimana's government, though because Mobutu's troops seemed more
interested in looting new territory than protecting it, they were quickly asked to
leave. French troops, ostensibly in Rwanda to train the Rwandan Armed Forces and
to protect French nationals and other foreigners, have been accused of playing a far
more active role in the war with the RPF.[9] Following the 1993 RPF offensive, the
size of the French contingent grew to 680 troops, which were deployed north of
Kigali, where there were no French nationals. Moreover, French troops were
reported to have played a direct role in the fighting, and French trainers advised
Rwandan officers in tactical combat situations.[10] The French also supervised the
expansion of the Rwandan armed forces from 5,000 prior to the beginning of the
1990 war to over 30,000 at the time of its defeat. As the military expanded and
obtained more sophisticated weaponry, older Kalashnikov rifles were distributed to
newly formed militias which were loyal to the regime, but operated outside the
framework of the military.[11]

Following the final signing of the Arusha Peace Accords, UN Security Council
Resolution 918 (1994) imposed a comprehensive arms embargo which applied to
both the government of Rwanda and the RPF. Following the adoption of the
resolution, France continued to supply the Rwandan government with weapons
through the Goma airport in eastern Zaire – the area destined to become the seat of
the FGOR.[12] As the then government was collapsing, the French intervened again,
in what has become known as Operation Turquoise. Here, French troops were
deployed through Goma into southern Rwanda where they created a safe zone
through which the defeated government could retreat, and where, under French
protection, the FGOR and its army were able to exert their control over the vast
population that was quartered there, and which subsequently fled to Zaire.

The French also facilitated the FGOR's move into exile. In the safe zone,
individuals accused of genocide, as well as those actually in prison, were released,
rather than turned over to the UN authorities. While the French had turned a blind
eye to arms flows from Zaire to the safe zone, when the FGOR moved into Zaire,
France claimed to have disarmed the departing troops.[13] Rather than turning the
weapons over to the UN troops, which according to the Arusha Accords were to
monitor the situation, the French turned them over to the authorities in Zaire, the

[9] Human Rights Watch Arms Project, 'Arming Rwanda: the arms trade and human rights abuses in
the Rwanda war', *HRWAP*, Vol. 6, No. 1 (January 1994), p. 23.
[10] *Ibid.*, p. 6.
[11] *Ibid.*, p. 27.
[12] Human Rights Watch Arms Project, 'Rearming with impunity: international support for the
perpetrators of the Rwandan genocide', *HRWAP*, Vol. 7, No. 4 (May 1995), p. 6
[13] *Ibid.*, p. 8; other material in this paragraph is taken from the same report.

very agency which had facilitated the supply of weapons to the FGOR in the first place. At more remote crossing points, little effort is said to have been made to disarm the troops. More directly, UN officials have argued that France facilitated the movement of crack troops and key commanders out of the region by flying them to French training centres in the Central African Republic (CAR). The government of the CAR requested a formal explanation from France as to why non-CAR soldiers, who were reputed to be linked to Hutu militias, were receiving training in French bases inside the CAR. In short, the French ensured that the FGOR possessed a large, well-equipped military and that it could escape to Zaire, with its command structure and key troops largely in place. If troops were disarmed at the border, they quickly rearmed on the other side.

Zaire also played an important role in guaranteeing the survival of the FGOR. In spite of its official neutrality and willingness to cooperate with the international community, events on the ground took a different turn. Two explanations are plausible for the discrepancy between the official and the actual policy. The first is duplicity. If access to the international community required that President Mobutu toe a particular line, he was ready to do so, but there was not necessarily any link between what was said and what was done. A second line of reasoning is that it might have been very difficult for Kinshasa to enforce its policies in eastern Zaire, even if it wished to do so, given the lack of institutional coherence in Zaire, and the strong tradition of autonomy which that region has maintained.

Perhaps the most important support Zaire provided was guaranteed safe passage into and out of its territory and residence for FGOR personnel, including those accused of crimes against humanity. At best, Zaire also turned a blind eye to the creation of some of the military training camps for FGOR soldiers, though in other cases, such as the Panzi camp near Bukavu, which was a former Zairean army/gendarmerie base, they obviously played a far more direct role.[14] Camps stretched from North Kivu, along the Rwanda–Uganda border, through Lake Kivu, where they were set up on islands in the lake, and into the area bordering Burundi. Throughout the region, the FGOR controlled refugee camps which were often strategically placed along the border with Rwanda and from which cross-border raids could easily be launched. Zaire likewise helped to ensure access to international arms supplies for the FGOR. Given that many of the Zairean troops were not paid, they often engaged in arms trafficking to raise funds. Larger-scale operations, such as the use of private air cargo carriers to transfer arms to the FGOR via Goma airport, were facilitated directly by the head of Zaire's secret police in Goma.[15] In an unpublished report which was leaked to the press, the United Nations asserted Zaire played a central role in creating an entire web of international contacts through which the FGOR purchased millions of dollars worth of arms from dealers in Britain, China, and South Africa to re-arm quickly and effectively.

The establishment of a viable FGOR within its territory was of great strategic value to Zaire. No longer of much value in Cold War terms, Zaire under President Mobutu had suffered from growing international political isolation in recent years because of repeated human rights violations, flagrant corruption within his regime,

---

[14] Human Rights Watch Arms Project., p. 13.
[15] *Ibid.*, p. 9.

and a dogged determination to avoid political and economic reform. Mobutu was able to recreate some of this value, and end his isolation, through the presence of the FGOR. By hosting a movement which threatened to perpetuate regional instability, Zaire became a key player in any attempt to achieve an internationally backed settlement to the crisis. Within Zaire's domestic political realm, the FGOR also played an important role. Eastern Zaire had long been one of the centres of opposition politics, and its economy operated independently of central government regulation. If pressures for democratization were effective, this region was most likely to lead opposition against the regime. The FGOR represented a strong authority which had a long pattern of cooperation with the central government of Zaire and which, because of its status as a foreign power on Zairean territory, was likely to strengthen rather than weaken the influence of Kinshasa.

The FGOR and Access to Resources

When the FGOR entered Zaire, it took with it enormous resources, including virtually all of Rwanda's skilled and educated manpower. This was, in part, because skilled and educated individuals who were members of the opposition, or who were Tutsi, had been killed during the genocide. It also grew out of the patronage base of Rwandan politics, in which virtually all institutions were linked to the state, which had been dominated by a single ruling party. This was superimposed upon a strong tradition of rigidly hierarchical social and political organization dating back hundreds of years. When the genocide was implemented at the top of a command-based socio-political structure, it was carried out not only efficiently, but also by a wide cross-section of the population. Moreover, whether they were directly implicated or not, many of the civil service, commercial, and intellectual elites were closely affiliated with those who were. Thus, when the RPF advanced to Kigali in July 1994, and corridors of escape to Zaire were opened, virtually the entire state structure fled.

As they fled, the departing Rwandans took with them nearly everything which was movable and of any value. Everything from corrugated steel roofing sheets, window frames, and door handles, to office and factory equipment, was exported to eastern Zaire's off-the-books economy.[16] Government property and military equipment, which the FGOR had received during the war with the RPF in growing quantities, faced the same fate. More importantly, the departing government took with it all of Rwanda's foreign exchange assets, as well as nearly all of the country's paper currency. Thus, when the FGOR arrived in eastern Zaire, it was well prepared to purchase those items it had not brought with it, or which were not provided by its allies.

The move into exile was both so swift and so massive that international humanitarian organizations were unable to set up adequate reception centres for the newly arriving refugees. Because the former government remained largely intact, it quickly assumed its old responsibility for organizing the population and distributing goods

---

[16] For the working of this economy, see Janet MacGaffey *et al.*, *The Real Economy of Zaire* (London: James Currey, 1991)

and services to them. In the process, the FGOR established effective control over the refugee camps. Movement into and out of the camps was regulated by the FGOR, which also controlled the movement of goods and services, including information. Because members of the FGOR had the administrative skills which were so sorely needed in such a humanitarian crisis, many of the individuals who had organized the genocide so efficiently became key employees of the very agencies which sought to gain access to the refugee camps.[17] Within the camps, markets for looted goods and international assistance quickly emerged. Here, again, the FGOR re-asserted its former role as regulator of the marketplace, thereby securing an additional source of income.

Internationally, the FGOR also used its former sovereign status to loot the country. Nearly ten months after its fall, diplomats representing the former regime in the Netherlands, Kenya, Tanzania, Cairo, Zaire and the United Nations continued to occupy diplomatic property, to draw upon embassy accounts, and to participate in international meetings designed to stop the crisis. In some instances, diplomats sold embassy property and emptied accounts to prevent resources from falling into the hands of the new authorities. In other cases, representatives of the new regime could only occupy their embassies after they had paid the back wages of the representatives of the FGOR![18] Prior to the arrival of the representatives of the RPF government, FGOR diplomats often participated in donor meetings to discuss strategies for dealing with the humanitarian crisis and the new government in Rwanda.

In short, the FGOR gained access to the resources it needed to sustain itself by using its former sovereign status to loot the country of human and physical resources. Utilizing well-established alliances with France and Zaire, the FGOR then exported these resources across the border to Zaire. Here, the FGOR built upon the hospitality of its pariah host by activating long-established international contacts to re-establish its military and to recreate its *de facto* authority over its now exiled population. In this way the FGOR was able to parley its control of a newly internationalized citizenry to obtain additional resources from the international humanitarian community. By early 1995, a government-in-exile had been established with a chain of command linking political leaders with military commanders. Within the military, ranks had been re-established, the former militias had been integrated into the regular forces, and because of the FGOR's control over the refugee camps, young recruits were constantly being added to the ranks. Now combined, the former military and the militias brought the total number of soldiers under the FGOR to 50,000.

Guerrillas in the Midst

Soon after consolidating their position in eastern Zaire, the FGOR began to pursue a policy of insurgency in Rwanda, while establishing links with other insurgent movements in the Great Lakes/greater East African region. As it became apparent

---

[17] African Rights, *Rwanda: Death, Despair, and Defiance.*
[18] Interviews.

that the policy of insurgency was not going to bear fruit immediately, the FGOR sought to secure its long-term security by forming an alliance with its hosts and becoming intertwined in the domestic conflict between the Banyarwanda and *autochtones* in eastern Zaire.

Within Rwanda, the FGOR used its geographic advantage of mountainous terrain in the north, and the close proximity to Rwanda's border of the camps on Ijwi Island in Lake Kivu and in the south, to infiltrate across the border with Rwanda.[19] Initial attacks, which began as early as October 1994, were limited to incursions just across the border. One year later, the attacks had increased in both number and scope. According to a November 1995 report by the Emergency Response Humanitarian Assistance Unit, there were 11 attacks in June and the number had tripled to over 30 in October.[20] While the majority of the attacks continued to be along the western border with Zaire, during the first two weeks of November attacks had occurred in the capital, Kigali, and in Rwanda's second-largest city, Butare, both of which are far removed from the border.[21] Subsequent reports uncovered plans by the FGOR for a full-scale invasion of Rwanda.[22] Such developments prompted Vice-President Paul Kagame, Rwanda's Minister of Defence and the head of the national Rwandan Patriotic Army (RPA), to declare the need to fight another war against the FGOR.[23]

The goal of the FGOR, as perceived by the RPF, was not a direct military victory, but the destabilization of the newly formed government of Rwanda by fomenting tension between the people and the government.[24] The strategy was to use guerrilla tactics to finish the genocide by attacking the *rescapés*, Rwandans of Tutsi origin who had survived the first genocide.[25] In so doing, the FGOR sought to provoke Rwanda's RPF-dominated army into retaliatory moves against those Hutu who had remained inside Rwanda. Such a strategy played upon two of the institutional weaknesses of the RPF. During the closing days of the war, its military wing had expanded rapidly by incorporating largely untrained recruits from inside Rwanda, many of whom were very young. Maintaining military discipline over these new troops was far more difficult than it had been over the smaller, more tightly organized armed wing of the RPF. Moreover, most of the original members of the RPF were raised in exile and their families were thus at least somewhat protected from the genocide in 1994. The new recruits came from inside Rwanda; many had seen their entire families massacred and were out for revenge. Further attacks against the Tutsi community by a Hutu-dominated force might be enough to provoke massive retaliation and drive an insurmountable wedge between the government and the people. Undoubtedly such a move would have contributed to the ongoing shift in world attention away from the crimes of genocide which the

---

[19] Kamanyola camp was only 800 metres from the border with Burundi and a few kilometres from the border with Rwanda. Camps on Ijwi Island were equally close to Rwandan territory.

[20] Report, Emergency Response Humanitarian Assistance Unit, November 1995.

[21] Amnesty International, 'Rwanda: alarming resurgence of killings', London, 12 August 1996.

[22] *International Herald Tribune*, 28 Nov 1996.

[23] Philip Gourevitch, 'Neighborhood bully: how genocide revived President Mobutu', *The New Yorker*, 9 September 1996, p. 57.

[24] Interviews.

[25] *Human Rights Watch*, Vol. 6, No. 12 (June 1994), p. 3.

FGOR had pursued and towards the human rights abuses which the RPF was alleged to be pursuing. Given the total absence of institutional linkage between the bulk of Rwanda's citizens and their government, such a wedge would have been very difficult to bridge in the short term. In order to sustain their new war, the FGOR also began an extensive propaganda programme which centred on the revision of Rwandan history.[26] In it, the FGOR attributed the catastrophic situation of the Rwandan people to the diabolical work of the RPF, which it held responsible for the genocide of the Hutu. It attributed its own exile to the arms embargo engineered by the US and the activities of that country as well as Belgium, the UN and Uganda.

The activities of the FGOR also involved a regional dimension, and were certainly viewed by neighbouring governments in a broader context of regional destabilization. To the south, the FGOR quickly established an alliance with the Hutu militia who had effectively limited the authority of the Tutsi-dominated army of Burundi to the major cities. By forming a pan-Hutu alliance, the FGOR hoped to strengthen the hand of the Burundian militias, and in the process gain access to the Rwandan Hutu refugees who had settled there. By operating through Burundi, the FGOR would then have been able to link up with the refugees in Tanzania and, in the process, to encircle two thirds of Rwanda.

To the north lay Uganda. While its central and southern parts were strongholds of the Museveni regime, his government had fought a continuous battle against armed insurgents in the country's northern and western territories. Movements in the north were linked to the former regime of Idi Amin, and also allegedly had links to some elements of the internal opposition. Virtually all received support from the government of Sudan and were widely believed to be using Zaire as a conduit between Uganda and their bases in Sudan. Sudan, in spite of growing international isolation, had also retained close relations with France. In one instance, France had provided satellite photographs of bases used by the Sudan People's Liberation Army (SPLA) in exchange for the return of a retired terrorist leader known as Carlos the Jackal. The result was a major setback for the SPLA, driving it back into Ugandan territory.

Domestically, Uganda was preparing for its first free elections since independence amidst a raging debate inside the country over whether parties should be permitted or not. One of the principal proponents of the formation of parties was Milton Obote, himself the head of one of Uganda's biggest parties and an exiled former head of state. With a low-intensity war on its northern front, the last thing Uganda wanted to see was a link established between the FGOR, the rebels in northern Uganda, and the internal opposition. Given the close ties which the FGOR maintained with France, and which that country maintained with Sudan, Uganda believed this to be a real possibility. By the summer of 1996, unconfirmed reports were circulating in security structures in Kigali that the very links which Uganda feared – between the FGOR, Obote and the northern rebel movements – were being established.

As the prospect of a quick victory over the RPF began to fade, the FGOR began to supplement its ongoing policies of forming regional ties and of destabilizing

---

[26] *Human Rights Watch*, pp. 3–4.

Rwanda, with another strategy of securing its long-term future in eastern Zaire, particularly in the North Kivu area of Masisi near the FGOR military headquarters at Goma. This it did by becoming directly embroiled in the conflict between the *autochtones*, who trace their lineage to groups which lie entirely within the territorial domain of present day Zaire, and the Banyarwanda, Kinyarwanda-speaking groups which trace their heritage, one way or another, to Rwanda. The latter are divided between those who were included in Zaire because of the colonial partition, which split the Kingdom of Rwanda between Rwanda, Zaire and Uganda, and a second group which migrated to Zaire after the turn of the century in response to incentives from the Belgian colonial authorities. While the *autochtones* are the numerical majority throughout eastern Zaire, the Banyarwanda have assumed the pre-eminent role economically. In North Kivu, and particularly Masisi, the Banyarwanda also formed the majority of the population, though they recognized their subordinate political status by paying tribute to local chiefs.

The political status of the Banyarwanda became a matter of conflict following the passage of a new citizenship law in 1981 which conferred citizenship only on those individuals who could prove that their ancestors resided in Zaire prior to the colonial partition. While many Banyarwanda had done so, the necessary documentation did not exist and thus, in the eyes of the authorities as well as those of many *autochtones*, they became inseparable from more recent arrivals. In short, the 1981 law threatened all Banyarwanda in eastern Zaire with statelessness. This was particularly important, in that participation in both elective and appointed posts in Zaire was limited to legal citizens. Thus, as pressure for democratic reforms mounted in the late 1980s, the Banyarwanda faced the prospect of deportation to Rwanda or being forced to live as guests under the political domination of the *autochtones*, even in those areas, such as Masisi, where they were in a numerical majority.[27]

Hutu Banyarwanda quickly formed organizations to protest their disenfranchisement, the largest of which was the Magrivi (Mutuelle des Agriculteurs et Eleveurs du Virunga – Farmers and Livestock Raisers Cooperative of Virunga). In addition to protesting their exclusion from the 1991 national conference to debate the political future of Zaire, the Magrivi also recommended the suspension of tributary payments to local chiefs. In the midst of ongoing conflict between members of the *autochtones* and Hutu Banyarwanda communities, which resulted in the loss of between 14,000 and 40,000 lives and the displacement of 350,000 people in 1993 alone, the Tutsi Banyarwanda stayed largely on the sidelines. Hutu viewed them as fellow Banyarwanda, but excluded them from the Magrivi, while *autochtones* communities did not see them as their principal opponents. By March 1994, much of the tension had been dissipated following the dispatch of a group of elite presidential troops, which was supplemented by a peace campaign led by a consortium of local NGOs and churches, to foster reconciliation. The programme was successful enough for displaced people to start returning to their homes. While NGOs called for the resolution of the citizenship issue, there was no official response.

---

[27] See Sheldon Yett, 'Masisi, down the road from Goma: ethnic cleansing and displacement in Eastern Zaire', Issue Brief, US Committee for Refugees (Washington DC: June 1996), p. 11.

While the tension in eastern Zaire had involved Hutu Banyarwanda and *autochtones*, it had not divided the Banyarwanda along Hutu–Tutsi lines. The 1994 genocide in Rwanda began this process, and the arrival of the FGOR in June guaranteed it. The FGOR quickly formed an alliance with the Hutu Banyarwanda, but rather than focusing upon the *autochtones*, began to focus their wrath upon the Tutsi. Initially, the activities of the FGOR and local Hutu focused upon theft, but later escalated to rape and murder which, according to one Tutsi Banyarwanda, the Hutu had learned in Rwanda.[28] By 1995, as it became clear that the FGOR would not be returning to Rwanda in the near future, attacks upon the Tutsi escalated and, for the first time, *autochtones* militia jumped on the bandwagon, attacking Tutsi as well. The arrival of poorly paid Zairean troops exacerbated the situation still further. With a monthly wage of less than $5, which was only paid occasionally, members of the Zairean Armed Forces (FAZ), rented themselves to the highest bidder, which was often the FGOR.[29] As the levels of violence increased, the troops extorted money from all sides. As the Tutsi began to flee to Rwanda to escape the violence, FAZ troops both demanded protection money and, for the equivalent of thirty pounds of beef, offered transport to the border, where the identity cards of the fugitives, and thus their citizenship, were officially destroyed.[30]

At the official level, the Governor of North Kivu supported the anti-Tutsi violence, inciting people to 'strike and strike now' against the immigrants.[31] Because of the violence, the government cancelled elections in 1995, and threatened to do the same for elections slated for 1997. In an area which had traditionally had the weakest links to President Mobutu and the strongest opposition to the central government, cancelling elections may well have been an effective way to camouflage state weakness.

The anti-Tutsi violence led to the displacement of between 100,000 and 250,000 individuals in Zaire, tens of thousands of whom crossed into Rwanda in March 1996 alone. Hutu–Tutsi violence also exacerbated tension between Tutsi and other groups, who sought to chase Tutsi from their midst, if for no other reason than to protect themselves from attack by Hutu militias.[32] By September, it was estimated that the entire Tutsi population had been displaced from the North Kivu province of eastern Zaire, where they had once been the majority. While many of the early refugees were treated as Rwandans who were returning to Rwanda, in April Rwanda announced that all new Tutsi arrivals from Zaire would be treated as refugees and housed in a camp 500 metres from the Zaire border, sandwiched between a military camp in Zaire and a gendarmerie camp in Rwanda. One refugee expressed the sentiment: 'My home is Zaire, not here in a camp; I will go home as soon as it is safe.'[33] If this is representative, as seems plausible, then the participation of Tutsi refugees in Rwanda in any organized movement to stop the violence would be highly likely. After completing their task in North Kivu, the FAZ/FGOR alliance turned their attention to the south.

[28] Yett, 'Masisi', p. 14.
[29] *Ibid.*, p. 15.
[30] Gourevitch, 'Neigbourhood bully', pp. 54–5.
[31] Yett, 'Masisi', p. 16.
[32] Gourevitch, 'Neighbourhood bully', p. 55.
[33] Yett, 'Masisi', p. 18.

International Impotence and the Rise of the ADFL

Throughout the two years that the FGOR operated from eastern Zaire, the international community debated the issue extensively, but took very little constructive action. Some international humanitarian agencies sought to devise ways through which the needs of the refugees could be met more effectively. This, in turn, contributed to the strength of the FGOR, which controlled the camps. Others sought to develop plans for the repatriation of the refugees and the prosecution of those elements which had perpetrated the genocide in the first place. To this end, the international community supported the establishment of the International Criminal Tribunal for Rwanda in Arusha, and the rehabilitation of the justice system in Rwanda.[34] At the same time, major powers repeatedly called for the removal of the refugee camps away from the Zaire–Rwanda border and the separation of the legitimate refugees from the criminals. With the onset of donor fatigue, some diplomats in Kigali suggested that the termination of international support for the refugee camps was inevitable, and that such a move would drive the refugees home and shut off international funding for the FGOR.[35]

Given the entrenched position of the FGOR, it was asserted that moving the camps and separating the two groups would have required a heavily armed and sizable military expedition which was authorized to use force. While the US actively supported the attainment of these goals, the crisis in eastern Zaire came after those in Somalia, Yugoslavia and Rwanda, and the Clinton administration simply was not willing to invest the necessary diplomatic, military and financial resources to undertake the project, nor was it willing to take such a risk just prior to an election.[36] While the French had a long history of direct military intervention in African affairs, they were also closely linked to the very group which the international community sought to dislodge, and which many (including the RPF) suspected France wanted to strengthen. While moving the camps might have been possible logistically (though an extremely expensive undertaking), separating the refugees from the criminals was thought to be far more difficult, because of kinship ties which linked the two; many of the refugees were the families of the members of the FGOR and its army. At the regional level, the heads of state of all the members of the Great Lakes region met regularly with representatives of the OAU, South Africa's Bishop Desmond Tutu, and former US President Jimmy Carter, though they too failed to draft an effective and implementable plan of action to deal with the crisis.

By the summer of 1996, the situation had grown increasingly serious. Diplomats in Rwanda fully expected that country to invoke self-defence as a justification for cross-border raids, which could well lead to direct war with Zaire. At the same time, violence supported by Zaire was increasing in northern Uganda, which was the only region in which the Ugandan opposition had had a strong showing in the recent

---

[34] When the RPF formed its government, the justice system had collapsed. With fewer than 20 qualified lawyers in the entire country, and virtually no magistrates, there was no way to deal with the growing numbers of individuals accused of crimes against humanity. It was not until early 1997 that the court system began to function again.

[35] Interviews, Kigali, 1996.

[36] Gourevitch, 'Neighbourhood bully'.

elections. At the UN, officials began to debate whether or not to invoke the Cessation Clause, which, because of improved conditions at home, would have revoked refugee status on Rwandans abroad.[37] All of this occurred within the context of a joint declaration in which the prime ministers of Zaire and Rwanda agreed to make operational the organized, massive and unconditional repatriation of all Rwandan refugees and the closure of the camps by Zaire. Thus, while the need for the FGOR to secure its position inside Zaire grew all the more pressing, depending upon the central government of Zaire for protection became more difficult. The FGOR and the FAZ therefore expanded their operations into South Kivu, where the Tutsi are known as Banyamulenge. Subsequent reports indicated massacres of Tutsi, using the same techniques which had been used in Rwanda two and a half years earlier.[38]

In response to the attacks, on 13 October the Banyamulenge in Zaire's South Kivu province began to fight back. The attack was led by Laurent-Desiré Kabila, a native of Shaba province with a chequered political background. Following the death of his erstwhile political leader, Patrice Lumumba, Kabila participated in uprisings against Mobutu in Stanleyville (Kisangani) in 1963–4. He then established the Marxist People's Revolutionary Party and carved out a niche among the Bembe in eastern Zaire which, according to some, he ruled 'like a typical African warlord' – including maintaining his power through extreme punishments which allegedly included burying people alive and kidnapping tourists for ransom monies to fund his activities.[39] An even more important source of funding was gold produced amongst the Bembe, which Kabila marketed in Dar es Salaam, where he spent the bulk of the decade prior to 1996. Reviving his People's Revolutionary Party, Kabila formed an alliance with the Mouvement Revolutionnaire pour la Libération du Zaire, the Alliance Democratique des Peuples (dominated by Tutsi from North and South Kivu), and the Counseil National de Resistance pour la Democratie (whose members came from eastern Zaire and Kasai), creating the Alliance of Democratic Forces for the Liberation of Congo/Zaire (ADFL).[40] Resting on a regional base in three provincial areas – eastern Zaire, Shaba (formerly known as Katanga), and Kasai – the ADFL was to spearhead the battle against Mobutu.

All three regions had tremendous wealth and long traditions of seeking autonomy from Kinshasa. Shaba, the home to some of the largest copper mines in the world, attempted to secede from Zaire shortly after independence, and had been in a constant state of rebellion since the 1970s. East Kasai, a world leader in the production of industrial diamonds, had adopted a less confrontational and more successful approach. During colonialism, East Kasaians received preferential access to advanced training, and came to dominate executive and professional posts throughout the country. In 1992, following stiff opposition from a Kasaian, Etienne

---

[37] 'UNHCR to meet on Rwandan refugees', *Egyptian Gazette* (Reuters), 30 September 1996.

[38] United Nations Department of Humanitarian Affairs, Integrated Regional Information Network (IRIN) Emergency Update, 17, 11 November 1996. Internet version (http://www.reliefweb.int. emergenc/greatlak/source/dha).

[39] Cindy Shiner, 'Kabila: despot or democrat? Accounts of Kabila's odyssey contradictory', *The Washington Post*, 19 May 1997, p. A01 (http:www.washingtonpost.com/wp-srv/inatl/africa/may/19/kabila.htm).

[40] IRIN, Emergency Update, 16 November 1996.

Tshisekedi emerged as leader of the opposition, and then as Prime Minister. One of his first undertakings was to sack upwards of one million Kasaians from their posts throughout Zaire. As these individuals returned to East Kasai, they brought with them enormous skills and began to carve out their own independent spheres, including the regulation of an independent monetary system and university.[41] Eastern Zaire was not only a principal source of food production for Zaire, but also possessed major gold deposits. While the three regions possessed significant resources, the benefits of these had traditionally flowed to Mobutu and his allies in Kinshasa. When events in eastern Zaire provided an immediate opportunity to act, people from all three areas thus had deep-seated reasons to do so.

Given its base in Shaba and East Kasai, it was hardly surprising that the forces of the ADFL launched their first attacks from there into South Kivu, first attacking the town of Uvira and later Bukavu. Because the citizenship of its opponents had been called into question by the 1981 citizenship law, the government of Zaire defined the rebellion as Rwandan aggression. Indeed, under the circumstances, distinguishing between Rwandans and Zaireans became very difficult. Many Tutsi from Zaire had joined the RPF during the war in Rwanda and, together with Tutsi refugees in Rwanda, may well have jumped at the chance to fight. Certainly the level of discipline, the amount of armaments available to the rebels, and the effectiveness of their tactics over the coming weeks, would indicate that this was far more than a rag-tag militia.[42] Subsequent reports from Rwanda indicate that the RPA provided critical, if not decisive, support to the ADFL.[43]

In South Kivu, the governor gave all Banyamulenge one week to evacuate the country, after which they would be treated as rebels by the Zairean army. He also asked international aid agencies to open up corridors through which they could safely depart.[44] At the same time, radio broadcasts in the south claimed that the Tutsi wanted to kill local citizens and that UN workers were there to support the Tutsi against the regime.[45] Instead of fleeing through the non-existent corridors, however, the ADFL advanced, capturing the provincial capital of Bukavu. In the process, the ADFL routed Zaire's notoriously undisciplined army, causing most of the international aid workers to flee. Zaire and Rwanda exchanged artillery fire across their mutual borders,[46] while the rebels shifted their attention from Zaire army posts to the FGOR-controlled refugee camps. Within days, the largest of those camps had been emptied, and hundreds of thousands of former residents were on the move. Those refugees closest to the border fled to Rwanda, while others, including those thought to be the leading forces in the FGOR, retreated deeper into Zaire. The

---

[41] Howard French, 'As Zaire crumbles, a province secedes into stability', *International Herald Tribune*, 19 September 1996.

[42] See Wm Cyrus Reed, 'The New International Order: state, society, and African international relations', *Africa Insight* (Pretoria), Vol. 25, No. 3 (1995), pp. 140–8.

[43] John Pomfret, 'Rwanda admits it led drive to topple Mobutu', *International Herald Tribune*, 10 July 1997, and Mahmood Mamdani, 'Why Rwanda admitted its role in Zaire' (interview with Paul Kagame), *Mail and Guardian* (Johannesburg) 8 August 1997 (http://www.africanews/specials/glakes/rwanda_zaire.html).

[44] 'Workers fear all out war in Eastern Zaire', *Egyptian Gazette* (Reuters), 10 October 1996.

[45] 'Chaos envelops Central Africa', *Guardian* (UK), 3 November 1996; 'A mounting crisis in Central Africa', *Guardian* (UK), 3 November 1996.

[46] 'Threat of war looms in Central Africa', *International Herald Tribune*, 31 October 1996.

United Nations High Commissioner for Refugees, Mrs Sadako Ogata, termed the situation a looming humanitarian catastrophe.[47] During the next two weeks, the ADFL advanced while the international community mobilized. In the end, the success of the former rendered the inertia of the latter irrelevant.

By the beginning of November, the ADFL had advanced to a position from which it controlled the three principal cities in eastern Zaire – Uvira, Bukavu and Goma – as well as a swathe of territory stretching from Burundi to Uganda, which included the entire Rwanda–Zaire border. The Zairean army kept to its tradition of looting and raping as it retreated, thereby ensuring that the advancing ADFL troops would be hailed as liberators in virtually every district they entered.[48] Within ADFL territory, displaced Zaireans began to return home, and the ADFL took the first steps towards recreating an administrative system. In order to demonstrate their difference from the former regime, newly appointed political commissars invited former civil servants to return to their jobs, but citizens were asked to identify those who should be retained and those who were corrupt. Because of the war, production and marketing structures in the region had collapsed. To address this, the ADFL declared Zaire's international borders with Rwanda open and abolished import duties, thereby not only increasing the availability of goods, but reducing their price as well.[49] At the same time, Kabila undertook negotiations with humanitarian agencies, including the UN, for the return of international workers and assistance. This time, though, the aid was distributed amongst the recently returned Zairean population and aid workers began to help rebuild the urban infrastructure in the rebel territory. Water and electricity were also restored and schools reopened. Representatives of the ADFL even went so far as to propose a regional system of taxation and the development of new programmes to address the problem of unemployment. Radio stations under ADFL control in Goma and Uvira began to refer to Kabila, the head of the ADFL, as the president. Even the head of the World Wildlife Fund praised the new attitude which the ADFL guerrillas had towards Zaire's endangered mountain gorillas. Rather than facilitating their extinction, the ADFL, with WWF funding, had begun a process of rehabilitating the infrastructure of the Virunga national park and the proper training of its staff.[50] In short, very soon after their arrival, the ADFL began to behave like a state and sought to demonstrate not only that their administration was better than that of their kleptocratic predecessors, but that they could deliver the goods to those who had become their constituents.

As the ADFL was establishing administrative structures in the south and inter- national contacts at the unofficial level, they advanced to the west from Goma and reached Mugunga, Kahindo, and Katale and other camps, which together housed upwards of half a million refugees, including the leadership of the FGOR. As the ADFL advanced, refugees poured out of surrounding camps and congregated in Mugunga. Faced with heavy artillery fire from Mugunga Camp, and warnings from the human rights community of a pending bloodbath, the ADFL sealed off access

---

[47] 'A jolt for Tutsi and Hutus', *Guardian*, 3 November 1996.
[48] Private correspondence from eastern Zaire, October 1996.
[49] *Ibid*.
[50] Reuters, cited in IRIN, Emergency Update, 148, 11 April 1997.

roads and it too called for the creation of humanitarian corridors, monitored by a neutral force (which did not contain French troops) through which the refugees could return to Rwanda.

With a US presidential election approaching on 5 November, the UN rather than the US became the centre for diplomatic activities, and the Canadian Ambassador to the US was asked to pursue a negotiated ceasefire. This was virtually impossible, in that Zaire refused to negotiate as long as Rwandans, meaning the ADFL and not the FGOR, occupied its territory. Regionally, Kenya called a summit of concerned parties,[51] at which member governments called for the territorial integrity of Zaire, the creation of humanitarian corridors through the use of force if necessary, an end to cross-border attacks, the inalienable rights of residents within internationally recognized borders to full rights of citizenship, and the separation of refugees from intimidators.[52] Building on the African call for intervention, but ignoring the calls to secure the rights of citizens of Zaire and to separate refugees from militants, the Security Council adopted a resolution calling for the creation of a multinational military force for humanitarian purposes in eastern Zaire, but failed to outline the operative dimensions of the force, including its mandate and goals.[53]

By the time member states agreed on 16 November to give the military force the right to use all necessary means to get aid to the refugees stranded in eastern Zaire, events on the ground had taken a different turn. Instead of the predicted bloodbath at Mugunga Camp, the residents separated themselves into two groups. While the heart and soul of the FGOR retreated further into Zaire, an estimated 250,000 refugees were expected to cross into Rwanda on the very day the Security Council provided the multinational force with its mandate. Rwanda immediately declared the force irrelevant. Inside Zaire, conflicts between local militias, the FGOR and the retreating Zaire army caused displacements as far south as Shaba Province, and as far north as Kisangani. Within days, nearly half a million refugees had repatriated themselves to Rwanda.

During its first phase of operation, the ADFL secured a large piece of territory stretching more than 500 km from Burundi to Uganda, within which it had displaced the authority of the government of Zaire and replaced it with its own. By forcing the closure of the principal refugee camps, the ADFL had also started the process of separating the intimidators from the refugees. Hundreds of thousands of refugees, and some of the FGOR, took advantage of the safe corridors and returned to Rwanda, thereby pre-empting any international military intervention, which would certainly have strengthened the hand of the Zairean government and weakened the ADFL.

Having secured its initial goals, the ADFL continued to advance to the north-west and south-west, routing the FAZ along the way. At the same time, rebel attacks in Uganda increased, in part because of the alliance between the FAZ and the

---

[51] Zaire refused to attend, and because of international sanctions, Burundi was not invited. Those in attendance included Eritrea, Ethiopia, Uganda, Kenya, Tanzania, Rwanda and Cameroon – the then Chair of the OAU.

[52] IRIN, Emergency Update, 9, 6 November 1996.

[53] IRIN, Emegency Update, 15, 9 November 1996.

Ugandan rebels. As the ADFL advanced into the areas from which the rebels operated, so too did the Ugandan army.[54] The result was the continued rapid northward expansion of the territory under ADFL control. By December 1996, ADFL territory stretched from Bunia in the north, to Walikale in the west, and south to Itomwe and Fizi, which lay 130 km south of the Burundi border. Within this territory lay the Sominki gold mines in Katamituga, 100 km south west of Bukavu. The area around Bunia was also heavily endowed with minerals, including gold. Three months later, Zaire's third largest city, Kisangani, had fallen into rebel hands. A regular supply of gold, exportable through an all-weather airport at Bunia, provided the ADFL with a secure source of income through which it could both continue to pursue its military goals and strengthen its grip over the re-emerging administrative structures, perhaps even reducing corruption by paying regular salaries.

The advances of the ADFL were a serious blow to the FAZ, whose 'authority' became demarcated by that territory which their opponents did not occupy. Upon Mobutu's return to Zaire after months in Europe for medical treatment, he appointed a new army chief, General Mahele Lyoko, whose main task was to overhaul the FAZ and to launch a major counter-offensive against the ADFL. One of Lyoko's principal strategies was reportedly to recruit mercenaries from Europe, South Africa, and Angola. The myth of the invincible white warrior, and those firms which provide them, vanished as Kisangani fell to rebel hands in mid-March. In a desperate move, Mobutu sacked the government for incompetence, later charging that the then Prime Minister had stolen the funds earmarked for the rehabilitation of the army. Kabila's statements that anyone who served Mobutu was his enemy, made the recruitment of a new government difficult. In April, Etienne Tshisekedi, Mobutu's long-time foe, accepted the nomination as prime minister, but immediately caused a stir. He not only appointed a new government and offered the ADFL six cabinet posts (which they rejected) but without the approval of his own party or Mobutu, he also dissolved the Transitional Parliament, which had been established by Mobutu under the 1994 constitution, and sought to replace it with the National Sovereign Conference, established in 1992. One week after his appointment, Tshisekedi was replaced by General Likulia Bolongo, who immediately declared a state of emergency throughout what was left of Mobutu's domain.

While politicians in Kinshasa manoeuvred, Kabila advanced, first into East Kasai and the city of Mbuji-Mayi, whose diamond mines alone were thought to produce annual revenues in excess of US$1 billion.[55] By the beginning of the second week of April, Kabila's forces received a 'hero's welcome' in Lubumbashi, the second largest city in Zaire and the centre of Zaire's cobalt and copper production. At the same time, De Beers, the South African diamond conglomerate, was reported to have initiated contact with ADFL leaders and by the end of the month a Canadian mining company, American Mineral Fields, signed an agreement with the ADFL for the investment of upwards of $1 billion in the rehabilitation of

[54] IRIN, Emegency Update, 68, 30 December 1996.
[55] IRIN, Emegency Update, 144, 5–7 April 1997.

existing and the development of new copper and cobalt mines in Shaba Province.[56]

The ADFL's advance into Shaba also brought to light the new regional alliances which Kabila had developed. As FGOR troops continued their retreat away from Kabila's forces, they moved closer to territory traditionally controlled by the UNITA movement in Angola, a movement closely aligned with Mobutu. To preclude any alliance, and to ensure UNITA's continued participation in Angola's newly formed government of national unity, that country was reported to have permitted ADFL troops to enter Zaire from its territory, and Angolan troops were later reported to have been seen inside Zaire. During the battle for Kolwezi, a mining town close to the Zambian border, ADFL troops were said to have entered Zaire from Zambia as well. The ADFL also developed close ties with Zimbabwe, which emerged as a major supplier of military goods and political goodwill. Indeed, on the seventeenth anniversary of that country's own successful armed struggle for independence, the ruling party, ZANU, issued a public statement hailing the victories of 'dear brother' Laurent Kabila, but also calling on him to 'extend the hand of reconciliation while swimming in victory'.[57]

By mid-April, Kabila controlled all of the sources of foreign exchange and revenue in Zaire.[58] It was thus clear that he could continue to pursue his demands for Mobutu's resignation prior to any negotiated settlement, and the conclusion of a negotiated settlement prior to any ceasefire. Such a position left very little room for the 'hand of reconciliation', precisely the policy which the international community began to pressure him to pursue while they themselves prepared for the evacuation of their own nationals. South Africa took up the challenge, and during a meeting with President Nelson Mandela, Kabila agreed to meet with Mobutu, but declined to set a time or a place, rejecting South Africa as too far away, while continuing his advance on Kinshasa.

On 5 May, Mandela hosted the first meeting between Kabila and Mobutu aboard a South African naval vessel. Mobutu called for the creation of a mutually acceptable transitional government prior to open elections in which everyone could participate. Kabila called for Mobutu to hand over power to the ADFL and assured everyone that there would be no ceasefire until the ADFL reached Kinshasa and formed a government. The search was now on for a face-saving method to remove Mobutu and avoid an armed battle for the capital. The first step in this direction was a Francophone summit in neighbouring Gabon which Mobutu attended and from which, to the surprise of many, he returned. At the same time, Tshisekedi called for a general strike and Kabila travelled to Cape Town, South Africa, where he was received as though he was a head of state. On 17 May, Mobutu agreed to withdraw from active involvement in affairs of state, while retaining the title President, and to leave the country for Togo. At the same time, Kabila declared himself President of

---

[56] The ADFL, which blames De Beers for funding Mobutu, broke the company's diamond purchasing monopoly in Zaire by selling to America Diamond Buyers the right to buy gold and diamonds in ADFL territory – a venture thought to be worth $100,000 per day in Kisingani alone. 'De Beers in secret deal with rebels', *Mail and Guardian*, 18 April 1997. Internet location: http://www.africanews.org/central/zaire/19970418_feat1.ht.

[57] IRIN, Emergency Update, 152, 19–21 April 1997.

[58] Mobutu controlled the production of money supply, which continued to grow with the production of larger notes, driving up domestic prices still further. *International Herald Tribune*, 22 April 1997.

the Democratic Republic of the Congo.

The acquisition of state power by the ADFL raises several fundamental questions which centre on the internal organization of the movement and its relations with other actors in the new Congo, not the least of which concerns the relationship between the Alliance and those parties which, for years, had waged a political struggle against Mobutu. Tension between the two mounted when Kabila announced that, in territory under its control, the ADFL would be the only party permitted to function – a ban effectively extended to the entire country in May. Subsequently, Kabila rejected calls to form a broad-based government by including Etienne Tshisekedi in the cabinet. Protests by Tshisekedi's supporters drew gunfire from the ADFL military and the government declared violators of the ban on public protests 'enemies of the liberation of the Congolese people' who would be 'punished to the fullest extent of the law'.[59] During a subsequent protest, one student chanted that Kabila should be given a chance, but condemned the presence of Rwandans within the ADFL.[60] The ban on political activities was similar to that imposed by Mobutu, though, because of the large Rwandan presence in the ADFL, one protester argued that the ADFL was a dictatorship 'by foreigners'.[61] How the ADFL would reconcile the relationship between its military, which was heavily dominated by ethnic Rwandans (of whatever nationality), and a civilian movement which would need to build a far broader political base if it was to expand its domestic and international political base, was critical to its ability to establish a stable and effective regime.[62]

The issue of civil–military relations also raised the question of whether the ADFL represented a new approach to African independence,[63] or simply a new group which sought power. The reported disappearance of the popular governor of Shaba Province – a strong advocate of regional autonomy – after a meeting with Kabila did little to strengthen the ADFL's democratic reputation, while the treatment of Rwandan refugees near Kisangani raised profound questions about the movement, its military, and Kabila's authority over it. Following their seven-month trek across Zaire, many of the refugees were near death when they arrived in Kisangani and the UNHCR had arranged for them to be airlifted back to Rwanda. Tension between the refugees and their Zairean hosts grew as international assistance to the camps increased, and as supplies destined for them arrived in Kisangani. Violence in the camps, coupled with the looting of international supplies, led the ADFL to cut aid workers off from the camps. By the time an assessment team was permitted back into Kasese, which had housed 50,000 refugees, it was empty.[64] Kofi Annan, the Secretary General of the United Nations, accused Kabila of attempting to kill the refugees by slow starvation,[65] while local farmers reported that mechanical digging

[59] 'Resist Kabila, opposition group urges', *International Herald Tribune*, 28 May 1997.
[60] 'Troops quell protest in Kinshasa', *International Herald Tribune*, 29 May 1997.
[61] *Ibid*.
[62] See Lynne Duke and James Rupert, 'Power behind Kabila reflects Congo war's Tutsi roots', *International Herald Tribune*, 29 May 1997.
[63] See Basil Davidson. 'Why Kabila could be welcome news for Africa', *International Herald Tribune*, 24 April 1997.
[64] IRIN, Emergency Update, 157, 24 April 1997.
[65] '50,000 flee refugee camp in East Zaire', *International Herald Tribune*, 25 April 1997.

machines had been used, perhaps to dig mass graves. These events overshadowed the ADFL's agreement to work with a UN Commission of Enquiry to probe alleged massacres carried out by the Alliance at the beginning of the war and to bring perpetrators to justice.[66] Relations between Kabila and the UN were strained over the issue of the massacres, with Kabila demanding that the UN look into the entire period from the movement of the FGOR into exile until the fall of Mobutu, while the UN sought to focus on the activities of the ADFL in Kisangani. Even after expanding the mandate of the UN team, Kabila blocked them from carrying out their investigation. This move, coupled with his earlier clampdown on the internal opposition, led most Western donors to withhold major pledges of international assistance until the extent of the massacres, and the role of various actors in them, had been determined.[67]

The events in Kisangani in turn hold much of the answer to the question of what happened to the FGOR. As already noted, those who fled westwards from Mugunga and other camps in eastern Zaire in November 1996 included a disproportionate number who were closely associated with the former government and the genocide, desperate to remain beyond the reach of the ADFL. Assuming that massacres did indeed take place as the ADFL caught up with them, members of the FGOR and its forces must have been the intended targets, although by no means all refugees could be equated with the FGOR, and many ordinary refugees, caught up in population movements over which they had no control, are likely to have died as well. Other less conspicuous FGOR members certainly returned with the flood of refugees to Rwanda, while continuing violence in eastern Zaire (now Congo) suggests that some at least may have remained at large there. Some leading members of the genocidal regime found refuge both in nearby African states and elsewhere, running the risk of arraignment before the UN's genocide tribunal in Arusha – a fate decidedly preferable to falling into the hands of the RPF. Whether an organized core of the FGOR continues to operate in the Rwanda/Congo borderlands, orchestrating attacks on the RPF government and its allies, remains at the time of writing uncertain.

Conclusion

The story of the ADFL and the FGOR is one of state creation, decay and recreation in Africa – and of the international consequences of these processes. Zaire, and the Mobutu regime, had been created and kept in place by the international community. In addition to maintaining close ties with the US and later with France, Mobutu's principal domestic task was to control revenue generated from mineral exports which he used to create local patronage networks. The FGOR also sought to use its access to the international community to keep itself in power after it had fled into exile, a flight which was caused by its inability when in power inside

---

[66] IRIN, Emergency Update, 156, 23 April 1997.
[67] James C. McKinley, Jr. with Howard W. French, 'Hidden horrors: a special report on Congo atrocities', *New York Times*, 14 November 1997 and Human Rights Watch/Africa, Report 9:5a, *Democratic Republic of the Congo: What is Kabila Hiding?* (October 1997).

Rwanda to incorporate disaffected groups in society into the state. Once it became clear that Mobutu was losing the backing of his international patrons, the absence of a meaningful domestic political base became clear, and the way was opened for the ADFL to attack. Similarly, when the FGOR lost access to the international community, it lost its ability to generate the resources necessary to pursue its cause. In the absence of a solid political base upon which they could rest, both Mobutu and the FGOR fell.

The most pressing challenge for the ADFL was the creation of a domestic political base and an effective sovereign state domestically, which both Mobutu and the FGOR lacked. The ADFL proved itself capable of defeating a state with little internal support, whose principal international ally was a former government living in exile inside its own borders. The task ahead was to become a government which could provide goods and services to its citizens and make effective demands upon them: in short, the transformation of the institutions of a guerrilla movement into those of effective governance. The extent to which the ADFL incorporated new groups into the state and created an effective domestic political base, would determine the extent to which Zaire could become the Democratic Republic of the Congo in fact, rather than just in name. If the ADFL, together with its regional allies, were to succeed, people in the region could well see no need to work outside the legal realm of the state to pursue their own interests. In short, the creation of domestically effective sovereign states in Rwanda and the Congo would be a critical component in helping to limit the extent to which guerrilla movements remained in the midst of regional politics.

10 STEPHEN ELLIS
Liberia's Warlord Insurgency[1]

On 24 December 1989 some 100 insurgents claiming allegiance to the National Patriotic Front of Liberia (NPFL) attacked a border town in Nimba County from neighbouring Côte d'Ivoire. This was the start of a war which was to last for more than seven years and spawn a confusing number of factions, of which at least seven were still in business by early 1997. In July 1997, victory in a national election by the NPFL leader, Charles Taylor, marked a clear end to the most violent phase of the struggle.

The NPFL fighters, joined by regular Burkinabe soldiers on secondment from their own government, met little resistance from the government's Armed Forces of Liberia (AFL) in their drive towards Monrovia. They advanced, handing out weapons, through areas whose populations had good reason to hate the government of President Samuel Doe, and within a few weeks the NPFL had thousands of armed but untrained civilians alongside its core of trained soldiers, most of whom were former Liberian army men who had deserted and gone into exile years earlier.

It was mainly the newcomers to the NPFL, victims of earlier abuses by the government army and now bent on revenge, who were responsible for the massacre of thousands of people, particularly Krahns and Mandingos, regarded as collaborators with the detested government of Samuel Doe. Doe, himself a Krahn, was a former army sergeant who had come to power via a lower-ranks coup in April 1980. Vying for power with other members of the military junta (most notably Thomas Quiwonkpa, a Gio man from Nimba County) Doe sought the collaboration of the Krahn and Mandingo communities by distributing jobs, commercial opportunities and other largesse to them. It was this which in 1990 made the Krahns and Mandingos so unpopular, especially in Nimba County. Reacting to the NPFL invasion, Doe killed Gio and Mano soldiers in his own army as well as Gio and Mano civilians in Monrovia, reproducing the cycle of ethnic massacres. Even before Doe's death in September 1990, many Krahns and Mandingos had fled from

[1] I am grateful to Christopher Clapham, Béatrice Hibou and Tom Kamara for comments on an earlier draft.

155

the threat of massacre by the NPFL to Sierra Leone and Guinea, where exiled army officers and politicians assembled from among the refugees the United Liberation Movement for Democracy (Ulimo), which in 1991 appeared as a new armed faction. From bases in Sierra Leone, supported by the Freetown government, it fought its way back into Liberia. Like all the militias, Ulimo in turn was soon to split and produce new armed groups.

Throughout mid-1990, as the insurgency came to the attention of the world's media, many Liberians hoped for intervention by the United States. The US, after all, was far more than the Cold War patron of Liberia: it was from America that the founders of the Liberian Republic, the oldest in Africa, had sailed to settle in West Africa in the nineteenth century. But, in the event, when US forces did intervene in June 1990, it was only to evacuate their own and European nationals. With the ending of the Cold War, the US government had lost the incentive to intervene in Liberia and was loath to take up duty as a global policeman.

In any case, it was not clear whom the US government should support if it were to stabilize Liberia. The State Department had for years been exasperated by Doe's corruption and brutality. But the alternative, in mid-1990, was Charles Taylor, the leader of the NPFL, a man wanted by US law enforcement agencies for escaping from a Massachusetts jail, an ally of Libya at the head of an unstable revolutionary force which was committing horrible atrocities. In search of new ways of maintaining international order after the Cold War, Washington encouraged the regional hegemon, Nigeria, to assume responsibility for maintaining peace in its own sub-region. When, on the night of 1–2 August 1990, Iraq invaded Kuwait, any lingering possibility of a US intervention to stop the Liberian war disappeared. The Nigerian government, operating under the umbrella of the Economic Community of West African States (ECOWAS), organized a military intervention force, the ECOWAS Monitoring Group or ECOMOG, which arrived in Liberia in August 1990, and was still present in 1997.

The ECOMOG intervention internationalized the Liberian conflict without putting a stop to the war. On the contrary, whatever the intentions of the Nigerian and other ECOWAS governments at the outset, the conflict created new economic opportunities which ECOMOG itself exploited, making the peace-keeping force a party to the war itself. Outside actors, including factions within ECOMOG, encouraged the emergence of a number of new armed groups within Liberia, such as Ulimo and the misleadingly named Liberia Peace Council (LPC). The result was that the war in Liberia soon became the field of competition of rival cross-border alliances.

Each of the seven or more identifiable armed factions which were active in Liberia by 1997 had its external allies, some of which were also providing soldiers to the ECOMOG peace-keeping force and were the main regional actors in various diplomatic initiatives designed to bring peace. This situation produced powerful conflicts of interest among putative peacemakers as Liberia became a zone of contention among military and commercial elites in Abuja, Abidjan, Conakry and other regional capitals, themselves allied with interest groups as far away as France, Lebanon and Ukraine. Just as, in the distant past, powerful West African kingdoms maintained themselves by raiding the hinterland for slaves, so the Liberian conflict stimulated the growth of a regional economy based on plunder and operated by networks of armed merchants or of warlords[2] with commercial allies. Liberia became a place of armed networks and factions rather than of parties and armies. Within the country, war became a form of business and a way of life, rather than an instrument for furthering any coherent ideological or even ethnic interest. In fact, after the widespread pogroms of 1990, the war lost most of its ethnic character.

This combination of factors defeated numerous peace initiatives by West African governments. One treaty after another broke down as new factions emerged in Liberia, often with the support of groups within various West African governments, and as the fortunes of individual warlords rose and fell. In April 1996, one peace initiative (the thirteenth, by most calculations) collapsed in an orgy of looting in Monrovia as unpaid fighters grabbed what they could and as rival factions struggled for control of the main diamond- and gold-producing areas of the country. By this time the most powerful of the warlords, Charles Taylor, had realized that he would never become president without the support of Nigeria, whose role he had earlier reviled and whose citizens and soldiers his fighters had killed. The Nigerian government, itself brazenly anti-democratic and contemptuous of civilian politicians, offered to the warlords a chance to form a new government if they could disarm at least most of their fighters and agree to an election. In July 1997, Liberians voted massively for Charles Taylor, in the belief that this was the best way of halting the war.[3]

The Origins of the War

In many respects, the origins of the violence which overtook Liberia lie in the coup which overthrew the True Whig government in 1980, making Samuel Doe the first of the country's modern warlords. Doe used his tenure of government to plunder the country's wealth blatantly and brutally; after the bloody suppression of a coup attempt by his rival Thomas Quiwonkpa in 1985, he resorted to a particularly poisonous form of ethnic manipulation which was to have consequences in the ethnic pogroms of 1990.

As thousands of people fled from the threat of massacre by one side or the other in 1990, the AFL and Ulimo were able to rally support by promising to protect Krahns and Mandingos, validating claims that these groups represented ethnic constituencies. But by 1993, at the latest, such claims had become largely spurious as armed factions ceased to represent credibly the interests of any ethnic group or any ideology. All were best identified by reference to the personality and public profile of their leaders and the identity of their external alliances. There was no distinction between the essential aims of the fighters. Most warlords changed alliances, sometimes more than once, and many of the rank and file fighters adhered to more than one group over the course of time.

The emergence of groups contesting for power, whose most obvious feature is

---

[2] On this term, see Quentin Outram, 'It's terminal either way: an analysis of armed conflict in Liberia, 1989–1996', University of Leeds, School of Business and Economic Studies, Discussion Paper E96/21, December 1996, pp. 11–19.

[3] A short chronology to 1996 is in Outram, 'It's terminal'.

their identification with a particular leader rather than with any ethnic identity or ideology, has a long history in Liberia. For decades the country's national politics were marked by a cult of personality centred upon the person of the president of the republic. The True Whig Party system of clientelism reached its height under President William Tubman (1944–71).[4] Tubman's centralization of patronage combined with the great increase in revenue which resulted from the commercial alliances with foreign companies inherent in his Open Door economic policy to produce a political system in which the leader was seen as the personalization of the nation. Several Liberian writers have attributed part of the blame for the malaise in their politics to the development of the cult of the presidency.[5] In fact, as in most patronage systems, the apparent omnipotence of the True Whig patronage machine, inherited by Tubman's successor President William Tolbert (1971–80), hid a variety of factional intrigues and local political struggles. In this case political competition occurred both between the rival families of American-Liberian origin which constituted the national oligarchy, and also within the local political cultures with roots in Liberia's various African societies, habitually referred to by Monrovians as 'country people' or 'tribal people'. The history of the interaction between national politics and those of the various areas of the country outside Monrovia is one in sore need of reinterpretation, and will briefly be referred to further in the present chapter.

The seizure of power by lower-ranking soldiers in 1980, although it marked a key moment in Liberian history, was not intended to disrupt the government patronage machine. On the contrary, Doe, who gradually emerged as the head of the military junta by murdering his former comrades-in-arms, was concerned to continue the workings of the old system subject only to its submission to himself. He had no hesitation in recruiting or rehabilitating certain members of the old elite of American descent which he claimed to have displaced, or employing other American-Liberians in his service. One such, in fact, was Charles Taylor, who became director-general of a government procurement agency under Doe until fleeing the country, accused of embezzlement, in 1983.

The manner of Doe's ascension caused him more than ever to emphasize the cult of the leader, particularly after he had formally assumed the presidency in the rigged election of 1985. It is notable that something similar was eventually to happen to the NPFL, the movement founded by Thomas Quiwonkpa in opposition to Samuel Doe, and later revived by survivors of Quiwonkpa's 1985 coup attempt. The revived NPFL was originally a collection of exiles who had little in common other than their hatred of Doe and his government, and Taylor emerged as the group's president only because he was the one with the best foreign contacts. Yet within a few months of the outbreak of war in 1989 the NPFL, just like the military junta which Doe had headed, was to turn from a collective into a presidential movement as one person murdered his potential rivals. This was a measure of the militarization

---

[4] On the True Whig patronage system, see Christopher Clapham, 'The politics of failure: clientelism, political instability and national integration in Liberia and Sierra Leone', in C. Clapham, ed., *Private Patronage and Public Power: Political Clientelism in the Modern State* (London: Frances Pinter, 1982), pp. 76–92.

[5] W. Nah Dixon, *In Search of a Leader* (Monrovia: publisher unknown, 1993), pp. 2–5; S. Byron Tarr, 'Founding the Liberia Action Party', *Liberian Studies Journal*, Vol. 15, No.1 (1990), pp. 42–3.

of Liberian politics which had taken place in less than ten years as a result of the 1980 coup. No matter how undemocratic Tubman and Tolbert may have been, there was a sharp difference between their autocracy, buttressed by a political patronage machine and using the revenue acquired from foreign corporations doing business in Liberia, and that of a Doe or a Taylor, achieved by the murder of their rivals and fuelled by plunder.

When the NPFL attacked Nimba County in December 1989, few Liberians had heard of the organization and fewer still had any idea who its leaders were. Within days of the attack Taylor phoned the BBC's *Focus on Africa* programme as a spokesman for the NPFL, and he was to become a regular performer on the BBC especially. Revealing a fine talent for public relations, Taylor used the media to build a national and international profile which gave him a vital advantage over other leaders of the NPFL in the early months of the war. Other opponents of Doe who had gone into exile, such as Moses Duopu, a former Minister of Labour who held the post of NPFL secretary-general, held a different view from Taylor of how the NPFL should function. As its forces advanced towards Monrovia during 1990 and opposition leaders began to jockey for places in a new government, Duopu publicly made known his view that the NPFL was run not by Taylor but by an Executive Council which should meet to choose the next president, and announced that he would be a candidate for this position.[6] Duopu attacked Taylor for his extravagantly pro-capitalist pronouncements, which included describing himself to the London *Financial Times* as 'a cold-blooded capitalist'.[7] Moreover, in the early months of the war several well-known public figures took refuge behind NPFL lines to escape the carnage in Monrovia. The most prominent among these was Jackson F. Doe, widely regarded as the real winner of the 1985 presidential election which had been rigged by Samuel Doe (to whom Jackson Doe was not related). Jackson Doe was himself from Nimba County, like many of the NPFL rank and file.

By mid-1990, then, with the NPFL apparently on the verge of taking Monrovia, Taylor found that his leadership of the NPFL was being contested by insiders like Duopu and by figures from outside the organization such as Jackson Doe. To eliminate these rivals, between June and August 1990 Taylor organized the murder of Duopu, Jackson Doe and others.[8] This was the first time, but by no means the last, that the fragility of the NPFL's military hierarchy was to become clear. After the purge of the NPFL leadership in mid-1990 Taylor eyed his generals with suspicion, and over the years several took opportunities to break away and set up their own factions. The NPFL's first major split came as Prince Johnson, a professional soldier and veteran of the 1985 coup, the training officer of the original 100 who had invaded Nimba County in December 1989, abandoned the organization to set himself up as an independent warlord, the first of many to follow this course. Taylor's 1990 purge turned the NPFL into an organization in which factional disputes or rival personal ambitions were resolved by violence rather than by

---

[6] Agence France-Presse despatch, 7 June 1990.

[7] Mobolade Omonijo, *Doe: the Liberian Tragedy* (Ikeja, Nigeria: Sahel Publishing, 1990), p. 29.

[8] The most succinct account of these murders is probably the press conference given by Tom Woweiyu, the former NPFL Defence Minister, in Monrovia on 19 July 1994, printed in *West Africa*, No. 4009, (1-7 August 1994), pp. 1342–4.

properly political means. Since Moses Duopu in particular had challenged Taylor partly on ideological grounds, Taylor's murder of his rival also emptied the NPFL of any real ideological debate. Charles Taylor himself, the holder of a degree in economics from Bentley College in Massachusetts, has never shown serious interest in questions of political ideology and has been notable for the diversity of his external alliances.

Methods such as these are not unique to Charles Taylor or to Liberia. Dictatorships, insurrections and coups have been the currency of West African politics for several decades, and, as Nigeria's President Ibrahim Babangida warned a meeting of his West African peers in 1992, 'Today it is Liberia. Tomorrow it could be any one of the countries represented here.'[9] Underlining the volatile nature of West African politics is the fact that nobody in early 1990 expected the general collapse of the Liberian state which was to occur. The general expectation of both African and foreign diplomats was that the uprising, after the crisis had passed, would lead to a change of government, leaving the machinery of state more or less intact and in the hands of new operators, as had happened from time to time in so many of Liberia's neighbours.

Liberia, however, shared with other countries in the region a profound crisis of legitimacy as patronage-based systems of government allied with overseas business interests failed to deliver economic benefits in new circumstances. Even before Liberia's war, popular dissatisfaction with incumbent governments throughout West Africa had led to the growth of radical populist leaders like Thomas Sankara in Burkina Faso and Jerry Rawlings in Ghana. Expatriate radical militants from all over West Africa, some of them intellectuals and university graduates, others soldiers who had fled after failed coup attempts, had gathered in Libya, whose government saw itself as the natural home of Third World revolutionaries. It was in Libya that Taylor recruited his initial military force, containing not only Liberian army deserters but also Ghanaians, Gambians, Nigerians and others. In 1991 the NPFL, fulfilling the fears of President Babangida and many of his fellow-presidents, indeed spread the Liberian war abroad by its attack on Sierra Leone and its support for the Revolutionary United Front (RUF) there. The RUF, too, was largely the creation of dissidents exiled in Libya. Also among the NPFL's sprinkling of revolutionary adventurers from elsewhere were veterans of the bloody 1981 coup attempt in the Gambia.[10]

The Shadow State[11]

Although Liberia's collapse threatened other states, there was nothing particularly novel about the figure of Charles Taylor. Other heads of state had had broadly similar careers, in the sense of using revolutionary or other ideological credentials to

    [9] Quoted in Ademola Adeleke, 'The politics and diplomacy of peacekeeping in West Africa: the ECOWAS operation in Liberia', *Journal of Modern African Studies*, Vol. 33, No. 4 (1995), p. 577.
    [10] Stephen Ellis, 'Liberia 1989–1994: a study of ethnic and spiritual violence', *African Affairs*, Vol. 94, No. 375 (1995), p. 168.
    [11] Cf. Christopher Clapham, *Africa and the International System: the Politics of State Survival* (Cambridge: Cambridge University Press, 1996), pp. 249–56.

achieve power, and had been similarly ruthless, like Blaise Compaore, President of Burkina Faso, who had murdered his friend Sankara to take power. Taylor's considerable intelligence and suavity enabled him to cultivate such dignitaries, and it was his personal links to heads of state and senior officials in Libya, Burkina Faso and Côte d'Ivoire which, in the vital early months of his campaign, gave him the funds and the weapons which he used to assert his supremacy within the NPFL. Thereafter Taylor kept personal control of commercial matters and entrusted the management of sales of diamonds, wood, gold and other commodities to members of his family and inner circle. Through its military conquests in early 1990, the NPFL had gained control of a large area and hundreds of thousands of people, in effect supplanting the weak bureaucratic state of Liberia with a patrimonial organization whose supreme head, Charles Taylor, used external commercial alliances as an instrument with which to control local social networks, the two being linked through informal markets.[12]

Although the NPFL's government-in-waiting, established in 1990, was a novelty in Liberian history, many of its features had antecedents, notably in the tensions between the logic of patrimonialism and that of bureaucratic government. But whereas the True Whig Party governments which governed Liberia before 1980 had also been patrimonial in nature, they had been able to ensure the modicum of bureaucratic discipline necessary to retain international recognition and to enable a political system which depended on personal patronage to survive changes of generation. It was under Samuel Doe that Liberia for the first time came under the control of a clique more interested in plunder than in managing power to their advantage and transmitting it intact to a successor chosen by political means. In part this was due to a mixture of greed and inexperience on the part of Doe and his inner circle, but it may also be because, as Reno has pointed out, the logic of a 'shadow state' may cause a warlord actually to destroy the bureaucratic state not only through a desire for plunder but also in order to eliminate it as a base for potential rivals.[13]

All the armed factions which emerged after the start of the war were personal militias formed by rival leaders who used external commercial alliances so as to dominate social networks. The resulting entity was then given the superficial appearance of a government-in-waiting or a liberation movement. Ulimo, founded in Freetown in 1991 among Liberians who had fled from the NPFL, was split from its earliest days between rival leaders. The two main Ulimo factions, which by 1992 had taken to carrying out selective murders of each other's personnel, consisted of a small group of Mandingos and of Krahns respectively, both cliques dominated by people who had held official appointments or military commands under Doe. By early 1994 the squabbles at the top of Ulimo had turned into a comprehensive split, with former Information Minister Alhaji Kromah leading one faction (generally labelled Ulimo-K) and the ex-civil servant Roosevelt Johnson the other (Ulimo-J). Perhaps the least faction-ridden of the main warring groups was the AFL, the rump of Doe's old army, and the LPC faction, which was little more than AFL soldiers

---

[12] William Reno, 'Foreign firms and the financing of Charles Taylor's NPFL', *Liberian Studies Journal*, Vol. 18, No. 2 (1993), pp. 175–87.

[13] William Reno, 'The reinvention of an African patrimonial state: Charles Taylor's Liberia', *Third World Quarterly*, Vol. 16, No. 1 (1995), pp. 111–12.

out of uniform. The leaders of both the AFL and the LPC were almost all Krahn, and they were able to capitalize on the fact that the atrocities perpetrated indiscriminately on Krahns in 1990 had the effect of convincing many of them that they needed the protection of one or other armed group if they were to survive. Thus the main Krahn warlords – General Hezekiah Bowen, chief of staff of the AFL, Dr George Boley, president of the LPC, and Roosevelt Johnson, head of one faction of Ulimo – were generally able to coordinate their strategy, despite the rivalry between them, against the greater danger posed by other leading groups, the NPFL and Ulimo-K.

The Causes of Fragmentation

Liberia's collapse was hastened by the decisions and actions of a handful of key players, the most important of whom was Charles Taylor. Particularly fateful was Taylor's rejection of the ECOMOG intervention in August 1990, which set him against the government of Nigeria. Taylor overestimated his own ability to out-manoeuvre his Nigerian enemies, one of several occasions on which he demon-strated a lack of strategic vision and real political skills, as opposed to a mere talent for manoeuvre, which he showed in abundance. By accepting ECOMOG in 1990, Taylor could have become president with Nigerian support since he controlled most of Liberia at that juncture and already had some international backing. His failure to do this meant that, once ECOMOG had intervened to secure Monrovia and had installed a puppet government, the conflict became intractable. Taylor was obliged to rethink his assumption of imminent victory and to make other plans. Each side (ECOMOG and the NPFL) sought to outflank the other by enlisting surrogate forces, Taylor by encouraging the RUF invasion of Sierra Leone in March 1991, and ECOMOG and the government of Sierra Leone by supporting Ulimo as an auxiliary force and, later, contributing to the revival of the AFL as a faction. The resulting *logique de guerre* crippled the Liberian state as an organ of administration and created a new set of economic opportunities based on plunder. By 1995 Taylor had come to accept that he would never become president without Nigerian acquies-cence, but by that time he had lost some of the advantages he held six years earlier.

Looting was a feature of the war from the beginning. 'Many of the Liberian youths who joined Charles Taylor's NPFL to overthrow the Doe administration saw the civil war as an opportunity to acquire properties and riches,' noted the pentecostalist Bishop W. Nah Dixon. 'Their motive was not liberating the people but looting their properties by use of the gun.'[14] The 1989 irruption into Nimba County by the NPFL, and the distribution of arms there, set off a wave of killing in which revenge and looting were inextricably mixed, especially as one of the insurgents' main targets, the Mandingo community, were often traders or small businessmen with cash and goods to hand. Subsequently, unpaid fighters developed a routine approach towards looting. The various warlords, and the foreign businessmen and politicians who supported them, acquired substantial interests in various forms of trade to which their use of armed force gave them access. The

---

[14] Dixon, *In Search of a Leader*, p. 30.

destruction of the peacetime economy resulted in a shortage of mechanized transport, which in turn caused warlords to impress civilians for forced labour as porters. At times, something close to a system of slavery operated whereby armed bands sought to control the movements of civilians and forced them to perform arbitrary unpaid service.

Although the war caused a massive increase in the scale and violence of looting, the use of force (or at least the threat of it implied by political power) to acquire goods illicitly was not new to Liberian public life. True Whig Party governments before 1980 were formed by ministers and public officials who enriched themselves at public expense and used part of the proceeds to run patronage machines. After 1980, Doe and his colleagues had neither the time nor the political base necessary to milk the system as systematically as Tubman and Tolbert had done; moreover, the sustained economic boom and the high commodity prices of the 1950s and 1960s had receded, depriving the government of revenue. One result was much greater use of coercion to acquire wealth, resulting, in the words of one well-informed observer, in 'years of rape and plunder by armed marauders whose ideology is to search for cash and whose ambition is to retain power to accumulate and protect wealth'.[15] Small wonder, then, that the citizens of Nimba County and others who had suffered under Doe's government engaged in a campaign of looting of their own when an opportunity arose. Charles Taylor's hope in 1990 was to displace Doe as soon as possible and assume the presidency himself, at which point he might hope to end the war, receive international recognition and run the state patronage machine in his turn. But the ECOMOG intervention of August 1990 and the murder of Doe the following month thwarted Taylor in this ambition and forced him to improvise a means of existence as an independent authority. Controlling most of the country outside Monrovia, and with access to the valuable resources of gold, diamonds, hardwood, iron ore and other commodities, he discovered that he could export the goods with which to maintain his rule over the territory he called Greater Liberia.[16] Other warlords – of the LPC, Ulimo-J, Ulimo-K and others – vied for control of the most productive areas. There were large reserves of gold, diamonds and hardwood to work, although these were largely finite resources. The looting of consumer goods, the destruction of infra-structure for exportable scrap metal and other forms of pillaging diminished as the quantity of lootable goods declined, and as foreign aid agencies learned the folly of importing goods which would only fuel the war. Hence, the peace process of 1996–7 was facilitated by the warlords' realization that looting by force had become subject to diminishing returns, and that a new political dispensation might open up new economic possibilities.

Many ECOMOG soldiers derived incomes of their own from similar means. The Nigerian contingent soon developed a particular reputation for rapaciousness. ECOMOG soldiers enriched themselves through plunder and receipt of bribes while senior Nigerian officials used funds earmarked for the expeditionary force, according to one Nigerian critic, as 'an excuse to engage in all kinds of extra-

[15] Amos Sawyer, *Effective Immediately: Dictatorship in Liberia 1980–1986: a Personal Perspective*, Liberia Working Group Paper No. 5 (Bremen, Germany: Liberia Working Group, 1987), p. 8.
[16] Reno, 'Foreign firms'.

budgetary spending, secret deals and corrupt practices'.[17] Senior officers of ECOMOG supplied various factions with weapons and other war material in return for looted goods or the exportable produce of the country.[18] Although many Monrovians made a sharp distinction between the practices of the Nigerian and other contingents, often singling out Ghanaian troops as the most orderly and the least venal, it is clear that the would-be peacemakers of ECOMOG themselves profited from the continuation of the war. The security which they brought to Monrovia was paid for by stripping the country's assets.

Nor was the profit motive limited only to foreign forces which actually occupied territory in Liberia. As long as Charles Taylor maintained a rear base in Côte d'Ivoire there was money to be made in supplying him with weapons and other necessities and brokering the exports of Liberia. Senior officials of the Ivorian government and associates of President Henri Konan Bedié made money from commercial deals linked to various Liberian factions,[19] just as various courtiers of his predecessor Félix Houphouët-Boigny had done. In 1995 one outraged Ivorian customs officer wrote an open letter to the press accusing a local administrator whom he named of trafficking with the LPC faction and of ordering the murder of customs officers who attempted to intercept the illicit trade.[20] Other Ivorian officials, with protection in high places, were reported to own rubber plantations inside NPFL-held territory.[21] On the north-western side of Liberia, similar relationships, particularly concerning diamonds, developed between senior Guinean officials and the Ulimo-K militia which they supported. Mandingo traders, most numerous in Guinea but with commercial connections in Liberia and elsewhere in West Africa, formed a financial link between the Liberian conflict and other insurrections, in Mali and even Senegal.[22]

The International Dimension

The war in Liberia has been instrumental in a larger redefinition of commercial and political space throughout West Africa. Since the colonial period, the region has been divided officially into French-speaking and English-speaking states, corresponding to discernible fields of commercial and political influence. Most of West Africa's French-speaking countries have remained closely aligned to the former metropolitan power and, in particular, have continued to use as their currency the CFA franc, which has a fixed rate of exchange with the French franc.

From the time of the Nigerian civil war of 1967–70, in which Côte d'Ivoire

[17] Beko Ransome-Kuti, quoted in Baffour Ankomah, 'The killing of Brian Garnham', *New African* (April 1997), p. 46.

[18] Josh Arinze, 'They looted my country', *Tell* (Lagos), 3 July 1995, pp. 24–7; Stephen Ellis, 'Liberators or looters?', *BBC Focus on Africa*, Vol. 5, No. 4 (October–December 1994), p. 14.

[19] 'Trafic du latex libérien par des Barons du PDCI', *Le nouvel horizon* (Abidjan), No. 253 (21 July 1995).

[20] *La Voie* (Abidjan), No. 1148 (22–23 July 1995).

[21] Freedom Neruda, 'Un lourd tribut', *La Voie*, No. 1110 (8 June 1995).

[22] Author's interviews in Conakry, April 1995. Cf. Barki Gbanaboma, 'The Guinea connection', *West Africa*, No. 3919 (26 October–1 November 1992), p. 1823.

supported the breakaway of Biafra from Nigeria, the rivalry between the French-speaking West African bloc and the English-speaking countries, Nigeria especially, was impelled more by economic than political factors. The formation of ECOWAS in 1975 represented an attempt by Nigeria, then enjoying a massive influx of new oil wealth, to create a common market of which Nigeria would be the centre. Despite the failure of ECOWAS as an economic unit, the sheer size of the Nigerian economy upset the stability of the CFA franc used in neighbouring countries. Particularly after English-speaking West African states had adopted World Bank-supported liberal economic policies in the 1980s, devaluing currencies which were not linked to a 'hard' currency like the French franc, the discrepancy between the devalued Nigerian naira and the over-valued CFA franc induced Nigerian traders to change their naira, legally or otherwise, into CFA francs which could be traded internationally. Low-priced Nigerian goods or re-exports flooded the region, very often through the mechanisms of the international underground economy rather than through formal trade structures.[23]

Nigeria was a major re-exporter of goods as well as a source of domestic manufactures sold throughout West Africa. In both fields Nigerian exports included large quantities of 'pirated' goods (cosmetics, medical drugs, electrical goods and so forth), often marketed under internationally known brand names without permission, and sometimes using adulterated ingredients. From the late 1970s Nigeria also became a major importer and re-exporter of narcotics, and Nigerian criminal syndicates used facilities in neighbouring countries for the transport of contraband goods as well as for money laundering. Even before the outbreak of war in 1989 Liberia, whose own currency was traditionally the US dollar, had become an important regional centre of money laundering and assumed a significant role in the underground economy which had burgeoned in West Africa since the 1970s.[24] For decades Liberia had been an attractive site for offshore transactions, most notably the registration of foreign-owned ships and offshore companies. President Tubman was a business associate of at least one major international criminal, a banker to the US mafia and the Israeli secret services.[25]

Even before the outbreak of the war in Liberia created new opportunities for smuggling guns, diamonds, drugs and so forth, the international underground economy was of rapidly increasing importance in the configuration of power in West African states. Heads of state and others with access to the machinery of government could use their positions to engineer commercial relationships which were either illegal in nature or which were more lucrative or of greater political usefulness when carried out clandestinely.[26] Among those who developed a business relationship with Samuel Doe was President Ibrahim Babangida, who

---

[23] Abdoulaye Diagne, 'Les travaux de recherche sur l'UMOA: un aperçu', *Africa Development*, Vol. 16, Nos 3–4 (1991), pp. 5–26; for a specific case study, Emmanuel Gregoire, 'Les chemins de la contrebande: étude des reseaux commerciaux en pays hausa', *Cahiers d'études africaines*, Vol. 31, No. 4 (1991), pp. 509–32.

[24] For a list of banks operating in Monrovia in 1990, see *Liberian Studies Journal*, Vol. 15, No. 1 (1990), pp. 140–1.

[25] Robert Lacey, *Little Man: Meyer Lansky and the Gangster Life* (London: Arrow Books, 1991), p. 309.

[26] Cf. Stephen Ellis and Janet MacGaffey, 'Africa's unrecorded international trade: some conceptual and methodological problems', *African Studies Review*, Vol. 39, No. 2 (1996), pp. 19–41.

became a part-owner of the Liberian national oil company. According to Charles Taylor, Doe was also a business partner of Gambia's President Sir Dawda Jawara.[27]

The personal interests which linked various West African heads of state were both the sinews of political relationships and a reflection of national aspirations, like the dynastic marriages and alliances of European princes of old. As Presidents Babangida and Doe cemented an alliance with their joint business ventures, so a rival potentate, President Houphouët-Boigny of Côte d'Ivoire, had a similar system of personal foreign relations. His god-daughter had married A. B. Tolbert, the son of Doe's predecessor. The Tolberts, father and son, both perished during the 1980 putsch which brought Doe to power, after which A. B. Tolbert's widow married Captain Blaise Compaore, later president of Burkina Faso. The Doe–Babangida axis during the late 1980s was therefore seen by Houphouët-Boigny not only as the perpetuation of the personal humiliation he had suffered when the upstart Doe had been responsible for the murder of his son-in-law, but also as the reversal of a previous diplomatic alliance linking Abidjan and Monrovia. The ramifications of these alliances went beyond the West Africa region. A former head of the French external secret service has recalled how Houphouët-Boigny in his last years, embittered by failure in his monumental struggle for domination of the world cocoa market,[28] was convinced that the economic difficulties faced by the Ivorian economy were engineered in large part by Anglo-American business interests working through Nigeria.[29] Houphouët-Boigny also attributed the ECOWAS intervention of August 1990, accurately enough, to US pressure.[30] Control of Liberia could bring access to the iron ore deposits in Nimba County, the most valuable in the world, coveted by both French and other European and US investors.[31] Hence Houphouët-Boigny's support for the NPFL insurgency in the early months of the war was in part intended to wrest control of an economic resource, and in this he had the support particularly of French businesses anxious to gain access to Liberia's raw materials.

By late August 1990, each of the two major armed forces then deployed in Liberia (the Nigerian-dominated ECOMOG and the Ivorian-backed NPFL) was working closely with a regional ally whose interests were partly political and partly economic. The Nigerian expeditionary force later formed alliances with various local warlords who emerged after 1990 (especially the Krahn warlords Roosevelt Johnson, George Boley and the collective leadership of the AFL), while Guinea's interests were articulated through Ulimo-K. Liberia became a prime example of how a collapsed state may lose political autonomy but extend its sphere of economic influence as an informal economy comes to dominate.[32] A major realignment of

[27] 'Face to face with Charles Taylor', interview by Baffour Ankomah, *Ghanaian Chronicle*, 12–18 October 1992, pp. 6–7.

[28] Jean-Louis Gombeaud, Corinne Moutet and Stephen Smith, *La Guerre du cacao : histoire secrète d'un embargo* (Paris: Calmann-Levy 1990).

[29] Claude Silberzahn with Jean Guesnil, *Au Coeur du secret: 1500 jours aux commandes de la DGSE, 1989–1993* (Paris: Fayard, 1995), p. 206.

[30] *Ibid.*, p. 206.

[31] Patrick de Saint-Exupéry and Sophie Roquelle, 'La montagne de fer que convoite l'Elysée', *Figaro*, 8 January 1992.

[32] William I. Zartman, ed., *Collapsed States: the Disintegration and Restoration of Legitimate Authority* (Boulder: Lynne Rienner, 1995), p. 9.

alliances in 1995 brought Taylor closer to Nigeria while different factions in Côte d'Ivoire continued to support either the NPFL or the LPC.

Social Breakdown

The origins of most civil wars can be traced, at least in part, to some shift in society which frustrates certain people and social groups in their expectations; their ultimate recourse is to violence.[33] In Liberia, the process by which an oligarchy of American-Liberian families cemented alliances with international business concerns and extended its reach into the country's hinterland in the early twentieth century produced profound social changes. The consequences convinced even President Tubman, the great architect of the True Whig system, that in order to secure the power he wielded in Monrovia he would have to offer further opportunities to the hinterland elites which had emerged from the earlier system of indirect rule and as a consequence of missionary education. He dubbed this the Unification Policy. It is widely recognized that the downfall of his successor, President Tolbert, and the putsch of 1980 were closely related to the political strains produced by this process. Individuals from outside the American-Liberian elite who aspired to a share in national political life through their completion of an elite education (including the later warlords George Boley and Alhaji Kromah), were a product of the True Whig Party's change in policy towards the hinterland. So too were the far greater numbers of people who had grown up in hinterland areas without ever achieving the level of higher education necessary to penetrate the ranks of the national elite, but who aspired to the opportunities provided by wage labour in the mines and plantations. Their expectations were dashed by the economic depression and the change in the terms of trade which affected the country, like other parts of Africa, during the 1970s.[34]

President Tolbert, Tubman's successor, aimed to create other new employment opportunities for the excluded. Crucially, one of the measures he chose was a change in the pattern of army recruitment, which had a notable effect on the composition and political stance of the military at an early stage.[35] Doe and those who took power with him in 1980 were broadly typical of a generation of young men who had entered the army with certain expectations, and found their path to promotion blocked by an officer corps dominated by American-Liberian families. The ambitions of this group, given full rein after the 1980 coup, and allied to the factional rivalries set in motion by the coup, transformed the AFL from the servant of the ruling party into a near-piratical establishment. Former street urchins who had risen from nowhere comported themselves with arrogant brutality and a complete disregard for the norms of any sort of government.[36]

[33] Cf. Ted Robert Gurr, *Why Men Rebel* (Princeton NJ: Princeton University Press, 1970).
[34] Robert Kappel, Werner Korte and Friedegund Mascher, eds, *Liberia: Underdevelopment and Political Rule in a Peripheral Society* (Hamburg: Institut für Afrika-kunde, 1986); Max Bankole Jarrett, 'Civil War in Liberia: a manipulation of chaos?', MA thesis, School of Oriental and African Studies, London, 1996, pp. 39–49.
[35] Sawyer, *Effective Immediately*, p. 5.
[36] *Ibid.*, pp. 4–8.

The events of 1990 illustrated further the potential consequences of arming unemployed and disaffected youths. Taylor armed hundreds of people from Nimba County, including young boys orphaned by the government counter-insurgency campaign who were formed into the NPFL's Small Boy Units, the first generation of Liberian child soldiers. Doe responded by arming indiscriminately Krahn and Mandingo civilians who could be counted upon to resist the NPFL, which was massacring people from their communities. Armed adolescents recruited by one or another faction were generally responsible for the most arbitrary atrocities of the war. War captains often kept their young fighters dosed with cane spirit, marijuana and cheap amphetamines, known as 'bubble'. Fighters could attack people on a mere whim.[37] 'It's a fratricidal war,' noted the US organization Human Rights Watch. 'A poor or low status villager joins, say, Ulimo. Then he kills the teacher who flunked him, the man who beat him. Other women were raped by friends of their sons.'[38]

Such discipline as existed in the fighting bands was harsh, with captains beating and torturing their own combatants as punishment. A survey of 354 high school children in Monrovia conducted by the World Health Organization in February 1994 reported that 61 per cent had seen someone tortured, killed or raped. Seventy-seven per cent had lost a friend or relative in the war, which in some cases caused extreme trauma.[39] 'It's a children's war,' according to the chief of operations of the United Nations Observer Mission. 'Kids get promoted in rank for committing an atrocity; they can cut off someone's head without thinking. The troops move into a village; they take everything and kill and rape. They stay there a couple of weeks and then move on.'[40] One man, a chief, recalled bitterly:[41]

> There was a time when we sent our children to the bush, where they learned to respect their elders.[42] With the war, we cannot send our children to the bush. It's too dangerous. None of the children have been initiated.... We have no jails for our bad children. We have no forest where we can send bad children. We have to live with them.

Some young fighters recognized their own exclusion from any wider society, like two soldiers of the NPFL who became accomplished performers of American-style rap music, calling themselves MC Ram Dee (aged 15) and Colonel Mike Maclean (aged 16):[43]

> Like most young Liberian fighters they can escape reality at will and pass into an imaginary world whose contours appear to be shaped by violent American films where the heroes are rapping black narcotics barons.
>
> Colonel Mike laid down the rap rhythm, a booming sound resonating through the bush and solely achieved with his mouth and his two hands, the left one of which is always covered in an oven glove, perhaps for improved percussion.
>
> Ram Dee started up.

[37] Leonard Brehun, *Liberia: the War of Horror* (Accra: Adwinsa, 1991), *passim*.
[38] Human Rights Watch Africa, *Easy Prey: Child Soldiers in Liberia* (New York: 1994), p. 18.
[39] *Ibid.*, p. 16.
[40] *Ibid.*, p. 32.
[41] Quoted by Jeffrey Goldberg, 'A war without purpose in a country without identity', *New York Times* colour supplement, 22 January 1995, p. 39.
[42] This is a reference to the initiation schools organized by the secret societies, Poro (for men) and Sande (for women).
[43] Nick Kotch, 'Rebel rappers join the cast at Liberia's war front', Reuters Dispatch, 1 April 1993.

I am a rebel
I fought off the trouble
I took in the bubble [amphetamines]
I said double trouble. I'm a man who's not stable.

Stateless Societies

It is only with hindsight that it becomes easier to detect the underlying patterns which form a given historical context. At the same time, the study of deeper historical patterns carries risks of its own, one of which is that it can easily create an impression of determinism: what actually happened, had to happen. In fact, the individual decisions of Doe, Taylor and others, as well as coincidental events in other parts of the world, played a crucial part in prolonging the war in 1990 at a point when it might easily have been curtailed.

The actual sequence of events, depending as they did on the conjuncture of a variety of factors, occurred in a historically constituted society, one whose attitudes, beliefs and values were rooted in cultural patterns inherited from the past, to constitute Liberia's 'governmentality'. In considering the ideas and dispositions of which this governmentality consists, it is necessary to recall the longer history of the area marked on the map as Liberia. This includes the history of Monrovia, the American settlement on the coast whose leading families dominated the True Whig Party and founded the Republic of Liberia. But it also includes the much larger territory of the Liberian hinterland, whose history prior to the twentieth century has generally been recorded as that of what Liberians call the 'tribal people'. The incorporation in the early twentieth century of the vast majority of the population of this area into a putative modern state (or, in other terms, their subjugation to the political elite in Monrovia) created specific patterns of relations between power holders and others, and specific traditions of political leadership, which continue to affect Liberia today.

One aspect of the historical dynamics affecting the ways in which elites have been formed, and an important one for the present discussion, is suggested by the many well-attested historical examples from various parts of Liberia before the twentieth century of young men successful in battle using plunder to reward their followers, and eventually rising to become leaders of some description.[44] (We know of no cases of women doing this, which is not to say that they had no role in traditional politics.) There is an obvious echo of this historical tradition in the practices of present-day warlords. This is not tantamount to saying that history is repeating itself, or that Liberians have reverted to doing things the way they did a century ago. The interest of the comparison between the activities of modern Liberian warlords, one of whom has a doctorate from an American university and several of whom have university degrees, and those of a hundred years or more ago, is that it suggests the existence of dynamics of Liberian history which shape political

---

[44] Svend E. Holsoe, 'Zolu Duma, ruler of the Southern Vai, 17??–1828: a problem in historical interpretation', *Liberian Studies Journal*, Vol. 15, No. 1 (1990), pp. 91–108; cf. Richard M. Fulton 'The Kpelle traditional political system', *Liberian Studies Journal*, Vol. 1, No. 1 (1968), p. 15.

leadership but which have often been obscured in the extensive literature on modernization and development. Deeper consideration of the way in which these historical trends have been transmitted would require a more extensive essay than the few remarks which follow.[45]

In the so-called stateless societies which abounded in much of Liberia before the twentieth century, political leadership above the level of households was often acquired by ambitious young men who could achieve a degree of power by their own enterprise, especially in war, but who were unable to turn this into any form of institutional hegemony.[46] Much of northern Liberia was in a constant state of petty warfare before the present century: raids for slaves and rivalry between towns were an important mechanism of political and economic regulation in the societies of that time and place, which had little or no tradition of durable, centralized political authority.[47] Clearly, there is a vast difference between the generally small-scale wars of four or more generations ago – whose size, duration and destructiveness were regulated by custom, by the institutional control of the Poro and Sande and other secret societies, and by the prevailing technology of war – and the massive destruction of the war of the 1990s. This change of scale occurred as a result of the conquest of the hinterland of Liberia by the forces of the republic in the early twentieth century, after which the government in Monrovia suppressed the practice of inter-town warfare. In doing so it eliminated many of the traditional mechanisms in stateless societies for individuals to rise to prominence and for small political units to combine for specific purposes, including defence and offence, in larger agglomerations. Instead, the hegemony of the republic provided new mechanisms for ambitious individuals to rise through access to new patronage systems dominated by the national government, and especially by the manipulation of notions of ethnicity and tenure of the administrative rank of chief, which the True Whig government turned into a salaried post. After the implementation of President Tubman's Unification Policy, further opportunities were created for ambitious people from outside the American-Liberian elite. Whether these opportunities were able to satisfy the demands they anticipated depended crucially on the success of the central government in managing its alliances with foreign businesses which sought access to Liberian raw materials. As one far-sighted analyst observed at the time, 'Few have recognized the character of the forces which have been unleashed by President Tubman's Unification Policy or identified them with processes which have been at work in Liberian culture throughout the history of the nation.'[48]

The incorporation of local societies into the ambit of Liberian politics enlarged the scale of operation of provincial notables by placing local politics within a national framework, itself enshrined in international law, whose ultimate arbiter was the President of the Republic, formally regarded as the supreme patron. It became

---

[45] Something of the sort was attempted almost three decades ago by Warren d'Azevedo. See his four-part series 'A tribal reaction to nationalism', *Liberian Studies Journal*, Vol. 1, No. 2 (1969), pp. 1–22; Vol. 2, No. 1 (1969), pp. 43–63; Vol. 2, No. 2 (1970), pp. 99–115; Vol. 3, No. 1 (1970-1), pp. 1–19.

[46] cf Robin Horton, 'Stateless societies in the history of West Africa', in J. F. Ade Ajayi and Michael Crowder, eds, *History of West Africa*, 2 vols, 3rd edition (Harlow: Longman, 1985), I, pp. 87–128.

[47] David G. Blanchard, 'The impact of external domination on the Liberian mano economy', PhD thesis, Indiana University, 1973, pp. 143–56.

[48] D'Azevedo, 'A tribal reaction to nationalism', Part I, p. 1.

impossible for ambitious individuals to achieve success through local war, now stigmatized as rebellion, or through the acquisition or sale of slaves, now illegal, but they could do so by participating in a patronage system in which coercion and forced labour played a leading role. Old factional struggles between rival towns or households were now incorporated into the administrative structures provided by the Liberian state. 'Processes of tribal territorial expansion and consolidation, interrupted more than a century ago', noted d'Azevedo in 1969, 'have reappeared within the context of national administrative policy and under the banner of national unification.'[49] Factional struggles occurred both between rival families of the American–Liberian elite which governed until 1980, and also in local or 'tribal' politics, reflecting the interests of local groups. After Samuel Doe and his comrades seized power in April 1980, the spirit of factionalism among the indigenous peoples escaped the institutional controls which had previously contained them.

This does not mean that Liberia's war was inevitable. The purpose of referring to the pre-colonial past, and the manner in which Monrovia secured the allegiance of the indigenous peoples of the hinterland over a long period, is to suggest only that Liberia's collapse, actually brought about by a conjuncture of events national and international and as the consequence of individual judgements and actions, is fully comprehensible only by reference to the *longue durée* of West African history. Just as a man who has been initiated into the Poro society bears the scars of the ritual throughout his life, to indicate that he has been eaten by the spirit of the forest, so does Liberia bear the scars of its own initiation into the modern family of nations.

[49] D'Azevedo, 'A tribal reaction to nationalism', Part I, p. 4.

11

IBRAHIM ABDULLAH & PATRICK MUANA
The Revolutionary United Front
of Sierra Leone

A Revolt
of the Lumpenproletariat

After waging a brutal and protracted war against three successive regimes, the Revolutionary United Front of Sierra Leone (RUF/SL) triumphantly marched into Freetown on 25 May 1997 amidst anarchy, mayhem and widespread looting.[1] The armed insurgency which began on 23 March 1991 had in six years displaced more than half the country's population and resulted in an estimated 30,000 deaths. A peace agreement, signed on 30 November 1996 by President Ahmad Tejan Kabba of Sierra Leone and Corporal Foday Sankoh of the RUF, failed to bring an end to the war. The RUF leadership subsequently became fractured, as a result of the peace plan – about which its military wing was ambivalent – and its leader was 'deposed' and subsequently incarcerated in Lagos, Nigeria, where he had gone in pursuit of the much-needed peace.

Central to an understanding of the war in Sierra Leone is the role of alienated youth, especially alienated lumpen youth in the urban and rural areas, for whom combat appears to be a viable survival alternative in a country with high levels of urban unemployment, where the economy is dominated by a precious minerals sector in long-term decline. This chapter discusses the evolution of the RUF and the dynamic of the civil war.[2] The analysis is structured in parts: an account of the background and emergence of the RUF; a discussion of the dynamics of the conflict; and an evaluation of the RUF as a guerrilla movement.

---

[1] On the *coup d'état* of 25 May 1997, see the following: Steve Riley, 'Sierra Leone: the militariat strikes again', *Review of African Political Economy*, No. 72 (1997), pp. 287–92; Lansana Gberie, 'Sierra Leone: a "militariat" coup?', in Ibrahim Abdullah and Yusuf Bangura, eds, *African Development*, Vol. 22, Nos 2 and 3 (1997), special issue on 'Youth Culture and Political Violence: The Sierra Leone Civil War'; A. B. Zack-Williams, 'Kamajors, "sobels" and the militariat: civil society and the return of the military in Sierra Leonean politics', *Review of African Political Economy*, No. 73 (1997), pp. 373–98; Ibrahim Abdullah, 'Kamajos, "sobels" and the militariat: a critique of Zack-Williams', *Leonenet: A Discussion of Sierra Leonean Issues* (Leonenet@mituma.mit.edu, 1 December 1997).

[2] See Paul Richards, 'Rebellion in Liberia and Sierra Leone: a crisis of youth?' in Oliver Furley, ed., *Conflict in Africa* (London: I. B. Tauris, 1995); Richards, *Fighting for the Rain Forest: War, Youth and Resources in Sierra Leone* (Oxford: James Currey, 1996). For a critique of Richards, see Ibrahim Abdullah, 'Violence, youth culture and war: a critical reading of Paul Richards', *Leonenet*, 19 May 1996; Yusuf Bangura, 'Understanding the political and cultural dynamics of the Sierra Leone war: a critique of Paul Richards' *Fighting for the Rain Forest'* in Abdullah and Bangura, *African Development*.

The Background to the Rebellion

Youth culture in Sierra Leone

The roots of the RUF lie in Freetown, where a rebellious youth culture began to evolve in the 1940s, based on the lumpen 'rarray boys'. These first-generation lumpens were predominantly foot soldiers for the politicians of the time. Due to defective education and an ill-formed political consciousness, they were hardly aware of their political manipulation. Mostly unlettered, these young lumpens were predominantly second-generation city residents.[3] Their popular resort was the *pote*. *Potes* are peri-urban spaces constructed around the *odelay* (masquerade). Lumpen habitués were known for their anti-social behaviour – marijuana smoking, petty theft and violence – that put them at odds with the community. Their periodic carnivals on public holidays were always under the watchful eyes of the police. Permits were needed to 'pull debel', first from the city officials and later from the police.[4] Revelry and riot alienated them from the sober citizenry; they were a good-for-nothing bunch, best avoided.

This picture of lumpen culture began to change in the late 1960s and early 1970s, when middle-class youths and other participants entered this popular cultural milieu and became key players. The character and composition of the *pote* was transformed, and *odelays* emerged as a more reputable element in the urban cultural landscape. Yet the change was replete with all the contradictory tendencies inherent in lumpens as a social category. Politicians continued to try to control the wilder elements, seeking a ready supply of thugs to do their dirty work, at the same time as the emergence of middle-class youths as keen participants in periodic carnivals transformed the *pote* from an abode of anti-social elements to an arena for a more broad-based political socialization.[5] Most of the middle-class youth element were still in high school but participated in the drug culture and gradually absorbed the mannerisms of the emerging popular culture. Others 'dropped out' of school entirely, following the footsteps of the original 'rarray boys'. This period coincided with the arrival of reggae music, and a definite turn to the political.

The influence of music was at first local – the beat was that of local bands, drugs and political talk, starting in 1971 with Purple Haze, a Freetown group, and Super Combo from Bo, later followed by Afric Jessips, Superb Seven (from Liberia) and Sabanoh '75. Of all these groups in the early 1970s, it was Super Combo that 'became youth champions' of the rebellious culture.[6] The reggae music of Bob Marley, Peter Tosh and Bunny Wailer, and the more directly political lyrics of West African musicians like Fela Anikulapo-Kuti and later Sonny Okosun, added a further dimension to the repertoire of youth rebelliousness. Liberation struggles

---

[3] Ibrahim Abdullah, 'Context, culture and crisis: changing identities of urban youth in Sierra Leone,1945–1992', forthcoming.

[4] Masquerade is popular referred to as 'debel'; James Nunley, *Moving with the Face of the Devil* (Urbana: University of Illinois Press, 1987).

[5] 'Youths held at ministerial building', *Sierra Leone Daily Mail* (Freetown), 1 January 1969.

[6] Chris Stapleton and Chris May, *African All-Stars: The Pop Music of a Continent* (London: Quartet, 1987), p. 52.

against settler colonialism in Southern Africa also contributed to the development of a 'culture of resistance'. The *pote* became an arena for political discussions centred on 'the system'. 'System dread', a refrain from popular reggae music of the period, became a slogan and rallying call for alienated youth, mostly unemployed. The RUF leader, Foday Sankoh, recently echoed this discourse in an interview: 'I said when I come out [from prison] I will organize the system.'[7]

The popularity of marijuana – the drug of choice – brought many participants to the *pote*. *Pote* language began to filter into mainstream society. Lumpen youth culture was suddenly at the cutting edge of the development of Krio language, the vocabulary expanding to incorporate *pote* terms for gambling, petty theft and hustling. 'Rarray boy' now became 'service man', complete with a new and spreading 'militant' language and iconography of resistance. In the 1970s the group included many high school drop-outs and a handful of unemployed 'O' and 'A' level leavers. Some later went to university (Fourah Bay and Njala College), but the others joined the city's swelling army of unemployed youth. As a group they knew the outline of the history of the slave trade and the dehumanization of the African it entailed, and could make connections between the colonial past and neo-colonial present, generally espousing some form of pan-Africanism. *Pote* discussions in this period were spiced with liberal helpings of Marcus Garvey, Kwame Nkrumah, Wallace-Johnson, and at times Haile Selassie. Some of the *pote* types had read a little Frantz Fanon and Walter Rodney, bits of Che Guevara and Fidel Castro, swallowing undigested passages of Marx and Lenin from cheap or free volumes from the Soviet Progress Publishers.[8]

Student politics

By the early 1980s the university students in the *pote* had become a respectable reference group for their more unfortunate brothers, their prestige enhanced by their role in the 1977 demonstrations against the All People's Congress (APC) government. In the *pote* code of honour, an extension of the *bra–bobor* (patron–client) relationship) found in the wider society, special regard was given to the *pote*-frequenting 'service man' who was also a university student. Their more unfortunate brothers listened to them with respect as they preached, smoked and politicized from the safe confines of the *pote*. In this environment, a change from 'service man' to *man dem* took place.[9] Camaraderie came full circle; 'one love' and 'brotherhood' became the new slogans of the group, apparent in the popular support the students received for their 1977 actions, notwithstanding APC youth wing attempts to mobilize the 'lumpens' against the students. Here we have a vantage point from which the series of student protests in the 1980s become intelligible. Students immersed in the rebellious youth culture became the articulate mouthpiece of a disaffected youth cohort attacking APC rule and calling for fundamental change.

[7] Interview with Foday Sankoh, 'The war would have started in 1988', in *Concord Times*, 10 December 1996.

[8] See Ishmail Rashid, 'Subaltern reactions: student radicals and lumpen youth in Sierra Leone, 1977–1992', forthcoming; Abdullah and Bangura, *Africa Development*.

[9] This change signified a collective identity: *man dem* refers to the group as opposed to the individual.

One of the first student groups to organize opposition to the APC was the maligned Gardener's Club, central to a number of demonstrations in the late 1970s and early 1980s. During the 1980s, however, other politically oriented student groups had emerged: the Green Book study club, the Juche Idea group, the Socialist Club and the Pan African Union (Panafu). These groups debated strictly political matters and sought to use the student union as an effective medium to channel grievances at national level. Some of these groups eschewed the drug culture, a central feature of the more rebellious world of the *pote*. Students had earlier been involved in political protest – against the One-Party Regime proposal of Sir Albert Margai, for example – but only as foot soldiers. What was distinctive about the events in 1977 is that they were planned and led by the radical students, received popular support, and forced Siaka Stevens to make concessions. The protests exposed the fragility of the regime.

The lesson of student power was not forgotten as the country entered the turbulent 1980s. Dwindling mining revenues, worsened by rampant smuggling, caused a sharp economic downturn, exacerbated by lavish spending on the 1980 Organization of African Unity (OAU) conference. Student scholarships and spending on health and social services declined. The swelling ranks of the young unemployed fuelled subversive discourse in the *pote*. Muted talk of organized protest in 1977 now gave way to open talk of revolution. How this revolution was to be prosecuted was never systematically discussed, nor were other options explored. But talk of revolution, vague and distorted as it was, remained alive in the discourse of rebellious youth. The language shifted from *man dem* to 'comrade', and finally to 'brothers and sisters', symptomatic of change among the *pote* intellectuals as well as among numerous study groups in Freetown, Bo, Kenema, Njala and Kono. From this period anti-imperialist slogans became an element in the iconography of youth.

Meanwhile there had been a sharp deterioration of relations between students and the administration on the Fourah Bay College (FBC) campus. Student demonstrations in January 1984 led to a three-month lock-out. A Commission of Enquiry report apparently favourable to the student position was never published.[10] By 1985 the administration had taken upon itself the task of disciplining students on extra-academic grounds to keep state interference to a minimum. The appointment of an ex-police chief, Jenkin Smith, as warden of students reflected the change of policy. It was in this context that a radical student leadership emerged to channel accumulated student grievances. The movement was a coalition of student groups with a populist platform attractive to radicals as well as democrats. The Mass Awareness and Participation (MAP) student union president, Alie Kabba, was elected unopposed, while away in Libya attending the annual Green Book celebrations. MAP was a loose coalition involving members of the Green Book club, the Gardener's Club, Panafu and the Socialist Club. Its fierce, at times adventurist, rhetoric alarmed the administration at FBC. A product of links with the world of the *pote*, the new union leadership was no longer reactive; imbued with a growing sense of the power of youth as a political force, it was prepared to seize the initiative. Anti-government posters and graffiti were spawned all over campus and city. A

---

[10] The 1984 Kutubu Commission Report.

people's tribunal adjudicated between students and regulated bad behaviour – an experiment in popular government reflecting alleged 'People Power'. Such activities, along with rumours that the leadership was sponsored by the Libyans, did not endear it to the authorities.

The alleged Libyan link led to the expulsion and suspension of 41 students in 1985. It was claimed that a group of students had held on to their room keys during a university break, intending to encamp Libyan mercenaries in their hostels. Neither the government nor the university investigated the charge. Instead, the college invited the notorious State Security Defence (SSD) on to campus, literally to 'flush' the students out of the hostels. When the college reopened, the authorities were faced with a militant student demonstration over the expulsions, degenerating into widespread vandalism, looting and affray. In the ensuing melée the principal's car was set on fire. Three members of the teaching staff judged 'friendly' to students – Olu Gordon, Jimmy Kandeh and Cleo Hanciles – lost their jobs.[11] Gordon and Hanciles were founding members of Panafu. The Union president, Alie Kabba, and four other students were arrested, detained for two months, and later charged with torching the car.[12]

The students' action might be described as infantile. They were neither politically mature enough nor sufficiently well disciplined to realize the shortcomings of whatever leverage they imagined they might have on administration or state. They appear naively to have believed that rhetoric would deliver 'people's power' without a solid organizational base. Comparing the 1985 leadership with that of 1977, one might say the 1985 group was better organized but less politically percipient, failing to understand the difference between student and national politics. The expulsion of this student group from FBC marked the end of a phase in the making of an informal, youth-oriented, opposition in Sierra Leone. Henceforth the baton passed to the 'lumpen' youths and pote-affiliated 'organic intellectuals' (some ex-students of FBC and the second campus of the national university at Njala) in numerous study groups and revolutionary cells scattered around the country.

The Making of the RUF

In addition to Alie Kabba, a number of other radicals attracted to populist conceptions of political action already had some Libyan connections. Some of these groups, mostly unemployed youths, were recruited in Sierra Leone – through networks established by some of the expelled students now resident in Ghana – for guerrilla training in Benghazi, Libya. Among those recruited was an older man, Alfred Foday Saybana Sankoh, once a corporal in the Sierra Leone army, cashiered and jailed in a 1971 for a coup plot against Siaka Stevens. Trained in the army as a signals technician, Sankoh found work on release as an itinerant freelance photographer in the south-east, which was to become the major theatre of war. He later found his way into a radical study group in the Bo-Kenema area, whose coordinator, Ebiyemi Reader, was an organic intellectual from Freetown west end. It was through him that Sankoh was able to make the trip to Libya.

---

[11] Jimmy Kande took the university to court and won; Hanciles and Gordon were never reinstated.
[12] They were subsequently released without bail and the matter was dropped by the administration.

All those who went to Libya for military and ideological training in 1987–8 and later, like Sankoh, became involved in the RUF, returned to Sierra Leone before the launching of the armed struggle. Back in Freetown, an attempt was made to recruit cadres for training at a farm in the vicinity of Yele, a small road junction settlement in Tonkolili District, on the provincial boundary between northern and southern Sierra Leone. The project was abandoned as too risky.

It could hardly be said that there was an organization. 'At the beginning, there was no leadership. All of us were [sic] all organizers,' Sankoh has revealed.[13] At this stage the movement was little more than a loose collection of individuals returned from military training in Benghazi. Of the 35 people who were trained in Libya, only three had any form of regular employment. There was a high school teacher, an engineer, and Sankoh, an itinerant photographer. Most of those who took part in the military and ideological training later opted out of the counter-insurgency project, partly because it was too risky. Even the expelled student radicals from FBC who had gone to Ghana to continue their education abandoned the project as a result of their experiences in Ghana and Libya.[14] Their exit from the project, according to Alie Kabba, who was the coordinator, opened the way for the 'wrong kind individuals'.[15] These individuals included Foday Sankoh, Abu Kanu and Rashid Mansaray, all of whom had gone to Benghazi for insurgency training, via Accra.

Forming a tight-knit group in Freetown, the three embarked on another recruitment drive among 'lumpens'. This time they decided to leave the city and settle in the provinces. From the time they left Libya in 1988 until they entered Sierra Leone as armed combatants in 1991, this trio travelled extensively throughout the country and in Liberia, quietly promoting their dream. In 1988 Sankoh met Charles Taylor, recently released from detention in Freetown. This meeting appears to have been the beginning of Sankoh's links with Taylor. Some RUF members, notably Mansaray and Kanu, fought alongside National Patriotic Front of Liberia (NPFL) combatants in Liberia, so that by 1991, when the RUF entered Sierra Leone, they were supported by an NPFL group – 'special forces' – under the command of Mansaray. They were also joined by lumpen Sierra Leoneans resident in Liberia.[16]

Paul Richards has suggested that the RUF planned to imitate a number of features of the initial successful incursion by NPFL forces into north-eastern Liberia, where the local population in Nimba County were ardent opponents of the Doe regime.[17] This could have been the case, for the early RUF appropriated most of its strategy and tactics from the Liberian experience.[18] Sankoh and the RUF obviously hoped to repeat the trick in eastern Sierra Leone, where the Kailahun people in particular were long-term opponents of the APC regime.

---

[13] Sankoh, *Concord Times*, 10 December 1996.

[14] For details see Ibrahim Abdullah, 'Bush path to destruction: the origins and character of the Revolutionary United Front(RUF/SL)', *Journal of Modern African Studies*, Vol. 36, No. 2, 1998.

[15] Alie Kabba, *Leonenet*, 19 December 1996.

[16] See the RUF propaganda pamphlet, *Footpaths to Democracy: Toward a New Sierra Leone*, Vol. 1, (1995), where this group is referred to as 'migrant workers'.

[17] See Richards, *Fighting for the Rain Forest*.

[18] This aspect of the RUF has led many observers to read the movement as the creation of Charles Taylor.

The Dynamics of War

Insurrection: first phase, 1991–3

The RUF entered Sierra Leone from Liberia, at Bomaru in Kailahun District and Mano River Bridge, Pujehun District, on 23 March 1991. Two small forces, about 100–150 in all, captured border towns and villages in what Richards has referred to as a pincer movement intended to encircle Bo and Kenema, the main regional centres in the east and south of Sierra Leone.[19] The RUF failed to take the strategic Moa bridge at Daru, or establish a link between the two groups at Joru south of Kenema. The southern group later pushed across Pujehun District to infiltrate Bo District from the south.

Envisaging support in a border region opposed for many years to the government of the APC, the RUF seized and summarily executed chiefs, traders, village elders, agricultural project workers and other government agents, NPFL style, but also made attempts forcibly to recruit individuals known locally for their opposition to the APC regime.[20] Some of these later became prominent in the leadership of the RUF.

The original insurgency forces which took Kailahun and Pujehun Districts were charged with the responsibility of establishing training bases and securing a swathe of territory, to facilitate the deployment of RUF forces which would advance further into Sierra Leone and bolster the border areas against anti-NPFL United Liberation Movement for Democracy (Ulimo) forces that were being recruited and re-armed by Nigerian and Sierra Leonean instructors.[21] Although forewarned by military intelligence, the APC regime failed to deploy substantial defensive troops and materiel in the vulnerable border area.[22]

The reaction of the civil population amongst whom the RUF hoped to foster their 'revolution' was at best ambiguous, notwithstanding the fact that these two border districts had been the scene of violent political opposition to the APC regime. On one hand alluvial diamond mining and the rich pickings of a parallel smuggler's economy had attracted lumpen youth to these areas, despairing at the malaise of economic and political exclusion but bristling with an overweening determination for self-advancement and prosperity. Here was a reserve army of fighting men who were attracted by the simplistic 'emancipatory' rhetoric of the RUF's ill-defined ideas, and motivated by the acquisition of wealth through looting, and of authority by wresting control from both the local and national political authorities whom they blamed for their predicament and the agony of the nation as a whole. The 'freedom-fighter' mantle – idealized in *pote* culture and given resonance by the RUF's appeal and initial success – coupled with the reversal of social hierarchy through the possession of the means of violence, had long been perceived

---

[19] Richards, *Fighting for the Rain Forest*.

[20] This contrasts sharply with the Liberian experience, where individuals willingly joined the invading forces. See Stephen Ellis's chapter in this volume.

[21] P. K. Muana, interview with ex-combatants, October 1996.

[22] See Abdul Karim Koroma, *The Agony of a Nation* (Freetown: Afromedia, 1996).

in the lumpen world view as a necessary route to heroism and self-actualization. On the other hand, the apprehension of a settled civil population was reinforced by testimonies of brutality from the Liberian crisis, and flight from RUF fighters became the ultimate security option for self-preservation. There was little scope for the transformation of political dissent in these areas into revolutionary fervour. Instead, the empowerment of the socially excluded with access to the instruments of violence and therefore power in a state teetering on the brink of collapse was more conducive to unbridled violence than was consistent with an agenda for revolutionary change.

Young people with some schooling – girls as well as boys – were taken for guerrilla training. Those without education were assigned labouring tasks. The Freetown *pote* culture already present in the hinterland provided a natural recruiting ground for the movement. The number of *potes* in Bo, Kenema and Koidu had increased from three or four in the early 1970s to a dozen or more in the early 1990s. Some, like those in Bo, were controlled by APC youth leaders as potential sources for the recruitment of political thugs. Others, such as those in Koidu and Kenema, had occupational linkages, serving as a centres for unemployed drivers awaiting casual work. As in Freetown, the hinterland *potes* were centres where school drop-outs and the young unemployed converged, took recreational drugs and exchanged political ideas. They also supplied drugs and served as meeting places for illicit diamond miners, locally referred to as '*san-san* boys'. It was from this group of alienated lumpen youths, who were engaged in what was probably the oldest form of collective lumpen resistance in Sierra Leone, illicit diamond mining, that the RUF recruited the bulk of its combatants during this phase. The current RUF strong man, Colonel Sam Bockarie (Maskita) was an illicit diamond miner, before moving to Liberia, where he was recruited by the RUF.

Recreational life in these illicit diamond enclaves reproduced the *pote* culture in the urban centres. In forcibly recruiting barely literate hinterland school children and the likes of diamond–digging *san-san* boys, the RUF had a confident expectation that it would be able to turn a significant number of captives into enthusiastic supporters of the movement, based upon a shared lumpen culture and political consciousness. The evidence is that many captives were quickly convinced by the movement's simplistic political analysis. The RUF's consistent 'political' message to recruits was simply that the country was immensely rich in mineral wealth controlled by a few Lebanese and business men with political connections, that the time for reasoned debate had passed, and that lasting solutions to the country's chronic economic and political problems could be found only through an explosion of destructive violence.

A significant portion of the Liberia border region into which the RUF incursion spilled is forested boundary enclave with considerable scope for clandestine smuggling, logging and diamond digging activities.[23] One of the options for young lumpens seeking a job was to drift into this off-limits frontier area and participate in illicit activities. The RUF pincer movement encircled this zone, and found within it considerable numbers of potential recruits sharing the lumpen worldview of the RUF leadership.

---

[23] See Richards, *Fighting for the Rain Forest*

If the RUF was able to garner support from the alienated and uprooted youth engaged in illicit mining as a result of shared culture and worldview, it could not gain ready acceptance among the settled civilian communities of the region, despite their political alienation from the APC regime. Any potential civilian enthusiasm for the RUF was stifled by the looting and indiscriminate violence of the Liberian 'special forces', an integral part of the original invading force. Sankoh, the RUF leader, justified looting by Liberians as 'reward' for their support. His dependence on these Liberians had great political costs for the RUF, since civilians in regions under RUF control, already alienated from the APC regime in Freetown, quickly came utterly to detest the RUF as well. This double alienation paved the way for the emergence of the popular Kamajo militia, eventually to prove a decisive factor in the war.[24]

Many captives perhaps only grudgingly accepted the anti-social political violence of the RUF in the first instance, but in order to survive they had little option but to adjust to its lumpen vision. Once sucked into the RUF, young border-zone captives found it impossible to quit. Deserters tattooed with RUF 'ID' risked summary execution by both RUF and the Sierra Leone army. Throughout the war and into the ceasefire period, those who sought to demobilize themselves were trapped by this suicidal double jeopardy, and by the expectation of revenge at the hands of rural civilians who judged all members of the movement by the values of its lumpen leadership.[25]

Counter-insurgency operations, 1991–2

The RUF guerrilla operation bogged down in mid-1991 after the failure of early attempts to take Bo in a conventional military operation and establish a regional centre similar to Charles Taylor's base, Gbarnga. This provided the APC regime with some brief respite. Lacking confidence in its own army, the APC began to arm anti-NPFL irregulars from among Liberian refugees living in the border region. Some of these refugees were ex-soldiers in the Liberian army with combat experience against the NPFL in the war in Liberia. The Sierra Leone army also began recruitment of irregular forces from among border-zone youth, teaching them guerrilla tactics as deployed by both the NPFL and the RUF. The lead was taken, as early as April 1991, in Kailahun, by a young lieutenant from Segbwema, Prince Ben-Hirsch. Some recruited youths had lost parents or guardians in the first wave of RUF attacks and were keen for revenge. Others were seeking, in military training, a substitute for educational opportunities disrupted by the conflict. Older recruits were inducted into the army. Very young irregulars were taken on as 'apprentices', personally loyal to their recruiting officer, without army identification. A combatant refers to this officer as his or her *bra* (big brother). Like the rebels, the government side also recruited young girls, some of whom proved highly effective combatants. These juvenile and under-age combatants became the canon fodder in the war, with drugs being used as 'morale boosters' to get them into action.[26]

---

[24] See Patrick Muana, 'The Kamajo militia: civil war, internal displacement and the politics of counter-insurgency', in Abdullah and Bangura, *African Development*.
[25] Interview with demobilized under-age combatants, Freetown, October 1996.
[26] *Ibid*.

Strengthened by Guinean troops, under a defence pact between Sierra Leone and Guinea, and later by a contingent of Nigerians (deployed in Sierra Leone essentially to protect the rear bases of the Nigerian-dominated ECOMOG peace-keeping operation in Liberia), the national army, assisted both by local irregular recruits and by Liberian irregulars later reorganized as Ulimo, began to counter-attack RUF positions from July 1991. Expecting an easy walk-over, RUF units were surprised by this offensive and several times evacuated positions, especially in Pujehun District, without a fight. By September, government troops had recaptured Pujehun Town and were in control of main roads and some larger settlements as far as the Liberian border. From early 1992 the RUF was mainly confined to the inaccessible south-eastern corner of Pujehun District (parts of Soro-Gbeima and Barrie Chiefdoms), and that part of Kailahun District north of Pendembu.

Young officers seize power: the military coup of 1992

Exactly a year after the insurgency started, a group of young military officers from the war front trooped to Freetown and seized power. This began as a revolt over pay and conditions by young officers from the front.[27] Calling itself the National Provisional Ruling Council (NPRC), the group declared a 'revolution', and a commitment to end the war, revamp the economy, and restore multi-party democracy. Contacts between the RUF leadership and the NPRC were characterized by general mistrust. Whereas the junta considered the formation of a broad-based and inclusive transitional government, the RUF leadership called for the exclusion of former APC functionaries and a total purge of the civil service. The RUF also demanded the dismantling of all foreign military bases, the withdrawal of all foreign troops, and the immediate incorporation of their representatives into the new regime. Fearing a backlash from civilians, and deeply suspicious of the request to dismiss all foreign troops as a precursor to a large-scale offensive by the NPFL in a bid to install the RUF and destroy forces opposed to it, the NPRC suggested a compromise plan for a phased withdrawal, to be preceded by a disarmament of the RUF forces. But under increasing military pressure from Ulimo forces in Cape Mount and Lofa counties in Liberia, the NPFL is thought to have advised their RUF allies to dismiss the proposal for peace as a foreign ploy to destroy the movement. The RUF leadership declared the ceasefire null and void, and condemned the NPRC as a continuation of the APC regime. Henceforth, they were to be fought like their 'masters'.

The NPRC enthusiasm to end the war waned as the young officers became mired in the very corruption that had characterized the APC regime. The comforts of being in power ensured that the more battle-tested officers were now drawn to Freetown, far away from the war. The replacement of these officers by a group of relatively inexperienced ones turned the tide in the RUF's favour. The RUF mounted several successful raids and ambushes on these inexperienced commanders.

---

[27] See Cecil Magbailey Fyle,'The military and civil society in Sierra Leone: the 1992 military *coup d'état*', in Abdullah and Bangura, eds, *African Development*, pp. 127–46; A. B. Zack-Williams and Steve Riley, 'Sierra Leone: the coup and its consequences,' *Review of African Political Economy*, No. 56 (1993), pp. 91–8.

Perhaps disgruntled by their treatment under the NPRC, officers abandoned positions that might have been better defended. Some appear to have paid more attention to diamond mining than to basic defence.[28]

Much more important was the expansion of the army to bring a speedy end to the war, and to reward its predominantly youthful constituency. Those recruited in this hasty exercise were 'mostly drifters, rural and urban unemployed, a fair number of hooligans, drug addicts and thieves'.[29] They came from the same social group as the RUF combatants. It is therefore not surprising that these lumpen recruits and the irregular elements in the new and expanded army freely admit to living off the brutal exploitation of civilians in the war zone. Control by officers was often minimal. For civilians caught in the war zone, conditions on the government side came increasingly to resemble those for civilians on the rebel side of the conflict. Overnight, the army became indistinguishable from the RUF.

Paranoid about the threat of an APC counter-coup, the NPRC executed a large group of political detainees at the end of December 1992, provoking a major outcry over human rights, and losing the country international support. The regime also lost local popular support as civilians began to suffer the consequences of a new enlarged, ill-trained, under-paid lumpen army scattered around the country in makeshift barracks and roadside checkpoints. RUF units began to exploit their knowledge of various smugglers' tracks and pathways linking the Kono diamond fields and the Liberian cross-border region where they had their main bases. Several effective incursions in September 1992 were followed by a major attack leading to the capture from government troops of Koidu, the main town in the Kono diamond region, in October 1992. As one of the country's main sources of foreign exchange, control of Kono was hotly contested. The RUF infiltrated the diamond-rich areas of Kono not so much as a way of establishing operational bases deep within Sierra Leone, but as a way of looting the rich bounty in that part of the country.

Outside the actual war zone, civilians quickly came to loathe the lumpen recruits in the NPRC-expanded army, suspecting them of causing as much mayhem as the rebels, and coining the term 'sobel' to account for the criminal behaviour of these ill-disciplined recruits. But in the eastern war zone, close to the RUF main concentrations along the Liberian border, matters were rather different. Here the activities of army-linked irregulars often had the support of local civilians. Civil defence groups were formed, with input from local hunters, and alliances began to develop between army irregulars and civil defence groups. Unable to control civilian enclaves except through coercion and fear, the RUF was denied access to any similar pool of local tactical and combat knowledge, and was dependent on the less certain bush knowledge of dragooned captives.

With the army concentrating its efforts on retaking and securing the Kono diamond fields, the by now well-armed Border Guard and other irregular units, supported by specialist hunters, many by origin from northern Sierra Leone, brought increasingly effective pressure to bear on RUF bases in the border zone

---

[28] See Arthur Abraham, 'War and transition to peace in Sierra Leone: a study of state conspiracy in perpetuating armed conflict', in Abdullah and Bangura, eds, *African Development*.

[29] Koroma, *The Agony*, p. 144.

during 1993. By the end of the year, eye witnesses describe a bedraggled RUF leadership contingent quitting Kailahun town with a couple of broken-down vehicles, driving a group of displaced civilians ahead of them to spring any ambushes on the road, heading in the direction of the border forest reserves to the south.[30] Here they fetched up in a last redoubt – Nomo Chiefdom, an inaccessible finger of land along the Liberian border, partly cut off from the rest of Sierra Leone by the forested curtain of the Gola North reserve. The country at large, increasingly disillusioned with the NPRC, decided that the war was over, and that only 'banditry, looting, maiming and raping' remained.[31] An army commander echoed similar views: 'there are rebels among us [soldiers], there are mercenaries among us, some of them our own people. The problem is not the RUF alone.'[32] It was widely assumed that lumpen recruits in the national army were reverting to criminal behaviour.

At this point, the RUF leadership contemplated abandoning its struggle to return to Liberia.[33] But after Charles Taylor's attempt to take Monrovia – Operation Octopus, December 1992 – ran up against stiff ECOMOG opposition, this line of retreat was blocked by Ulimo control of the Liberian side of the border zone. To survive as a guerrilla movement, tactics had to be changed. The organization was too weak and poorly equipped to risk direct confrontation with a much better-armed enemy. Small towns were evacuated, vehicles were abandoned, and the leadership adapted to life in a series of secure forest hide-aways. Henceforth, combat operations were limited to ambush and hit-and-run raids. RUF units were instructed to strike 'softer targets' – positions not heavily defended – and seize arms and ammunition. Contact with enemy forces was to be avoided, and RUF units were ordered to infiltrate enemy territory by way of 'by-passes' or bush paths, to raid villages and ambush government forces. Small units began a pattern of deploying knowledge of bush tracks to strike at all parts of the country, apparently at will. Terror tactics, such as hostage taking and mutilation of civilians, were used to signal the desperate determination of the movement to survive and enter negotiation with the regime.

Cheated of its lumpen constituency, the RUF meanwhile opened up the wedge between civilians and the NPRC by disguising many of its own attacks as raids by army personnel, having obtained army-pattern combat fatigues and identity in raids and deals with corrupt army officers. Most weapons and ammunition came from raids on the national army forward supply posts. Some were imported by selling diamonds across the border to Liberia and Guinea.

War without front-line: the second phase, 1994–7

During this period, a reinvigorated RUF duplicated its initial secure border-zone forest camps in strategic parts of the country, connecting them by movements along secured bush trails towards Freetown. This scatter of camps then provided a platform for a second expansive phase of RUF operations: a nation-wide campaign

[30] See Abraham, 'War and transition'; Lansana Gberie, 'War and state collapse: the case of Sierra Leone' (MA dissertation, Wilfred Laurier University, 1997).
[31] Chairman Strasser, Head of State, cited in *Vision* (Freetown), 22–29 July 1994.
[32] Brigadier Kellie Conteh,'Open letter to His Excellency Captain Strasser', December 1995, cited in Abraham, 'War and transition'
[33] See *Footpaths To Democracy*, 1995.

of hit-and-run raids reaching all parts of the country in late 1994 to early 1995. There was no front-line; and the national army was spread thinly across the country.

Key targets included direct attacks on the major hinterland centres of Bo and Kenema at Christmas 1994, a series of ambushes on main roads leading from the hinterland to the capital, and strikes against the Njala campus and the economically vital bauxite and rutile mines in the south of the country. Small raiding parties – at times no more than a platoon, accompanied by unarmed juveniles carrying equipment and stores – carried out hit-and-run raids far and wide, and returned to base camps with looted items. Captive youngsters, rounded up initially to carry looted items, were inducted as potential new recruits. One long-distance strike on Kabala, a town in the far north of Sierra Leone, was apparently intended to challenge the power of a powerful hunter magician based in Kabala, who had been advising the NPRC war effort in Kailahun. The raiding party encountered two British volunteer workers in a house at the edge of the town who were seized as hostages. Subsequently more foreign hostages were taken, the RUF using negotiations over their release as a means to bring the movement publicity. But the immediate political objective was to make the country ungovernable, and therefore force the military junta to yield and include them in a transitional government. Thus commenced the bloodiest phase in the civil war.

Hit-and-run raids on all parts of the country, including the town of Kambia in January 1995, at the furthest provincial extremity from the RUF's initial point of entry into Sierra Leone, conveyed an impression of remorseless advance across the country towards the capital. So effective was this message that by early 1995 aid agencies began to evacuate personnel from Freetown, apparently convinced the RUF now had the upper hand. The national mood swung from the view that the violence was all the work of disloyal soldiers to a belief that the renascent RUF was all-powerful.

There can be little doubt that there was civilian disillusionment with the NPRC military government, aided by the RUF in its renaissance and advance on Freetown. There was much justified public disquiet at the way in which members of the NPRC regime had begun to enrich themselves from the war.[34] The suspicion grew that the regime was prolonging the war in order to create further opportunities for enrichment. This was reinforced by evidence that some war-front officers, perhaps to save their skins in vulnerable forward positions, were fraternizing with the enemy. Some appear to have abandoned materiel to RUF attack, perhaps by prior arrangement and for financial gain. Equally, there seems little doubt that ill-disciplined elements among the junior ranks were routinely harassing citizens and engaging in extensive looting. Civilians in the war zone became familiar with two-phase attacks: first a lightning raid by RUF forces in which weapons, medicines and young people might be carried away, and then a second wave in which defending troops would descend on an area with trucks to carry away heavy items, including zinc roofing materials, abandoned by fleeing civilians. Kellie Conteh and Joy Turay, force commanders under the NPRC, were on record as admitting that the regime did not control large sections of the army. The popular perception was that the country had fallen victim to a new species of armed men – 'sobels'.

[34] See Abraham, 'War and transition'.

Two new strategic factors on the government side began increasingly to make their mark on the conflict from mid-1995. The first was the introduction of a private South Africa-based security firm, Executive Outcomes (EO). The second and more decisive factor was the strengthening of the civil defence units, known as the Kamajo militia. With never more than a few hundred combat personnel in Sierra Leone (and latterly as few as 82), the main significance of EO was to provide training in counter-insurgency to the army, and helicopter air support for pinning down troops close to RUF camps. EO also helped locate RUF base camps by tracking and triangulating rebel radio communications.

The Kamajo intervention appears to have had a decisive impact on the war. The bush knowledge of the *san-san* boys and city lumpens, who were by now in control of the fighting forces, was mainly confined to by-pass routes associated with smuggling and clandestine diamond mining operations. Long-distance raiding parties, although guided by captives from the local area, not infrequently lost their way in trying to stay away from suspicious individuals. Guides with real bush knowledge were often only reluctant converts to the cause, and sometimes led parties up the wrong path only to cut and run. What made a decisive difference to the campaigns against the RUF from 1993-4 onwards was the mobilization of a mass civil defence movement with superior local knowledge of the terrain. This began with the formation of the Eastern Region Defence Committee by the late Dr Alpha Lavalie, and continued on a large scale as a mass movement in 1996, when regent chief Captain Hinga Norman was appointed as Deputy Minister of Defence. These Kamajo forces were groups of local youth with a shared knowledge of local bush tracks and ambush points, often far superior to that of the enemy. Unlike the army and the RUF, they enjoyed the support of local civilians.

By early 1995, displaced people had begun to realize that deserting their respective chiefdoms gave the RUF a huge strategic and political advantage, since their control of the 'footpaths to democracy' was unchallenged. Chiefs and other chiefdom elders decided that they had to occupy and re-settle their vacated chiefdoms in the war zone. Unable to trust the government troops, Pujehun chiefs initially inquired about the availability of Nigerian peace-keeping forces. A more durable alternative was to expand the training of the kinds of Kamajo civil defence units organized by Hinga Norman, which had proved effective in controlling RUF incursions in Gbongor Chiefdom, adjacent to the diamond-rich Sewa area. The idea of resettling chiefdoms accompanied by Kamajo militia forces rapidly became popular among the displaced population of camps in Bo and Kenema. Displaced civilian groups nominated and sponsored many of their own young people for Kamajo training and initiation. Units were organized in such a way that combatants were posted only to their own chiefdoms, to ensure loyalty, discipline and a bush knowledge superior to that of the RUF. The revered and ancient esoteric Mende cult of invincible and heroic hunters was revived as a communal militia, chosen from, trained within, and responsible to the people. Only lightly armed with shotguns, knives and the occasional captured AK47, Kamajo combatants went into battle against the hitherto invisible RUF.[35] Armed thus with social as well as with technical combat skills, Kamajo units began to track and counter-attack RUF groups moving over bush

[35] See Muana, 'The Kamajo militia'.

paths to carry out raids or secure supplies, limiting RUF freedom to organize and exchange supplies.

The Kamajo battle song captures the collective imagination about the war and people's perception of the RUF. In this collective representation the RUF is depicted as a criminal organization that deserves to be fought at all cost.[36]

Who set the *dambi*?
Who set the *dambi* on our forefathers' land?
Who set the *dambi* along our rivers?
Who set the *dambi* in our bushes?
Please tell me, who set the *dambi*?

We set the *dambi*.
We, the Kamajo, set the *dambi*.

Why did you set the *dambi*?
Please, tell me, for whom did you set the *dambi*?
Which animal do you hope to trap with the *dambi*?
Please, tell me, why you set the *dambi* on our forefather's land?

We set the *dambi* before the rebels.
Because the rebels killed our forefathers.
Because the rebels killed our mothers.
Because the rebels raped our wives.
Because the rebels raped our mothers.
Because the rebels raped our sisters.
Because the rebels have made us into a displaced people.

Tell me, again, why you set the *dambi* before the rebels.
Please tell me why you set the *dambi* before the rebels.
Tell me why it was necessary to set the *dambi*.
Please tell me again why it was necessary to set the *dambi* on our forefathers' land.

We set the *dambi* in order to return to our homes.
We set the *dambi* in order to farm in our forefathers' land.
We set the *dambi* in order to protect our wives.
We set the *dambi* in order to protect our mothers.
We set the *dambi* in order to protect our sisters.
And we kill rebels in order to make our land safe.

The *dambi* is the Mende word for trap, which essentially portrays how the people see the RUF, or the rebels, as they are locally called. As animals preying on the land of their 'forefathers', they are seen as fair game to be hunted down and killed in order to protect the community.

The Kamajo offensive was so devastating that the RUF had to admit that their enemy was the Kamajo, not the army. It forced the RUF to resort to a series of appalling atrocities intended to break the cooperative link between rural civilians and the civil defence militia. But the evident need to protect isolated groups of civilians from these barbaric attacks only served to boost recruitment and deploy-

---

[36] We are grateful to Professor Kelfala Kallon for calling our attention to this song, and for supplying the translation from Mende to English.

ment. Supported by more conventional forms of military intelligence provided by Executive Outcomes, the superior bush knowledge of the Kamajo had a decisive impact, in allowing army-Kamajo units to locate and surround the main RUF camps during the latter half of 1996. The RUF headquarters camp, the Zogoda, and several other key camps in the south-east were overrun in September– October 1996, and several thousand RUF combatants killed or put to flight. Many RUF combatants fled over the border into Liberia. Peace negotiations, which started under Brigadier Maada Bio in February 1996, were resumed under the popularly elected government of President Kabba, leading to a comprehensive peace agreement signed on 30 November 1996.

The RUF as a Guerrilla Movement[37]

Leadership: Sankoh and the War Council

The RUF lumpen guerrilla force was first recruited by a small team: Sankoh, Kanu and Mansaray. At the outset Sankoh was first among equals, claiming the title 'head of ideology', and acting as spokesman for the group in speaking to the BBC African service in London, while disclaiming presidential ambitions. The initial trio was augmented by other leading figures, some recruited in Liberia, but others captured or abducted once the movement was in Sierra Leone. One Philip Palmer from Bonthe District, an engineering graduate from FBC working in Liberia, who fought in the southern (Pujehun) sector in 1991, later emerged as an influential figure in the peace process.[38] Once the war started there were some defections, as the violent impact of the Liberian special forces on Sierra Leonean civilians became clear. The RUF also lost leaders both in combat and through internal dissension. Blamed for military reverses against the NPRC, Rashid Mansaray and 'Commander' Fengbeh were executed in 1992 in Kailahun for 'technical sabotage' (failure to defend a position).[39]

Just as the lumpen guerrilla force was augmented by rounding up potentially amenable *san-san* boys and school drop-outs in the border zone, so the depleted leadership group was later augmented by capturing and enlisting local opponents of the APC regime. Two such figures were I. H. Deen-Jalloh, a lecturer from the rural teacher's training college at Bunumbu, and his wife Agnes Deen-Jalloh, a Segbwema school teacher. Another captive recruited to the leadership was Fayia Musa, from one of the Kissi chiefdoms in Kailahun District. Noted from his early school days for his contentiousness, Musa had crossed paths with authority at Njala, where he became a student in the 1970s. Twice failing his exams and repeating years, he was

---

[37] The information contained in this section is taken from a collective study commissioned by the Sierra Leone Ministry of National Reconstruction, Resettlement and Rehabilitation: Paul Richards, Ibrahim Abdullah, Joseph Amara, Patrick Muana, Teddy Stanley and James Vincent, *Reintegration of War-Affected Youth and Ex-Combatants: a Study of the Social and Economic Opportunity Structure in Sierra Leone*, 1996.

[38] Palmer led the coup against Sankoh in March 1997; he and other members of the group, all educated, are presumed dead.

[39] Abu Kanu, a leading vanguard and founding member, was executed in 1991 for conniving with the enemy. See Richards *et al.*, *Reintegration*.

finally sent down without graduating. When taken by the RUF in 1991, Musa was a low-paid agricultural assistant in a rural secondary school in Kailahun. He claimed that his conversion to RUF-style violent radicalism was precipitated by a speech in which APC president Momoh announced that the government considered education a privilege, not a right. As 'Minister of Agriculture', Musa was in charge of the so-called state farms established in the early phase of the war, which turned out to be a thinly disguised system of slavery.

It is difficult to ascertain how influential these educated members were in the movement in general, or how much leverage they had on the fighting forces. They certainly contributed to its development, particularly in the sphere of public relations and in publicizing the struggle, especially during the hostage crisis and the negotiations in Ivory Coast. But the important question remains: why did they fail to attract any support from the battle group and battle front commanders when they deposed Sankoh for blocking the implementation of the peace proposal? The answer may well be that the civilian members who were not lumpen did not share the world view of the predominantly lumpen commanders. It is therefore not surprising that, apart from Philip Palmer, all of them joined the movement after it entered Sierra Leone. In the absence of Sankoh, who was detained in March 1997 by the Nigerians in growing frustration at the failure of the peace process, the future of the conflict rested solely with the lumpen vanguard battle group commanders, especially Colonel Sam Bockarie and Lieutenant Collins, and their new-found allies in the Armed Forces Revolutionary Council (AFRC), formed after the bloody take-over of 25 May 1997.

Officers and other ranks

RUF 'battalions' are made up of combatants in the following categories: 'vanguards' (instructors in RUF ideology, consisting of guerrilla trainers, senior battle group commanders and more junior battle front commanders); Special Forces ('Liberians', latterly perhaps mainly persons of Liberian origin but with a family connection with Sierra Leone, who accounted for a significant number of senior officers in the RUF); *Salon wosus* (rank-and-file combatants, recruited mainly by capture but converts to the cause, trained, and allowed to carry weapons); 'standbys' (captives under training, of unproven loyalty and competence); and 'recruits' (fresh intake).

Any combatant selected to command a mission is known as 'CO'. Those leading attacks on major RUF targets are 'battle front commanders', and typically hold RUF ranks of Lieutenant and Captain. The more senior 'battle group commanders' are responsible for coordination and command of all battle front commanders in their sectors. Holding the rank of Major or above, battle group commanders have a voice on the War Council. Until 1996, the most senior of these commanders was Lieutenant-Colonel Mohammed Tarawallie ('Colonel Zino'), a fair-complexioned man of medium height in his late 20s or early 30s, who was killed when the Kamajo overran the Zogoda.

The 'vanguard' and *wosu* groups contain some female combatants. The greater number of women in the RUF, however, belong to two groups known as Combat Support and Combat Wives Units. Most young women were recruited by capture.

Women in the Wives Unit and later Combat Wives Units were armed with 'sista beretta' (mainly Beretta submachine guns); they were charged with responsibility for policing gatherings of the captive population and occasionally acted as body-guards. Some were later involved in 'special missions' – infiltrating 'enemy territory', and running 'survival missions' into large civilian settlements behind enemy lines in order to purchase essential commodities and medicine.

The Internal Defence Unit (IDU) is the 'intelligence' arm of the RUF. Tasks include carrying out reconnaissance (infiltration of target areas, procurement of vital supplies), target assessment (estimating army strength and materiel, and prospecting possible routes to targets and new camps from which to mount attacks), general military intelligence, liaison between commanders of battle groups and battle fronts, monitoring movements of civilians and RUF personnel in RUF-controlled enclaves (informing HQ for action), liaison with RUF head of ideology (Foday Sankoh), and monitoring deployment of civilian captives. Headed by I. H. Deen-Jalloh, the unit was once known as G-2, but the name was changed at a conference in Kailahun in 1992, after an operational mix-up with a similarly named NPRC organization. IDU representatives are present in all operational areas, even during combat.

RUF combat groupings

During the 1994 revival the RUF established a national network of six or more main combat groupings or 'battalions', based in camps in isolated and readily defended forest enclaves in strategic parts of the country, as a basis for its attempted advance on Freetown. The main concentrations so far identified were to be found as follows: Malal Hills (overlooking the Freetown–Makeni highway) was responsible for attacks on Kambia District in January 1995, during which a small group of expatriate nuns and a hundred or so children from Kambia Town were taken hostage. Fearing air attack (the NPRC government had at this time acquired the services of two or three Russian-built helicopter transports), the group rebuilt its camp at the other end of the Malal Hills, and then advanced to a new site in the vicinity of Rotifunk, from where the army post at Mile 38 on the Freetown road and villages close to the capital were attacked. Some ambushes on vehicle convoys on the Bo–Freetown road appear to have been made from a forward position at Makeni-Rofula.

Others were located around Kangari Hills, Geima, close to the Liberian border in Kailahun, and at Peyeima, based in the forested country behind Panguma, with access to the Tongo diamond field; the Sendumei-Jui group was located in a forested ridge south of the Kambui forest reserves; the Sulima group was in the south-east of the country where it could control supplies in and out of Liberia and on the coast. In addition, the RUF maintained a headquarters camp, where Sankoh and many of the War Council appear to have been based, at the Zogoda, an elaborate defensive installation in flat forested country east of the Moa and north of Zimmi. Site descriptions from visiting combatants suggest a location in the Gola forest west reserve. It was from here that Foday Sankoh was airlifted by helicopter to begin the peace negotiations in Abidjan in January 1996. The base was overrun and destroyed by units of the army and Kamajo militia in October 1996. On entry the government and the Kamajo forces discovered large numbers of severely malnourished civilian captives and only very limited supplies of munitions. Anti-aircraft guns at the site were non-operational.

Guerrilla operations

The RUF was never a formidable military force. Whenever a position was seriously defended by the army, as at Daru and Joru in 1991, the rebels ran into difficulty. When operating in remote and lightly defended forested terrain the RUF expanded rapidly, not through fighting but through imposing itself by spooking small and isolated army units and then controlling civilians through fear. Among the tactics used, the RUF particularly favoured letters written to village chiefs, warning of dates of attack and consequences of resistance. Alleged opponents of the rebels were rounded up and beaten, tortured or publicly executed. Some of the methods – beheading by knife, for example – were intended to terrorize witnesses. Body mutilation (carving the letters RUF into the skin, or amputation of hands, ears, fingers and genitals) was also used to punish recalcitrants and signal certain kinds of messages to civilians. Amputations and mutilations were used to deter women from harvesting in areas outside RUF control, to 'punish' civilians for attempting to vote in the 1996 elections, and to 'mark' potential runaways so that they would not abscond again. Some specific forms of punitive torture were imported from the Liberian civil war. To *tabay* people meant to tie them so tightly (with wet ropes) that arms and shoulders were permanently damaged. Civilians were also sometimes stripped naked, arms and feet tied, and then beaten from point to point while lying prone, a punishment known as *halaka*.

Post-1993 guerrilla operations emphasized small units making long-distance hit-and-run raids, using RUF command of bush 'by-pass' routes. RUF units were especially skilled at spying out the ground, camping for periods in the bush, and mounting ambushes. A 'relay' system was used, known as 'soldier replaces dead soldier'. Combat reserves were termed 'standbys' (young recruits not yet qualified to carry arms in their own right). On operations, units might make temporary bush camps, with a main section for *wosus* and a separate section for officers. Burning vehicles and seizing and eating cooked food in villages were forbidden (the latter perhaps a measure to avoid poisoning). Commanders were under orders to control rape, looting and drug abuse, and some ruled their potentially unruly lumpen troops with an iron rod of summary execution. The movement's leadership insists it had a well-disciplined guerrilla force at its command, and that RUF discipline prevented unsanctioned rape, looting or drug abuse. Abuses are laid at the door of government troops and 'sobels'. But in many cases it is absolutely clear that commanders sanctioned rape and torture of civilians as a means to control local populations. It is also clear from talking to combatants that both sides in the war tolerated and in some case actually encouraged use of drugs like amphetamines and crack cocaine, as ways of preparing terrified young combatants for battle. Combatants on both sides also report having used marijuana extensively. Before major battles RUF fighters were officially 'de-sensitized' with a concoction of amphetamines and herbal intoxicant in order to eliminate a sense of fear on the battlefield.

RUF 'civil administration'

After the resurgence of the bush war in early 1994, RUF units avoided residing permanently in villages, especially roadside settlements where the army could counter-attack. Isolated civilian enclaves were controlled from the secure forest camps where the combatants were based. These civilian enclaves were administered under the RUF's so-called 'ideology system'. The head of ideology, Foday Sankoh, reportedly lectured recruits on the reason for the insurrection. At the RUF's vocational secondary school training base at Pendembu, his tirade against the APC regime effectively convinced most recruits to embrace the RUF motto 'arms to the people, power to the people, and wealth to the people'.

The ideology system involved appointing civilian collaborators – often young people with some lumpen sympathies – to act as civil authorities under the RUF. These civilians were known as 'town', 'area' and 'section' commanders, and 'town mothers' (women chiefs), assisted by 'civil police' and 'military police'. Under the ideology system, combatants were reportedly ordered not to take 'even a single needle' from the local population. In spite of this injunction, looting was widespread. Members were instructed to refer to one another as 'brother' or 'sister'. This policy was designed to effect a kind of lumpen bonding to replace the networks which connected members to the wider society. It was reinforced by the total exclusion of RUF fighters from the civilian population in what were referred to as 'Zoe' bushes (militarized camps). Some were even forced to witness or even participate in atrocities against captives or family members in their own towns and villages. The main duties of civil 'commanders' seem to have been to organize agriculture in the RUF interest, and maintain village discipline. They were empowered to oblige civilians to pay tax in kind and provide labour for RUF 'state farms', and could carry out summary executions. Town commanders were also obliged to look out for and return deserting rebel combatants. Deserters were either killed or their bodies marked with tattoos (mutilations in which the letters RUF were cut into the body with a razor and rubbed with lime). Some RUF civil commanders eased their plight by giving daughters to rebel combatants as wives.

The RUF in Comparative Context

The RUF has defied all available typologies on guerrilla movements. It is neither a separatist insurgency rooted in a specific demand, as in the case of Eritrea, nor a reformist insurgency with a radical agenda superior to the regime it sought to overthrow.[40] Nor does it possess the kind of leadership that would be necessary to designate it as a warlord insurgency. The RUF has made history; it is a peculiar guerrilla movement without any significant national following nor ethnic support. Perhaps because of its lumpen social base and its lack of an emancipatory programme to garner support from other social groups, it has remained a bandit organization solely driven by the survivalist needs of its predominantly uneducated and alienated

---

[40] For a typology of insurgency movements, see Christopher Clapham, Introduction to this volume; Clapham, *Africa and the International System* (Cambridge: Cambridge University Press, 1996), Chapter 9.

battle front and battle group commanders. Neither the peasantry, the natural ally of most revolutionary movements, nor the students, amongst whose ranks the RUF-to-be originated, lent any support to the organization during the six years of fighting.

This lack of support begins to explain the initial isolation of the organization and the lack of knowledge about its activities. As Olu Gordon recently observed, the RUF is 'an armed movement with a political objective' not 'a political movement with an armed wing'. The RUF has emphasized the importance of military victory rather than a solid programme of societal transformation, precisely because it does not have such a programme or the wherewithal to produce one. For what marks the RUF is the chronic lack of cadres to disseminate its alleged egalitarian ideology, for which it has come to depend on the those whom it abducted in the course of the war.[41]

The propaganda pamphlet hurriedly produced by the organization, *Foot Path to Democracy*, is a pathetic and well-worn criticism of the APC regime, culled from an original document produced by some of the expelled students in Ghana.[42] Unlike UNITA or any of the liberation insurgencies, the RUF does not have any programme of societal transformation. All it could do at the peace negotiations in Abidjan was to make *ad hoc* populist demands about free education, free health care services, rural development and a people's budget. The movement does not have the intellectual capital that movements such as Renamo and UNITA had at their command, nor does it have a group of dedicated intellectuals: hence its reliance on a few captured educated members to negotiate on its behalf and run its intelligence unit.

The singular importance of the RUF as a guerrilla organization is that it has defied all radical pronouncements about the political importance of the lumpen proletariat in taking political action in its own interest. Originally a product of Freetown youth culture, the movement entered Sierra Leone with combatants, mostly urban lumpens, who were joined by another group of lumpen Sierra Leoneans resident in Liberia. Failing to receive the anticipated support from the people, the RUF turned for support to its natural allies, the *san-san* boys, illicit diamond miners in the communities of the south-east, the major theatre of war. This alliance is the secret of the movement's survival and the major reason for the continuation of the war. Once the Kamajo militia was formed, the movement lost some of this support, so that it had to depend on another group of lumpens in the military who shared the same lumpen culture and interest as the RUF commanders: uncertainty about what an end to the war would mean for their collective well-being. This congruence of interest between the two erstwhile enemies provided the basis for the alliance which led to the overthrow of the elected government of Ahmed Tejan Kabba on 25 May 1997.

The RUF's presence in the capital took away much of the mystery surrounding the movement. The ideas of the original vanguard leadership were shaped by the urban lumpen milieu portrayed at the outset of this chapter. This lumpen world was

---

[41] Olu Awoonor-Gordon, 'A nation held hostage,' in *For Di People* (Freetown), 12 June 1997.
[42] The second volume of this propaganda tract is still not published; some parts of it were taken from 'The Basic Document' produced in Ghana. For an elaboration of these issues see Abdullah, 'Bush path'.

transformed by the specific social conditions of Freetown in the 1970s and 1980s, in which a middle-class student element came into contact with the young un-employed in the *potes* associated with *odelay* masquerade. A lumpen rebellion was hatched as a result. The movement set out to round up and convert rural youths sharing aspects of this lumpen world view, and some isolated and angry individuals opposed to the decadent APC regime. Setting no limits on the use of violence for social destabilization, using techniques imported from the Liberian civil war, the original rebellion failed in its attempts to gain any significant civilian support in the border zone.

But an NPRC military regime, fired by some of the same simplistic views about revolutionary change, was soon mired by the same lumpen violence responsible for the political failure of the RUF. New recruits into a rapidly expanded army became as great a menace to rural civilians as the RUF. This gave the RUF, bogged down in forest reserves on the Liberian border, a second chance. It re-emerged from the forest, driven by the desperate ingenuity of its lumpen leadership and the stop-at-nothing propensity for shocking violence of its young combatants, cut off from a hostile and vengeful civil society and convinced that only victory would secure its readmission to that wider society. Finally, rural civilians came to realize the vulnerability of a movement based on shock tactics but without local support and legitimacy. The civilian Kamajo militia began to better the RUF at its own game of surprise attack based on unopposed movement through the bush. 'Footpaths to Democracy' soon became 'Bush Paths to Destruction' for the RUF.

Despite the limitations and failures of the RUF, the country – indeed the continent – will have to pay more attention to the frustrated energies of its lumpen 'revolutionaries' who are asking a poignant question about how the nation is being governed: 'Is it not more sensible to pull the rug from under such pampered feet by establishing our own self-subsisting habitation?'[43] Establishing their own self-subsisting habitation – that is to say, moving onto the centre stage in the historical process, as opposed to being marginal – is not only a RUF agenda but the lumpen project writ large.

[43] Wole Soyinka, *The Open Sore of a Continent*, Cambridge, Cambridge University Press, 1996, p. 130.

Bibliography

Abdullah, Ibrahim, and Yusuf Bangura, eds, *African Development*, Vol. 22, Nos 2 and 3 (1997), special issue on 'Youth Culture and Political Violence: the Sierra Leone Civil War'.

Abdullah, Ibrahim, 'Bush path to destruction: the origins and character of the Revolutionary United Front (RUF/SL)', *Journal of Modern African Studies*, Vol. 36, No. 2 (1998).

Adeleke, Ademola, 'The politics and diplomacy of peacekeeping in West Africa: the ECOWAS operation in Liberia', *Journal of Modern African Studies*, Vol. 33, No. 4 (1995).

African Rights, *Rwanda: Death, Despair, and Defiance* (London: 1995).

———, 'Great expectations: the civil roles of the Churches in Southern Sudan', Discussion Paper No. 6, April 1995.

———, *Facing Genocide: The Nuba of Sudan* (London: July 1995).

———, 'Imposing empowerment? Aid and civil institutions in Southern Sudan', Discussion Paper No. 7, December 1995.

———, *Food and Power in Sudan: A Critique of Humanitarianism* (London: May 1997).

Amnesty International, 'Rwanda: alarming resurgence of killings', London, 12 August 1996.

———, 'Zaire: lawlessness and insecurity in North and South Kivu', London, November 1996.

———, 'Crisis in eastern Zaire: Amnesty International's appeal for the protection of human rights in the crisis in eastern Zaire', London, 1996.

Andargachew Tiruneh, *The Ethiopian Revolution 1974–1987: a Transformation from an Aristocratic to a Totalitarian Autocracy* (Cambridge: Cambridge University Press, 1993).

Bazin, J. and E. Terray, eds, *Guerres de lignage et guerres d'états en Afrique* (Paris: Archives Contemporaines, 1982).

Behrend, H., 'Is Alice Lakwena a witch? the Holy Spirit Movement and its fight against evil in the north of Uganda', in M. Twaddle and H. B. Hansen, eds, *Changing Uganda: the Dilemmas of Structural Adjustment and Revolutionary Change* (London: James Currey, 1991).

————, 'Violence dans le nord de l'Ouganda: le mouvement du Saint-Esprit (1986–1987), *Politique Africaine*, 48 (1992).

————, *Alice und die Geister: Krieg im Norden Ugandas* (Munchen: Trickster, 1993).

————, 'The Holy Spirit Movement and the forces of nature in the north of Uganda', in M. Twaddle and H.B. Hansen, eds, *Religion and Politics in East Africa* (London: James Currey, 1995).

————, 'Power and women as spirit mediums', in M. Reh and G. Ludwar-Ene, eds, *Gender and Identity in Africa* (Munster/Hamburg: Beitrage Zur Afrika-forschung, 1995).

Behrend, Heike and Meillassoux, 'Krieg in Ruanda: der Diskurs über Ethnizitiät und die Exploision des Hausses', *Lettre 26* (1994).

Bhebe, Ngwabi, and Terence Ranger, *Soldiers in Zimbabwe's Liberation War* (London: James Currey, 1995).

Cerulli, Enrico, *Somalia: scritti vari inediti ed inediti*, 3 vols (Roma: Istituto Poligrafico dello Stato, 1957, 1959, 1964).

Charlton, Roger, and Roy May, 'Warlords and militarism in Chad', *Review of African Political Economy*, Nos 45/46 (1989).

Clapham, Christopher, *Africa and the International System* (Cambridge: Cambridge University Press, 1996).

Clarke, Walter S., *Humanitarian Intervention in Somalia* (Carlisle: US Army War College, 1995).

Cliffe, L. and B. Davidson, *The Long Struggle of Eritrea for Independence and Constructive Peace* (Trenton, NJ: Red Sea Press, 1988).

Compagnon, Daniel, 'Ressources politiques, régulation autoritaire, et domination personelle en Somalie: le régime de Siyaad Barre (1969–1991)', PhD thesis, Université de Pau, France, 1995.

————, 'Les limites de l'ingérence "humanitaire": l'échec politique de l'ONU en Somalie', *L'Afrique Politique 1995* (Bordeaux/Paris: CEAN/Karthala, 1995).

————, 'Somaliland, un ordre politique en gestation?', *Politique Africaine*, No. 50 (1993).

————, 'Dynamiques de mobilisation, dissidence armée et rebellion populaire: le cas du Mouvement National Somali (1981–1990)', *Africa* (Rome), Vol. 47, No. 4 (1992).

————, 'The Somali opposition fronts: some comments and questions', *Horn of Africa*, Vol. 13, Nos 1–2 (1990).

Connell, D., *Against All Odds: a Chronicle of the Eritrean Revolution* (Trenton, NJ: Red Sea Press, 1993).

Crocker, Chester A., 'The lessons of Somalia: not everything went wrong', *Foreign Affairs*, Vol. 4, No. 3 (1995).

Dawit Wolde Giorgis, *Red Tears: War, Famine and Revolution in Ethiopia* (Trenton, NJ: Red Sea Press, 1989), p. 277.

Delumeau, J., *Le Pêche et la peur* (Paris: Fayard, 1983).

De Mars, William, 'Tactics of protection: international human rights organizations in the Ethiopian conflict, 1980–1986', in E. McCarthy-Arnold, ed., *Africa, Human Rights and the Global System* (Westport: Greenwood Press, 1994).

De Waal, Alex, *Evil Days: Thirty Years of War and Famine in Ethiopia* (New York: Human Rights Watch, 1991).

────, *Famine Crimes: Politics and the Disaster Relief Industry in Africa* (Oxford: James Currey/Bloomington: Indiana University Press, 1997).

De Waal, Alex, and Raakiya Omar, 'Doing harm by doing good? The international relief effort in Somalia', *Current History*, No. 5 (1993).

────, *Operation Restore Hope: a Preliminary Assessment* (London: African Rights, 1993).

Duffield, Mark, 'The political economy of internal war: asset transfer, complex emergencies, and international aid', in Joanna Macrae and Antony Zwi, eds, *War and Hunger: Rethinking International Responses to Complex Emergencies* (London: Zed Books, 1994).

Ellis, Stephen, 'Liberia 1989–1994: a study of ethnic and spiritual violence', *African Affairs*, Vol. 94, No. 375 (1995).

Enosa, Abe, 'The East African revival among the Kakwa of the Sudan', paper presented at the Fourth International Sudan Studies Conference, Cairo, 13 June 1997.

Farah, Ahmed Y., and Ioan M. Lewis, *Peace-Making Endeavours of Contemporary Lineage Leaders: a Survey of Grassroots Peace Conferences in North-West Somalia/ Somaliland* (London: Action Aid, 1993).

Firebrace, James, and S. Holland, *Never Kneel Down: Drought, Development and Liberation in Eritrea* (Nottingham: Spokesman Books, 1984).

Firebrace, James, and Gail Smith, *The Hidden Revolution: an Analysis of Social Change in Tigray, Northern Ethiopia* (London: War on Want, 1982).

Furley, Oliver, 'Child soldiers in Africa', in O. Furley, ed, *Conflict in Africa* (London: I. B. Tauris, 1995).

Gebru Tereke, 'Continuity and discontinuity in peasant mobilisation: the cases of Bale and Tigray', in M. Ottaway, ed., *The Political Economy of Ethiopia* (New York: Praeger, 1990).

Geffray, C., *Les Causes des Armes au Mozambique* (Paris: Karthala, 1990).

Guichaoua, André, *Le Problème des réfugiés Rwandais et des populations Banyarwanda dans la région des Grands Lacs Africains* (Geneva: UNHCR, 1992).

Hansen, Holger Bernt, and Michael Twaddle, *Uganda Now: Between Decay and Development* (London: James Currey, 1988).

────, *Changing Uganda: the Dilemmas of Structural Adjustment and Revolutionary Change* (London: James Currey, 1991).

────, *From Chaos to Order* (Kampala: Fountain Publishers/London: James Currey, 1994).

────, 'Uganda: the advent of no-party democracy', in John Wiseman, ed., *Democracy and Political Change in Sub-Saharan Africa* (London: Routledge, 1995).

Hendrie, Barbara, 'Relief behind the lines: the cross-border operation in Tigray', in Joanna Macrae and Antony Zwi, eds, *War and Hunger: Rethinking International Responses to Complex Emergencies* (London: Zed Books, 1994).

Heywood, Linda, 'Towards an understanding of modern political ideology in Africa: the case of the Ovimbundu of Angola', *Journal of Modern African Studies*, Vol. 36, No. 1 (1998).

Hirsch, John L., and Robert B. Oakley, *Somalia and Operation Restore Hope* (Washington: US Institute of Peace, 1995).

Human Rights Watch Arms Project 'Arming Rwanda: the arms trade and human rights abuses in the Rwanda war', *HRWAP,* Vol. 6, No. 1 (January 1994).

———, 'Rearming with impunity: international support for the perpetrators of the Rwandan genocide', *HRWAP,* Vol. 7, No. 4 (May 1995).

Human Rights Watch/Africa, 'Democratic Republic of the Congo: what Kabila is hiding: civilian killings and impunity in Congo', Report 9: 5A (October 1997).

Hutchinson, S. E., *Nuer Dilemmas: Coping with Money, War and the State* (Berkeley: University of California Press, 1996).

Hyden, Goran, *No Shortcuts to Progress* (Berkeley: University of California Press, 1983).

Iyob, Ruth, *The Eritrean Struggle for Independence: Domination, Resistance, Nationalism 1941–93* (Cambridge: Cambridge University Press, 1995).

James, W., 'War and "ethnic visibility": the Uduk on the Sudan–Ethiopian border', in K. Fukui and J. Markakis, *Ethnicity and Conflict in the Horn of Africa* (London: James Currey/Athens OH: Ohio University Press, 1994).

———, 'Radio and conflict: Sudan', paper presented at a conference on 'African Broadcast Cultures: Radio and Public Life', University of London, School of African and Oriental Studies (SOAS), 12–13 June 1997.

Johnson, D. H., 'North-South issues', in P. Woodward, ed., *Sudan After Nimeiri* (London: Routledge, 1991).

———, 'Increasing the trauma of return: an assessment of the UN's emergency response to the evacuation of the Sudanese refugee camps in Ethiopia, 1991', in T. Allen, ed., *In Search of Cool Ground: Displacement and Homecoming in Northeast Africa* (London: James Currey/Trenton NJ: Africa World Press, 1996).

Johnson, D. H. and MacAskill, J., 'Eastern Bahr el-Ghazal evaluation', Oxford, Oxfam, May 1995.

Johnson, D. H. and Prunier, G., 'The foundation and expansion of the Sudan People's Liberation Army', in M. W. Daly and Ahmad Alawad Sikainga, eds, *Civil War in the Sudan* (London: British Academic Press, 1993).

Joseph, Richard A., *Radical Nationalism in Cameroon* (London: Oxford University Press, 1977).

Karim, A., et al., 'Operation Lifeline Sudan: a review', Geneva, Department of Humanitarian Affairs, July 1996.

Kibreab, Gaim, *Refugees and Development in Africa* (Trenton, NJ: Red Sea Press, 1987).

Kittsteiner, H. D., 'Das Gewissen im Gewitter', *Jahrbuch für Volkskunde*, Vol. 10 (1987).

Koroma, A. K. *The Agony of a Nation* (Freetown: Afromedia, 1996).

Kriger, Norma J., *Zimbabwe's Guerrilla War: Peasant Voices* (Cambridge: Cambridge University Press, 1992).

Kuol, M. L., *Administration of Justice in the (SPLA/M) Liberated Areas: Court Cases in War-Torn Southern Sudan* (Oxford: Refugee Studies Programme, February 1997).

Kurimoto, E., 'Civil war and regional conflicts: the Pari and their neighbours in south-eastern Sudan', in K. Fukui and J. Markakis, eds, *Ethnicity and Conflict in the Horn of Africa* (London: James Currey/Athens OH:Ohio University Press, 1994).

Laitin, David D., and Said S. Samatar, *Somalia: Nation in Search of a State* (Boulder: Westview, 1987).

Lan, David, *Guns and Rain: Guerrillas and Spirit Mediums in Zimbabwe* (London:

James Currey/Berkeley: University of California Press, 1985).

Lederach, Jean-Paul, 'The intervention in Somalia: what should have happened', *Middle East Report*, No. 2 (1993).

Lemarchand, René, *Rwanda and Burundi* (New York: Praeger, 1970).

Lewis, Ioan M., ed., *Nationalism and Self-determination in the Horn of Africa* (London: Ithaca, 1983).

Lewis, Ioan M., *A Pastoral Democracy: a Study of Pastoralism and Politics Among the Northern Somali of the Horn of Africa* (London: Oxford University Press, 1961).

Leys, Colin, and John Saul, *Namibia's Liberation Struggle: The Two-Edged Sword* (London: James Currey, 1995).

Lonsdale, J. M., 'The moral economy of Mau Mau', in B. Berman and J. M. Lonsdale, eds, *Unhappy Valley* (London: James Currey, 1992).

MacGaffey, Janet *et. al., The Real Economy of Zaire* (London: James Currey, 1991).

Malwal, B., 'In Kurmuk the thoughts are all about defeating the NIF regime', *Sudan Democratic Gazette*, September 1997.

Marchal, Roland, 'Les *mooryan* de Mogadiscio: formes de la violence dans un espace urbain en guerre', *Cahiers d'Etudes Africaines*, Vol. 33, No. 2 (1993).

——, 'La militarisation de l'humanitaire', *Cultures et Conflits*, No. 11 (1993).

——, 'La guerre à Mogadiscio', *Politique Africaine*, No. 46 (1992).

Markakis, J., *National and Class Conflict in the Horn of Africa* (Cambridge: Cambridge University Press, 1987).

——, 'Eritrea, the transitional period', *Review of African Political Economy*, No. 58 (1993).

Minter, William, *Apartheid's Contras: an Enquiry into the Roots of War in Angola and Mozambique* (London: Zed Books, 1994).

Museveni, Yoweri, *What is Africa's Problem?* (Kampala: NRM Publications, 1992).

——, *Sowing the Mustard Seed: the Struggle for Freedom and Democracy in Uganda* (London: Macmillan, 1997).

Nadel, S. F., *Races and Tribes of Eritrea* (Asmara: British Military Administration, 1944).

Ngoga, Pascal, 'Guerrilla insurgency and conflict resolution in Africa: a case study of Uganda', PhD thesis, Lancaster University, 1997.

Niehaus, I. A., 'Witch-hunting and political legitimacy: continuity and change in Green Valley, Lebowa, 1930–91', *Africa*, Vol. 63, No. 4 (1993).

Nunley, J. *Moving with the Face of the Devil* (Urbana: University of Illinois Press, 1987).

Nyaba, P. A., *The Politics of Liberation in South Sudan: an Insider's View* (Kampala: Fountain Publishers, 1997).

Ocan, M., 'The war currently taking place in northern Uganda', paper presented to the Sessional Committee on Defence and Internal Affairs, Parliament House, Kampala, Uganda, 1996.

Oduho, J. and W. Deng, *The Problem of the Southern Sudan* (London: Oxford University Press for the Institute of Race Relations, 1963).

Pirouet, L., 'Human rights issues in Museveni's Uganda', in H. B. Hansen and M. Twaddle, eds, *Changing Uganda: the Dilemmas of Structural Adjustment and Revolutionary Change* (London: James Currey, 1991).

Prunier, Gérard, 'A candid view of the Somali National Movement', *Horn of Africa*,

Vol. 13, Nos 3–4 and Vol. 14, Nos 1–2 (1990–91).

——, 'L'inconcevable aveuglement de l'ONU en Somalie', *Le Monde Diplomatique*, November 1993.

——, *The Rwanda Crisis: History of a Genocide* (London and Kampala: C. Hurst and Fountain Publishers, 1995).

Ranger, T., 'War, violence and healing in Zimbabwe', *Journal of Southern African Studies*, No. 18 (1992).

——, 'The invention of tradition revisited: the case of colonial Africa', in T. Ranger and O. Vaughan, eds, *Legitimacy and the State in Twentieth Century Africa* (Oxford: Oxford University Press, 1993)

Reed, Wm Cyrus, 'International politics and national liberation: ZANU and the politics of contested sovereignty in Zimbabwe', *African Studies Review*, Vol. 36, No. 2 (1993).

——, 'The New International Order: state, society, and African international relations', *Africa Insight* (Pretoria), Vol. 25, No. 3 (1995), pp. 140–8.

——, 'Exile, reform, and the rise of the Rwandan Patriotic Front', *Journal of Modern African Studies*, Vol. 34, No. 3 (1996), pp. 479–501.

Reno, William, 'Foreign firms and the financing of Charles Taylor's NPFL', *Liberian Studies Journal*, Vol. 18, No. 2 (1993).

——, 'The reinvention of an African patrimonial state: Charles Taylor's Liberia', *Third World Quarterly*, Vol. 16, No. 1 (1995).

Reyntjens, Filip, *L'Afrique des Grands Lacs en crise: Rwanda et Burundi (1988–1994)* (Paris: Karthala, 1994).

Richards, Paul, 'Rebellion in Liberia and Sierra Leone: a crisis of youth?' in Oliver Furley, ed., *Conflict in Africa* (London: I. B. Tauris, 1995).

——, *Fighting for the Rain Forest: War, Youth and Resources in Sierra Leone* (Oxford: James Currey, 1996).

Riley, Steve, 'Sierra Leone: the militariat strikes again', *Review of African Political Economy*, No. 72 (1997), pp. 287–92.

Roesch, O., 'Renamo and the peasantry in Southern Mozambique', *Canadian Journal of African Studies*, Vol. 26, No. 3 (1992).

Rosberg, Carl and Robert Jackson, 'Why Africa's weak states persist', *World Politics*, Vol. 35, No. 1 (1982), pp. 1–24.

Sathyamurthy, T. V., *The Political Development of Uganda 1900–1986* (Aldershot: Gower, 1986).

Stapleton, C. and May, C., *African All-Stars* (London: Quartet, 1987).

Steiner, R., *The Last Adventurer: From Biafra to the Sudan* (London: Weidenfeld and Nicholson, 1978).

Trevaskis, G. K. N., *Eritrea: A Colony in Transition 1941–52* (London: Oxford University Press, 1960).

Tvedt, T., 'The collapse of the state in Southern Sudan after the Addis Ababa Agreement: A study of internal causes and the role of the NGOs', in Sharif Harir and T. Tvedt (eds), *Short-Cut to Decay. The Case of the Sudan* (Uppsala: Nordiska Afrikanistitutet, 1994).

Van Crefeld, Martin, *The Transformation of War* (New York: Free Press, 1991).

Vaughan, Sarah, *The Addis Ababa Transitional Conference of July 1991: Its Origins, History and Significance,* Occasional Papers No. 51, (Edinburgh University: Centre of African Studies, 1994).

Wakoson, Elias Nyamlell, 'The origin and development of the Anya-Nya movement 1955–1972', in Mohamed Omer Beshir, ed., *Southern Sudan: Regionalism and Religion*, Graduate College Publications No. 10 (Khartoum: University of Khartoum, 1984).

Watson, Catherine, *Exile from Rwanda: Background to an Invasion* (Washington, DC: US Committee for Refugees, 1991).

Werbner, R. P., *Ritual Passage, Sacred Journey* (Washington: Smithsonian Institute Press, 1989).

Wilson, A., *Women and the Eritrean Revolution: the Challenge Road* (Trenton, NJ: Red Sea Press, 1991).

Wilson, K. B., 'Cults of violence and counter-violence', *Journal of Southern African Studies*, No. 18 (1992).

Woldemikael, T. M., 'The cultural construction of Eritrean nationalist movements', in C. Young, *The Rising Tide of Cultural Pluralism* (Madison: University of Wisconsin Press, 1993).

Young, John, 'The Tigray and Eritrean People's Liberation Fronts: a history of tensions and pragmatism', *Journal of Modern African Studies*, Vol. 34, No. 1 (1996), pp. 105–20.

——, *Peasant Revolution in Ethiopia: the Tigray People's Liberation Front, 1975–1991* (Cambridge: Cambridge University Press, 1997).

Zack-Williams, A. B., and Steve Riley, 'Sierra Leone: the coup and its consequences,' *Review of African Political Economy*, No. 56 (1993), pp. 91–8.

Zack-Williams, A. B., 'Kamajors, "sobels" and the militariat: civil society and the return of the military in Sierra Leonean politics', *Review of African Political Economy*, No. 73 (1997), pp. 373–98.

Zartman, William I., ed., *Collapsed States: the Disintegration and Restoration of Legitimate Authority* (Boulder: Lynne Rienner, 1995).

Index

Bold references indicate the principal discussions of the index subject concerned.

Abyei Liberation Front, 58
Acholi, 12, 103, 107, 108-18
Addis Ababa, 4, 25, 27, 33, 49, 77, 80
   agreement, 56, 57, 71
   conference, 87-8
Afabet, 27, 31, 46
Afar, 28
African National Congress (ANC), 53
Alliance of Democratic Forces for the Liberation
   of Congo-Zaire (ADFL), 4, 7, 105, **134-54**
Armed Forces of Liberia, 155, 157, 161-2, 166,
   167
Armed Forces Revolutionary Council, 188
African Rights, 66, 69
Aidid, Huseen, 84, 90
   Mahamed Farah 7, 80, 81-4, 87-90
AIDS, 114
Akalai Guzai, 24
Akol, Lam, 61-2
Ala group, 25, 28
Albania, 49
al-Bashir, Mahamed 105
Algeria, 2, 6, 23
Ali Mahdi Mahamed, 7, 78-9, 81, 83-4, 86-90
Alier, Abel, 61
Al-Ittihad, 81, 89
Americo-Liberians, 12, 158, 167, 170-1
Amhara, 37, 40, 48, 50
Amin, Idi, 3, 91-2, 94-5, 106, 108, 115-6, 122,
   125, 129, 142
Angola, 3, 6, 7, 15, 17, 150, 151
Ankole, 92, 98, 122-3
Annan, Kofi, 152
Ansar, 55
Anyanya, **54-7**, 58-9, 61, 70-1
Anyanya II, 60-2, 64
All People's Congress (APC), 174-5, 177-82,
   187-8, 191-3

Arab League, 79
Arabs, Arabism, 23-4
Aregowie Berhe, 38
arms supply, 137-8, 183
Arusha accords, 133, 137
   tribunal, 136, 145, 153
Asian insurgencies, 7
Asmara, 4, 25-8, 31-2, 48
'asset transfer', 16
Auma, Alice, *see* Lakwena
Awate, Idris Muhammed, 23

Babangida, Ibrahim, 160, 165-6
Bahr al-Ghazal, 68, 70, 72
baito, 30, 43-4
Bakuvu, 147, 149
Bani Amir, 21-4, 28
Banyamulenge, 141, 143-4, 146-7
BBC World Service, 17, 63, 159, 187
Bedié, Henri Konan, 164
Belgium, 120, 124, 142-3
Biafra, 165
Bio, Julius Maada, 187
Bo, 173, 175, 178-80, 184-5
Boley, George, 162, 166-7
Bonthe, 187
Boutros-Ghali, Boutros, 88
Bowen, Hezekiah, 162
Britain, British, 20, 55 67-8, 71, 96, 99, 138, 184
   Military Administration (Eritrea), 22
Buganda, 92, 94, 96, 100, 102, 111, 126
Bukavu, 138, 150
Burkina Faso, 155, 160-1
Burundi, 122, 124, 132, 142, 148-50
Bush, George, 87
Busoga, 112
Butare, 141

Cabral, Amilcar, 3
Cameroon, 3
Canada, 124, 148, 150
Cape Mount, 181
Carlos the Jackal, 142
Carmichael, Stokeley, 92
Carrington, Lord, 96
Carter, Jimmy, 49, 145
Casamance, 3, 6
Castro, Fidel,. 174
Committee for the Defence of the Republic
    (CDR), 132
Central African Republic, 138
Chad, 2-4, 6, 13
child soldiers, 11, 53, 98, 116, 168, 179-80, 184,
    190
chimurenga, 14
China, 2, 28, 74, 111, 138
Christianity, 3, 10, 13, 21-4, 28, 66, 112, 114,
    143
    Catholic, 114, 120, 122
    Orthodox, 3, 41-2, 49
    Protestant, 122
CIA, 39
civil society, 11
Clinton, Bill, 145
cobalt, 151
Cold War, 4, 7-8, 15, 19, 48, 53, 120, 129, 138,
    156
Commonwealth, 93
Compaore, Blaise, 161
Congo, 121
Congo DR, *see* Zaire
Côte d'Ivoire, 155, 161, 164, 166-7, 188-9, 192
Crocker, Chester, 87
Cuba, 11, 19, 28

Dankalia, 21, 24
Dar es Salaam, 92, 105, 146
Darfur, 55, 57, 61, 66
De Beers, 150
decolonization, 3
Derg, 36-8, 40-3, 45-50, 53, 57, 61-2
diamonds, 16, 146, 150-1, 157, 161, 163-5, 178-
    9, 182-3, 185, 189
Dinka, 55, 61, 64, 66, 68, 70, 72
discipline, 10, 19, 101-2
Djibouti, 3, 13, 74
Doe, Jackson, 159
    Samuel, 4, 7, 155-9, 161, 163, 165-6, 168-9,
    171, 177
drugs, 16, 165, 168, 173-4, 179-80, 182, 190
Duopu, Moses, 159-60

ECOMOG, 156, 162-4, 181, 183
ECOWAS, 156, 165, 166

education, 6, 9, 11, 20, 29, 30, 32, 55, 80, 99,
    173
Egypt, 21, 22, 55, 140
Endaselassie, 47-8
Equatoria, 63, 64, 65
Eritrea, 2-3, 6, 10, 13-4, 16-7, **19-35**, 36-7, 46-
    9, 55, 59, 65, 69-71, 77, 79, 106, 191
Eritrean Liberation Front (ELF), 10, 19-20, 22-6,
    32-4, 37, 59, 69
Eritrean Liberation Movement (ELM), 22
Eritrean People's Liberation Front (EPLF), 1, 4,
    9-10, 13, 16, **19-35**, 37, 39, 45-9, 70, 77,
    79
Eritrean People's Liberation Party (EPLP), 29
Eritrean Relief Association (ERA), 33, 44
Ethiopia, 3, 5-8, 10-3, 16-7, 19-23, 25-6, 31, 34,
    36-52, 55-6, 58-62, 64-6, 70, 72, 75, 77, 79,
    106
Ethiopian Democratic Union (EDU), 39, 40, 42
Ethiopian People's Democratic Movement
    (EPDM), 40
Ethiopian Peoples' Revolutionary Democratic
    Front (EPRDF), 4, 7, 13, 27, 36, 48-9, 53,
    62, 75, 81
Ethiopian People's Revolutionary Party (EPRP),
    37, 39, 40, 42
Ethiopian revolution, 27-8, 36
ethnicity, 13, 18, 21, 40, 53
Executive Outcomes, 185, 187
exit strategies, 6

factionalism, 73-4, **83-6**, 89, 157, 161-2
famine, 15, 16, 41, 45, 46
Forces Armées du Nord (FAN), 4
Fanon, Frantz, 92, 174
Fourah Bay College (FBC), 174-7, 187
Front de Libération de la Côte des Somalis
    (FLCS), 74, 89
Front de Libération Nationale (FLN), 23
foco theory, 106
Fort Portal, 96, 103
'frame of steel', 27, 31
France, 116, 124, 128-9, 131, 137-8, 140, 142,
    145, 148, 153, 156, 166
Freetown, 161, 172-3, 175-7, 179-81, 183-4,
    189, 192-3
Frelimo, 92-3
Frolinat, 6
Fronasa, 93-5, 98, 100, 125, 127

Gabon, 151
Gambela, 58
Gambia, 160, 166
Garang, John, 54, 58, 60-5, 69-71, 105
Garvey, Marcus 174
Gbarnga, 180

genocide, Rwandan, 119, 132-4, 139-41, 153
Ghana, 160, 164, 176, 192
gim gima, 43, 48
Gio, 155
Gojjam, 49
Gola, 183, 189
gold, 146-7, 150, 157, 161, 163
Goma, 137-8, 143, 149
Gondar, 39-40, 49
Gorbachev, Mikail, 48
gorillas, 149
governmentalities, 12, 169
Greater Liberia, 163
Guevara, Che, 106, 174
Guinea, 156, 164, 166, 181, 183
Guinea-Bissau, 2, 6
Gulu, 115

Habre, Hissene, 4
Habyarimana, Juvenal, 122, 126, 128-30, 132, 134, 136-7
Haile-Selassie, 32, 36, 40, 43, 50, 174
Hamasein, 26
Harer, 77
Hargeisa, 79, 80
Hausien massacre, 47
Holy Spirit Movement, **107-18**
Holy Spirit Safety Precautions, 110, 112, 115
Houphouet-Boigny, Felix, 164, 166
human rights, 142
Human Rights Watch, 168
Hutus, 119-33, 134, 138, 141-4

ideology, 5, 8, **9-11**, 20, 25-6, 29, 37, 50, 54, 120, 157, 189, 191-2
Igal, Mahamed Ibrahim, 85, 89
India, 80
Independent National Patriotic Front of Liberia (INPFL), 10
international politics of insurgencies, **15-7**, 32, 105-6, 135-6, 164-7
international economy, 16
inyenzi, 121-2, 128
Iraq, 23, 156
iron ore, 163, 166
Islam, 3, 7, 10, 13, 15, 21-4, 28, 30, 55, 57, 60, 65, 71-2, 81, 105
Israel, 56, 165
Issayas Afewerki, 4, 24-5, 28-9, 33
Italy, 22, 50
Itang, 63
ivory, 16

Jawara, Dauda, 166
Jees, Umar 76
Jijiga, 77

Jinja, 107
Johnson, Prince, 10, 159
Roosevelt, 161-2, 166
Juba, 62, 63, 65

Kabala, 184
Kabamba, 95, 98, 103, 105, 125, 127
Kabba, Ahmad Tejan, 172, 187, 192
Alie, 176-7
Kabila, Laurent, 105, 146, 149, 151-3
Kagame, Paul, 105, 125, 128, 130-1, 141
Kailahun, 177-8, 180-1, 183-4, 187-9
Kamajo, 180, 185-90, 192-3
Kambia, 184, 189
Kampala, 4, 91, 94, 96, 98, 101, 104, 107-8, 113, 125-6
Kasai, 146-7, 150
Kassala, 65
Katanga, *see* Shaba
Kayibanda, Gregoire, 126, 128
Kayira, Andrew, 93, 100
Kenema, 175, 178-9, 184-5
Kenya, 2-3, 6, 59, 74, 78, 86, 104, 109, 113, 140, 148
Keren, 26-7, 31
Kerubino Kuanyin Bol, 60, 64-5, 71
Khartoum, 49, 105
khat, 86
Khatmiyya, 23
Kigali, 4, 130-1, 134, 137, 139, 141
Kinshasa, 147, 151
Kisangani, 146, 148, 150, 152-3
Kisimayo, 78
Kittani, Ambassador, 87
Kivu, 138, 141, 143-4, 146-7
Koidu, 179, 182
Kolwezi, 151
Kono, 175, 182
Kony, Joseph, 9, 106-8, 113, 115
Kordofan, 55, 59, 66
Korea, 111
Krahn, 155, 157, 161-2, 166, 168
Krio, 174
Kromah, Alhaji, 161, 167
Kuti, Fela Anikulapo, 173
Kuwait, 156

La Baule speech, 128
Lagu, Joseph, 56
Lakwena, Alice, 17, **107-13**, 114-5, 126
land reform, 41-3
Langi, 103
Latin American insurgencies, 7
leadership, 8-10, 19, 26, 28, 36, 39, 52, 56-7, 96, 101, 104, 169, 170, 187, 191
Lebanon, Lebanese, 156, 179

liberation insurgencies, 6-7, 192
liberation movements, 135-6
liberation war, 4, 10, 18
Liberia, 2, 3, 4, 7-13, 16-7, **155-71**, 173, 177-83, 187-90, 193
Libya, 58, 95-6, 156, 160, 175-7
Lofa, 181
London, 80, 96, 118
    1991 conference, 49
looting, 10, 16, 85-6, 109, 123, 139-40, 149, 152, 157, 161-4, 169, 172, 178, 180, 182, 184, 190
Lord's Resistance Army (LRA), 64, 106, **115-8**
Liberia Peace Council (LPC), 156, 161-4, 167
Lubumbashi, 150
Lukoya, Severino, 107-8, 113-5
Lule, Professor, 93, 96-7
lumpens, 4, 172-4, 176-80, 182, 185, 187-8, 190-3
Lumumba, Patrice, 146
Luwero triangle, 96, 98, 103, 125

Makerere University, 98, 101
Mali, 164
Mandela, Nelson, 151
Mandingo, 155, 157, 161-2, 164, 168
Manifesto Group, 78, 81, 84
Mano River, 178
manqa crisis, 25, 32
Mao Tse Tung, 2, 7-8, 10, 14, 18, 26, 29-30, 39, 106, 119
Margai, Albert, 175
Marley, Bob, 173
Marxism, Marxism-Leninism, 7-8, 11, 33, 37-8, 43, 49, 53-4, 75, 96, 146, 174
Marxist-Leninist League of Tigray (MLLT), 38, 43
Mashar, Riek, 61-2, 64-6, 70-1
Massawa, 26-8, 34, 48
Mau Mau, 2, 109
Mbuji-Mayi, 150
Mouvement Démocratique Républicain (MDR), 129
Mekelle, 47
Meles Zenawi, 14, 38, 49
Mende, 185-6
Mengistu Haile-Mariam, 6, 27, 32-3, 48-9, 60-2, 80, 82
Mitterrand, François, 128
Mobutu Sese Seko, 105, 137-9, 144, 146-7, 150-4
Mogadishu, 77-9, 81, 86-7
Moi, Daniel arap, 104, 106
Momoh, Joseph, 188
Monrovia, 155, 157-9, 162, 164, 168-71, 183
mooryan, 79

Mozambique, 3, 6-7, 15, 92-4, 98, 100
Muki Somali African Organization, 89
Muntu, Mugisha, 95, 104
Museveni, Yoweri, 4, 9, 91-118, 123-7, 130-1, 142

Nairobi, 116, 125
Namibia, 3, 6, 14
Naqfa, 27, 31
Nasir group, 62-4, 69, 71
National Democratic Alliance (NDA), 65, 71
National Islamic Front (NIF), 53, 71
National Patriotic Front of Liberia (NPFL), 4, 10, **155-71**, 177-8, 180
National Provisional Ruling Council (NPRC), 181-4, 187, 193
National Resistance Army (NRA), 4, 7, 10, 13, 53, 70, **91-106**, 107-9, 123-4, 126, 130, 133
nationalities, *see* ethnicity
Netherlands, 140
non-governmental organizations (NGOs), 16, 33, 44-5, 86-7, 143
Northern Frontier District Liberation Front (NFDLF), 74, 89
Nigeria, 156-7, 160, 162-7, 172, 178, 181, 185, 188
    civil war, 164
Nimba, 155, 159, 162-3, 166, 168, 177
Nimeiri, Jaafar, 44, 57, 60-2, 67, 71
Njala University, 174-6, 184, 187
Nkrumah, Kwame, 99, 174
Norman, Hinga, 185
Nuba Mountains, 55, 58-61, 64, 66, 69, 72
Nuer, 55, 59, 61, 64, 66, 69-70
Nyerere, Julius, 92-3

Oakley, Robert, 87
Organization of African Unity (OAU), 4, 145, 175
Obel group, 24-5
Obote, Milton, 3, 56, 92-6, 98-9, 103-4, 106, 108, 122-3, 126-7, 130, 142
Ogaden war, 27, 40
Ogata, Sadako, 149
oil, 165-6
Okello, Basilio, 108
    Tito, 103-4, 108
Operation Lifeline Sudan (OLS), 63
organization of insurgencies, **8-11**, 19, 28, 54, 96, 98, 110, 152, 159, 188-9
Oris, Juma, 64, 106, 115-6
Oromo, 37, 48
Oromo Liberation Front (OLF), 49, 60, 62
Oromo People's Democratic Organization (OPDO), 48

PAIGC, 3
Palestine, 121
pastoralism, 21-2, 30, 73
peace-keeping, 156
peasantry, 30-1, 34-5, 39-41, 43-5, 50-2, 192
People's Front for Democracy & Justice (PFDJ), 35
People's Liberation Forces (PLF), 24-6, 28
'people's war', 2
Poro society, 12, 170-1
Portugal, 3
Popular Resistance Army (PRA), 95-7
Pujehun, 178, 181

Qadhafi, Muammar, 60, 79, 95
Quiwonkpa, Thomas, 155, 157-8

Rahanweyn Association (RRA), 89
Ramadan Muhammad Nur, 28-9, 33-4
Rawlings, Jerry, 160
Red Sea, 24, 26, 28
Red Star campaign, 27, 45
reform insurgencies, 7
refugees, 11, 29, 44-6, 121-3, 127, 129, 134-6, 138-42, 144-9, 152
Relief & Rehabilitation Commission (RRC), 41, 46
Relief Society of Tigray (REST), 44, 45
religion, 12, 21-2,
    see also Christianity, Islam
Renamo, 1, 7, 192
resettlement policy, 41
Restore Hope, Operation, 85-6
revolution, 36, 43, 51-2, 175, 178
Revolutionary United Front (RUF), 160, 162, **172-93**
Rodney, Walter, 92, 174
Rome, 80
Ruhengeri, 131
Ruwenzori, 100, 103
Rwanda, 1-2, 4, 7-8, 10-1, 13-4, 16, 94, 98, 105-6, 116, **119-33, 134-54**
Rwanda, Former Government, **134-54**
Rwandan Alliance for National Unity (RANU), 124-6
Rwandan Patriotic Front (RPF), 4, 9-10, 14, 105, **119-33**, 134, 136-7, 139-42, 153
Rwandan Refugees Welfare Association (RRWF), 124
Rwigyema, Fred, 9, 99, 103, 105, 125, 127-8, 130

Sabbe, Osman Saleh, 23-4
Sadiq al-Mahdi, 44, 60, 62
Sahel, 24-7, 30-3, 45
Sahnoun, Mahamed, 87

Salim Saleh, 100
Sande society, 170
Sankara, Thomas, 160-1
Sankoh, Foday, 9, 172, 174, 176-7, 180, 187-9, 191
Saudi Arabia, 39
Savimbi, Jonas, 8, 17
Sebhat Nega, 38
Senegal, 3, 164
separatist insurgencies, 6
Shaba, 146, 147, 151, 152
shadow state, 160-2
Sharia, 69
Shona, 12
Sierra Leone, 2, 9, 11-2, 156, 160, 162, **172-93**
Silanyo, Ahmed, 76, 82, 84
Siyaad Barre, Mahamed, 3-4, 7, 75-81, 83-5, 88
slavery, 16, 116, 156, 163, 170, 174, 188
smuggling, 179
'sobels', 182, 184, 190
Somali Democratic Alliance (SDA), 89
Somali Democratic Movement (SDM), 89
Somali National Alliance (SNA), 4, 7, 84, 88, 90
Somali National Democratic Union (SNDU), 90
Somali National Front (SNF), 90
Somali National Movement (SNM), 74-7, 79-85, 89-90
Somali National Union (SNU), 90
Somali Patriotic Alliance (SPA), 90
Somali Patriotic Movement (SPM), 76-7, 90
Somali Revolutionary Socialist Party, 75
Somali Salvation Alliance (SSA), 7, 88, 90
Somali Salvation Democratic Front (SSDF), 74-7, 79-81, 90
Somali Workers' Party, 75
Somalia, 2-13, 17, 27, 47, **73-90**, 93, 145
Somaliland, 76, 79-80, 82, 84-5, 89
South Africa, 3, 6, 11, 15, 17, 138, 145, 150-1, 185
South Sudan Independence Movement (SSIM), 61, 64-5, 70, 72
South Sudan Independence Army (SSIA), 66
South West Africa People's Organization (SWAPO), 14, 53
spirits, 12, 16, 107, 109-11, 113-4
state collapse, 7
stateless societies, 169
Stevens, Siaka, 175-6
structural adjustment, 129
students, 7, 22, 25, 33, 36, 40, 42, 50, 92, 174-7, 187, 192-3
Sudan, 2-4, 6, 10, 12-3, 16-7, 21, 24, 27, 31-2, 35, 39-40, 44-6, 49, **53-72**, 93, 95, 105, 108-9, 116, 142
Sudan People's Liberation Army (SPLA), 7, 10, 44, **53-72**, 105, 136, 142

Syria, 23, 28

Tanzania, 93-5, 108, 124-5, 131-2, 136, 140, 142
Taylor, Charles, 7, 9-10, 16-7, 155-69, 177, 180, 183
terror, 190-1
Tigray, 2, 12, 21, 33, **36-52**, 70, 77
Tigray National Organization (TNO), 37, 38
Tigray People's Liberation Front (TPLF), 6-7, 9-10, 13-6, 19, 33, **36-52**, 53, 70, 77, 79
Togo, 128, 151
Tolbert, A.B., 166
    William R., 158-9, 163, 166-7
Tombalbaye, President, 6
Tonkolili, 177
Torit, 61
Toronto, 80, 118
Touaregs, 2
tribalism, see ethnicity
True Whig Party (TWP), 4, 157-8, 161, 163, 167, 169-70
Tshisekedi, Etienne, 147, 150-2
Tubman, William V.S., 158-9, 163, 165, 167, 170
Turabi, Hassan al-, 53
Turquoise, Operation, 137
Tutsi, 98, **119-33**, 134, 136, 139, 141, 143-4, 147
Tutu, Desmond, 145
Tuur, Abdirahman Ali, 82, 84-5, 88
typologies, 5, 191

Uganda, 2-3, 7, 9-11, 13, 16-7, 56, 64-5, 70, **91-106, 107-18**, 121-32, 136, 138, 142-3, 145, 148-50
Uganda Freedom Fighters (UFF), 93, 96
Uganda Freedom Movement (UFM), 93, 116
Uganda National Liberation Army/Front (UNLA/F), 94-5, 99, 103-4, 108, 110, 113, 122
Uganda Patriotic Movement (UPM), 93
Uganda People's Army (UPA), 109, 113
Uganda People's Congress (UPC), 92, 98, 122-4
Uganda People's Defence Force (UPDF), 102
Uganda People's Democratic Army (UPDA), 108-10, 113, 116
Uganda People's Democratic Christian Army (UPDCA), 116
Ukraine, 156
Ulimo, 156-7, 161-4, 166, 168, 178, 181, 183
Umma party, 60
Union des Populations du Cameroun (UPC), 3

Unionist Party (Eritrea), 22, 31
UNITA, 1, 7, 151, 192
United Kingdom, see Britain
United Nations (UN), 46, 53, 63, 82, 87, 89, 120, 138, 140, 142, 146, 148-9, 152-3
    High Commission for Refugees (UNHCR), 121, 127, 149, 152
    Operation in Somalia (UNOSOM), 82, 85-6, 88-9
    Security Council, 89, 137, 148
    United Task Force (UNITAF), 87
United Somali Congress (USC), 74, 77-81, 83-4, 90
United Somali Front (USF), 90
United Somali Party (USP), 90
United States (US), 11, 17, 20, 33, 49, 63, 87-8, 124, 130, 142, 145, 148, 153, 156, 165-6, 168
    Congress, 97
Usman Ato, 84, 86
USSR, 11, 13, 15, 19, 25-6, 33, 37, 40, 84
UWONET, 117

Vietnam, 26
Virunga, 131

Wallace-Johnson, I.T.A., 174
Wardhigley, Ali Mahamed, 76, 80
warlords, warlord insurgencies, 7, 74, 157, 159, 162-3, 169, 191
Washington, 80
West Nile, 94
West Nile Bank Front (WNBF), 106, 115-6
Western Sahara, 2
Western Somali Liberation Front (WSLF), 74, 90
witchcraft, 107-8, 110
Wollo, 40, 49
women & insurgency, 32, 42, 111-3, 116-7, 169, 179, 188-9
Workers' Party of Ethiopia (WPE), 48
World Bank, 165
World Health Organization (WHO), 168
Worldwide Fund for Nature (WWF), 149
woyene, 50

Yemen, 24, 32
youth, 172-6, 178-80, 192-3
Yugoslavia, 145

Zaire, 2, 4, 7, 94, 105-6, 116, 124, 132, **134-54**
Zambia, 151
Zimbabwe, 3, 6, 12, 14, 49, 51, 151
Zimbabwe African National Union (ZANU), 12